Closely Observed Infants

Closely Observed Infants

edited by

Lisa Miller
Margaret Rustin
Michael Rustin
Judy Shuttleworth

Duckworth

Fourth impression 1995
Third impression 1993
Second impression 1991
First published in 1989 by
Gerald Duckworth & Co. Ltd
The Old Piano Factory
48 Hoxton Square, London N1 6PB

ISBN 0 7156 2311 7

British Library Cataloguing in Publication Data

Closely observed infants.
  1. Babies. Development. Assessment. Observation methods
  I. Miller, Lisa
  155.4

ISBN 0-7156-2311-7

Photoset in North Wales by
Derek Doyle & Associates, Mold, Clwyd.
Printed and bound in Great Britain by
Redwood Books, Trowbridge, Wiltshire

Contents

Preface

This book has been written in a tradition which began in 1948 when Esther Bick introduced Infant Observation to the Tavistock course for the training of Child Psychotherapists. Her inspired initiative has had an enormous influence. At the Tavistock Clinic approximately a hundred students are now engaged in this task every year, and the educational fascination and interest of the process has led to a remarkable spread in the practice of infant observation. The Institute of Psychoanalysis in London added it to their curriculum in 1960, and most of the organisations training psychoanalytically-oriented psycho-therapists in Britain have followed suit over the years. There has also been a striking growth of interest abroad, notably in Italy, but also in France, Spain, Norway, Germany, several South American countries, Australia, and now also in Canada and the United States.

Psychoanalytic infant observation is a very distinctive approach to the study of babies and their families. There has recently been a greatly increased interest in the academic study of infant development. The subtleties of its new research techniques have opened up a fresh basis for dialogue between clinicians and researchers, while in parallel there has emerged the new and important area of Infant Psychiatry. In this context, it seemed timely and worthwhile to publish an account of the Tavistock Clinic child psychotherapists' experience in this field. Three of the editors are members of the now large number of experienced child psychotherapists who have taught Infant Observa-tion over the last twenty years. The fourth is a sociologist with a particular interest in psychoanalysis. The book was first conceived in discussion with Martha Harris, whose exceptional ability to teach this approach to the study of human relationships has deeply influenced all the editors. The book is dedicated to her memory with profound gratitude.

To safeguard the privacy of the families described, the observers who have written the individual case studies are named as contributors but not as authors of particular chapters. One of the observers who was involved in early discussion of the project was Mary Barker. We are grateful to have been given permission to use an early draft of Mary's chapter as the basis for one of the case-studies, following her sad death in 1987.

The work of gathering together and making a book out of the

contributions of many writers has been slow, and we have been enormously helped by the intelligence and patience of those working on the typescript, in particular, Jane Raynor, Diana Bissett and Susan Fitzgerald. Patrick Lefevre helped us with computing problems. Our editor at Duckworth, Deborah Blake, made the final stages of work go smoothly. To all these people, to the families who offered us the privilege of observing their babies' development, and to our own families who have suffered with us we offer grateful thanks.

Introduction
Lisa Miller

This book introduces a wider public to the method of observing infants pioneered in the training of child psychotherapists. The authors draw their knowledge of this method from their acquaintance with the child psychotherapy training at the Tavistock Clinic in London, but infant observation of this kind is being developed not only for training therapists and psychoanalysts but also for enlarging and enriching the work of other professionals such as teachers, doctors and social workers. Moreover, these developments are not confined to London or indeed to England. They are taking place in Birmingham, Leeds, Oxford, Bristol and Edinburgh; in numerous cities in Italy; in France; and in the USA. However, although the method has been found to be capable of ever-widening application, it has its origins in the training of students in psychoanalytic psychotherapy with children. The training in child psychotherapy is rooted in systematic, intensive and concentrated psychoanalytical work with individual children, though the work which a child psychotherapist does in the National Health Service with children, young people and their families is of a broader nature. However, the movement is from the particular to the general – conclusions about development in infancy have been drawn from close, intimate, careful attention to the individual.

The core of this book therefore lies in the descriptions of particular infants. These descriptions are extracted from the series of regular weekly observations recorded after the event by the contributing Tavistock trainees. The cases have been chosen in order to describe a range of babies in differing circumstances. Although all come from families where two parents are present in the household, they vary in their positions in their families, in social class, in ethnic background, and in their attitudes, ideas and preconceptions about child-rearing. The material has been presented in slightly varying ways. In some of the cases distinct themes have been drawn out and illustrated. For example, in the case of Eric we have a graphic account of the turmoil and unheaval attending the early life of a first baby; as Eric's father as well as his mother throws himself into the fray we have an interesting contrast with the case of Oliver whose very different father thrusts himself into a prominent position in relation not only to his son but

1

also to the observer. The case of Suzanne and Kathy, the twins, raises its own questions about the experiences both of having and of being twins. In the case of Harry we watch as he accommodates himself to a mother whose own problems, at first barely perceptible, develop within the relationship to which Harry is making his contribution from the start. In other cases, Steven and Jeffrey for instance, we have accounts with an even tenor, giving us a chance to observe more quietly the way in which these babies grow up to be members of their individual families. Each family has its own flavour, a culture of its own.

In all cases comment is given rather sparingly. Our wish is for the reader not to be over-directed. There must be some sign-posts, and some selection and shaping has taken place. But the reader needs to be free to read the case material without too many preconceptions and without a heavy exegesis. Some may wish to read the case histories first and then turn in a different frame of mind to the three opening chapters. These deal with the use of infant observation in training and teaching, with the theory which lies behind it and with its methodology. While it would be only tantalising not to include these chapters, they still are in a sense subsidiary to the cases. The cases are the primary source. They are the text to be worked upon. They are intended to make an impact in their own right rather than to exemplify theoretical points. Their impact can be amplified and deepened through acquaintance with the theoretical chapters, but it should not be conditioned by them.

There is an analogy between creative reading of the case material and the creative reading of a literary text. The approach of the students who make these observations is similar to the approach of a reader who may have considerable knowledge of an author and his times and considerable acquaintance with literary criticism. But he will leave this lying at the back of his mind while he responds to the work he is reading with the fresh immediacy of direct mental contact. The students have all sorts of background knowledge about babies and varying degrees of acquaintance with theories about them. These are set aside during the acts of observing and recording in favour of allowing the experience to make its own impact. A similar process goes on in the seminars when the group discusses individual observations. Each observation is to be looked at as closely as possible so that it can generate thoughts and ideas, not so that it can exemplify theories. Readers of this book are being asked to do something like this, and to concentrate upon the infants, recalling Freud's observation that his case histories 'read like novels'.

One would not expect to read a novel without its evoking an emotional response. This method of infant observation attempts to take emotion into account. A new concept of the observer is being employed. Conventionally, the observer has tried to be an impartial recorder, putting aside feeling and involvement lest these interfere with the process of noting objective truth. But here the truths which interest us are themselves emotional truths. The observer cannot register or record them without being stirred, and the reader must expect something of the same. Perhaps we owe a debt to Freud here. Freud at first regarded 'the transference' – all the complicated and passionate feelings for the analyst which arise in the patient – as a sheer nuisance. However, rather than pushing this idea away, he seized and embraced it, seeing that the transference (the patient's feelings) and the counter-transference (the feelings aroused in the analyst) could be used in a central way to investigate what was happening in the patient's mind. Here too the observers are investigating mental activity, mental states. Intellectual and social development, the growth of a child's mind, character and relationships are all underpinned by emotional development in relation to the people who take care of it. Emotion holds a cardinal place; it has to be observed and recorded and it will occur in the observer and the reader. It is not a distraction or a contaminant. Correctly grasped, the emotional factor is an indispensable tool to be used in the service of greater understanding.

Direct contact with strong infantile feelings awakens similar emotions in those who make the contact. A lecture on the emotional development of babies prompted a woman in the audience to ask questions. These were based on something in her current experience which suddenly during the lecture had begun to worry her severely. She was thinking of a crying, perhaps neglected baby she could often hear in the flats where she lived. The lecture brought into focus serious questions in her mind. If we start to feel the force of early anxieties and to be aware of the importance of the experiences of infancy in this way, then the critical nature of our adult responsibilities becomes plain. The ideas raised in this book have wide political and social relevance. They add new dimensions to thinking about child care in all its aspects. There is much here not only to enlighten individual workers' understanding but also to feed into the process of making decisions and implementing policies in relation to medicine, the Social Services and education. For example, in cases of child sexual or physical abuse, in questions of adoption and fostering, in all matters of emotional damage or deprivation, it is important to think about ways in which adults can learn to bear to be sensitised to infantile anxiety and pain.

In this book we present observers concentrating in detail on dramas which usually slip away and are forgotten. There is the elegiac note in Jeffrey's experience of his mother's going, the faint feeling of resignation in Steven as something seems to disappear from his experience. There is the conjunction of sensitive tenderness and fearful knocks for Andrew, the turmoil which weaning stirs in Rosa and her parents, the episode of the gorilla mask which frightens Oliver. Freud said ruefully that it was his fate to discover 'what every nursemaid knows'; Melanie Klein was inspired to watch and listen to the detail of small children at play. Here too we are trying to look with an observing eye at an ordinary process, at the intensity and complexity in the development of children who are growing up to be more or less like their parents.

The editors felt that it was necessary to make some small adjustments to bring the recorded observations into line with each other so that readers would not be distracted by differences. For instance, the babies' parents are called 'mother and father'. In fact, students name the parents in various ways. They write about them as Mr and Mrs or Mum and Dad or they use the parents' first names. All these choices have significance, and the discussion of the observation in the seminar can bring out illuminating shades of meaning even in details like this. However, we hope that not too much subtlety has been lost in the interest of homogeneity, since alterations have been slight.

Part One
Theory and Method

1

Encountering Primitive Anxieties
Margaret Rustin

The practice of systematic observation of the development of infants provides the observer with an opportunity to encounter primitive emotional states in the infant and his family, and indeed in the observer's own response to this turbulent environment. The place that this experience can take in preparing potential therapists for clinical work is the focus of this chapter.

In order to establish the framework, I shall first describe the place of infant observation in the training courses for child psychotherapists. This particular technique of studying babies was pioneered by the child analyst, Esther Bick, in the post-war period when a specific training for child psychotherapists was under development. Students are asked to make an arrangement to visit a family on a regular weekly basis at a fixed time for an hour, and to record afterwards, in as much detail as possible, what they have observed. Inferences, speculations, and their own personal reactions usually are not part of the recorded material. Students are members of a small seminar of approximately five observers who meet weekly for 1½ hours with a seminar leader to study the material of the observations. Seminar leaders vary in their approach, but ordinarily the students will take it in turn to present 'their' babies, thus giving each member a full seminar twice a term for discussion of their experiences. Observations and seminars continue for two years.

The task of the seminar is to explore, on the basis of the available evidence, the emotional events between infant and mother and the other members of the family present during observations. There may also be a baby-minder or nanny sharing in the care of the baby and this might be part of what is directly observed. The aim is to describe the development of the relationship between infant and others, including the observer, and to try to understand the unconscious aspects of behaviour and patterns of communication. Over time, a picture emerges which embraces a good deal of knowledge of the characteristic dynamics of family interaction. Aspects of the inner world of the family members which underlie their personalities and relationships become manifest. In particular, the creation of the infant's personality, the interaction between constitutional and temperamental factors in the baby, and the particular strengths and weaknesses of the holding environment can be considered. Most observers feel they gain some real understanding of the observed infant from inside, becoming able not only to empathise with the baby's internal world but also to grasp its shape and structure, and to recognise the pattern of internalised object relationships. Infant observation therefore serves as a splendid introduction to the study of the early development of children, as well as to an understanding of family life. While infant observation is a central part of all the recognised trainings for child psychotherapists, it has also proved very valuable for professional development of other workers in a variety of roles with children.

The powerful rationales for devoting so much training time to this activity could be summarised as learning about early emotional development – that is, about the actual baby – and also learning from one's own response to the observations. In this latter category are the issues of how one finds a place for oneself in the family during visits, one's identification with different members of the family, one's response to anxiety and uncertainty and a large measure of helplessness, and one's exposure to some of one's own personal problems as a consequence of the emotional impact of the observations.

The observations take place in a non-clinical setting, where the observer has a responsibility only to maintain a reliable, non-intrusive, friendly and attentive presence, and this experience offers the student an opportunity to discover a great deal about her potential aptitude and appetite for clinical work. In this sense I would argue that it is an excellent component of a pre-clinical training programme, giving trainee and trainer a good basis for an assessment of suitability for work as a psychotherapist. Where that choice has already been made, the exposure to intense feelings, the impact of feeling oneself drawn into an emotional force-field and struggling to hold one's balance and sense of self, the encounter with the probably unfamiliar confusion and power of infantile emotional life, are especially valuable aspects of infant observation for beginning therapists. These aspects of learning are linked with W.R. Bion's distinction between 'learning about', an intellectual activity, and 'learning from experience', which leads to a kind of knowledge akin to the Biblical sense of 'knowing', being in touch with the core and essence of something or somebody. This is a form of knowledge imbued with emotional depth.

The work done in the seminar is crucial, especially in the gradual revelation to students of the elements of transference and countertransference in the observation situation. For example, students may find themselves treated in unexpected ways from the first exploratory telephone contact with the family onwards. They are encouraged to present themselves as people interested in studying the development of babies in their family setting, and wishing to undertake observation as part of a professional study of child development; reference to anything relating to therapy or mental health is avoided, with the emphasis being placed on the baby's growing relationships, capacities and activities, and the wish to watch the baby in his ordinary setting without any changes in the everyday pattern of family life in consequence of the observer's presence. However, the family's expectation, usually mediated by the mother, can range from viewing the observer as a child-care expert, endowed with all sorts of special knowledge, to treating her as needing to be taught the basic facts of life and in particular the fundamentals of baby-care. The seminar exchange of experience is very helpful in alerting observers to the position in which they are being placed by the family, and to a realisation that this is not solely based on a realistic perception of their capacities, but also on an expectation of them which derives from the inner world-view of the mother. Students are advised not to give more personal information than is absolutely necessary to establish a comfortable position as observer in the family, and are encouraged to interpret the role of observer as a receptive listening one, not blankly passive, rather following the leads of mother, baby and others. Of course, the observer's role develops considerably over time as she becomes increasingly well-known to the family, and there is a lot to work out about the role as the baby becomes able to take the initiative very directly in play and later also in conversation.

It seems useful to distinguish between those anxieties which tend to afflict observers new to their task from anxieties likely to be encountered by the mother and infant in their early weeks together in the post-natal period. These two different sources of anxiety do, however, intersect and reverberate in ways which may make the situation either more or less tolerable, depending on the containing capacities of all those involved.

Let us consider, first, some characteristic concerns of the new observer, and explore their more primitive aspects. Often a whole seminar group can be seized by immense worry about the intrusive potential of the observational setting. Observers are invited into the intimacy of people's homes, not just for a social visit, but to come close to the care of a tiny infant. Watching the feeding, bathing, holding and total responses of a mother to her new infant takes the observer to some of the most vulnerable moments in the lives of them both. Feelings are often not just near the surface, but bursting out. The observer is confronted starkly with the intimacy of mother and baby, often including the attempt to establish breastfeeding, and certainly involving the details of the physical care of the baby. The tiny size of the new-born, the wobbly head, the huge eyes, the tenderness of new skin, are often a shock to the observer, even to one with experience of a baby of her own or in a professional context. The position of observer removes the active role which adults expect to have in the presence of an infant, and this absence leaves a space in which the infant's sensations have a more intense impact. At the same time as potentially becoming deeply identified with the infant's experience, the observer new to this situation will also be drawn into identification with the mother who has the task of getting to know her baby. This task is particularly overwhelming for a first-time mother, but even for experienced mothers is always a new one because of the individuality of each infant.

Observers become very anxious that their watching may invade the privacy of intimate relationships in a damaging way. In the seminar group this anxiety can take the form of considerable criticism of the mode of study, as the group fears it will cohere in an aggressively voyeuristic attitude. The seminar leader has to work at describing the anxieties aroused by looking, helping observers to distinguish between what is being required of them by the task and how they fear this task might be perverted in the interests of, for example, smug judgments about the competence of parents designed to bolster the superiority of the group, sly investigation of the difficult areas of the family's experience without any balancing appreciation of their strengths and pleasures, or excited childish feelings about the physical, and particularly sexual, aspects of the experience.

The context of the observation is one which tends to elicit acting-out unless a great deal of careful thinking takes place, since the observer's own infantile self will be painfully stimulated by the observation of a mother-baby couple. There are many ways in which conflicts are stirred up inside the observer. For example she may, at times, feel herself to be invaded by the feelings of being a rivalrous mother, a neglected sibling, a benevolent grandmother, or an excluded third party. Memories in unconscious feeling of her own experience as a baby, or fears and wishes about herself as a mother, actual or potential, will be aroused. The position of a male observer is a particularly sensitive one in the early days if the mother is breastfeeding, as both mother and observer have to find a way to manage this physical intimacy, which remains unusual in western culture between a woman and a man who is not her partner. In fact, the presence of the husband may be needed to make this tolerable, or the mother may deal with it by arranging the observer's visits to avoid feeding times.

This range of concern arises from the unconscious significance of the use of our eyes, which can be felt to function with benevolence, interest and truthfulness, but which may also be felt to be used as weapons to attack (watching in order to pick holes), to project unpleasant feelings (like the well-known idea of eyes 'green with envy'), to intrude beyond the boundary of what is being offered (like peeking through a key-hole), or to pervert truthful looking by some kind of distortion (like the distorting mirrors of funfairs and waxworks).

Through the practical details of arranging the observation and of managing oneself appropriately in early visits, are revealed all kinds of uncertainty about first steps in a relationship, which can be thought about at length. This experience is a more helpful background when students approach their first clinical case. How to introduce oneself, where to put oneself in a room, when to sit down, whether to take off one's coat, whether to accept a proffered cup of tea, how to respond to the charming, bullying, interfering or needy approach of a young child in the family faced with the arrival of a new baby, how to deal with the arrival of other people during the observation, how to bring it to an end and take one's departure, are all important issues. How much to talk, how to deal with personal questions, and, in general, how to find and maintain a relationship which is something in-between the personal and the professional, are also recurrent and crucial items for the seminar. The experience of working out one's own personal solution and of living with or trying to shift the imperfections of one's solution can be quite a painful challenge.

For example, one observer found herself on her very first visit asked to take care of the baby while the mother ran out on some urgent errands. She felt caught in a dilemma. On the one hand, she wanted to respond to the desperation of a new mother, who could not see how she could combine sensitive care of her baby ('he'll wake up if I move him') with her domestic responsibilities, but on the other hand, she wanted to establish the parameters of the observational setting as one in which she could be with both mother and baby. How could she get across her interest in the relationship without seeming precious or odd, and without leaving the mother feeling unhelped and resentful? (Another quandary is that most mothers find it very hard to understand that an observer could be interested in a sleeping infant. Either they tend to assume that the observer should be entertained by conversation if the baby is asleep, or they incredulously leave the observer to take charge of the sleeping baby, expecting to be alerted when he stirs.) There is a difficulty in resisting becoming a baby-sitter once it has happened, and the observer had to struggle for months afterwards ever to see mother and baby together. This poorly supported mother felt she had found a reliable person who would help her out in this way, but at another level the mother felt that she had confirmed her belief that the observer came to see the baby, not her, and that she herself was not worthy of serious interest.

This example draws attention to a difficult aspect of the observer's task: how to respond adequately to the mother as an adult, while bearing in mind that at an infantile level she will respond on quite a different basis. The relatively common experience of observers finding themselves expected to function as baby-sitters reflects in part the pressured and inadequately socially supported lives of many mothers. It may also reflect important issues for the mother such as her underlying self-devaluation, her difficulty in being with her infant at all, or her hostility to the baby.

Another observer faced a similar situation when, on several occasions, she arrived at the appointed time to find the mother out, sometimes with a note on the door for her, indicating that the baby was in the house alone and that the mother would return shortly. On one occasion, this observer had to wait at the door hearing a very distressed baby inside, but unable to do anything until the mother returned. This sort of event raises acute anxieties in the observer about the level of distress or risk to which the infant may be exposed, and careful thinking about responsibility is then required. In the particular observation just mentioned, these early indications of the mother's difficulties in taking appropriate responsibility were accentuated further when the baby became mobile and was left in circumstances where obvious dangers were not being monitored by the mother. The observer had to sort out what intervention would be most helpful – to fill in for the mother's neglect, to try to find ways of alerting the mother to her problem without exacerbating the situation, and to consider the implications of the mother's need for more help and support as a prerequisite for improvement in the care of the baby.

In extreme cases, where there is apparent evidence of serious neglect, of abusive behaviour or of sexual abuse, seminar groups may find themselves discussing how the observer should tackle circumstances where the presence of an external agency with statutory responsibilities for the care of children seems required. More common are borderline circumstances where the observer is not in a position to know whether the dangerous behaviour is taking place in the knowledge of the observer's presence as a safety factor, and is to be understood as a communication about the mother's areas of vulnerability, or whether it continues at other times, placing the baby at actual risk. Very careful detailed observation of sequences can help to clarify these issues, but it will be evident that an observer visiting weekly may have to sustain considerable anxiety over a lengthy period. These extreme cases highlight the uncertainties of the observer's position. She is a visitor to the family, and it can be very painful to bear the tension between behaving, on the one hand, as a social worker or policeman and not as an invited observer, and on the other hand betraying the best interests of child or parent through cowardice, confusion or unthinking collusion. When the abuse of children is defined as including emotional abuse, the number of family settings with abusive aspects can become alarmingly large. The seminar takes on a crucial role of holding the observer's anxieties so as to allow for space in which the overall pattern of events can be thought about, and to represent the importance of reflection over time and thus diminish the anxious observer's impulse to take premature action one way or another. Occasionally, however, intervention may need to take place, and observers also find themselves viewed as people who can be asked how to get help of different sorts.

There is one area of negotiation between observer and family which provides an opportunity for thinking about response to changes and discontinuities, and which serves to provide future therapists with usually unforgettable evidence of the powerful unconscious rever-berations of apparently ordinary and reasonable matters. The rationale behind making a regular time for visiting the family is not based on an attempt to simulate clinical conditions, but rather on the need to behave in a considerate and thought-through way. It acknowledges the impact of an outside visitor on a family's life, and the family's need for prior knowledge of arrival, as well as the observer's need for a proper framework for the discipline of close observation. The regularity of visits does, however, tend to make the observation a focus for transference and countertransference reactions akin to those elicited in a clinical setting. This fact can come into sharp relief when there is a need to rearrange the time of the visit, and working out such a change can be very tricky.

One observer, for example, when faced with a request to change the time of her own analytic session, asked the mother for a shift from a late afternoon to an early morning time without allowing any weeks to sort things out. While this was not in fact inconvenient for the mother, and perhaps even had certain advantages for her, the precipitate request, while agreed to on the surface, led to confusion and a series of cancellations. In the ensuing muddle the observer was sometimes stranded on the doorstep, or found herself confronting the mother in a dressing gown, looking unprepared and bewildered. It seemed clear that the observer had passed on her own upset about the change of her analytic hour to the mother and baby in the way she had handled her request, by projecting some of her own unacknowledged feelings.

While the observer was able to re-establish a regular rhythm of visits after this considerable hiccup, there was evidence later to suggest that the painfulness of the situation had not been adequately resolved. This family was to move to a new flat, which was not in fact far away, but the mother made it clear that she did not wish the observation to be continued in their new home. This was despite the fact that the little girl (now sixteen months) very clearly enjoyed the observer's visits, and that the mother herself had a considerable attachment to the observer and enjoyed talking over her daughter's development. This family's move was at the time of the approaching summer holiday break, and it seems likely that the mother was determined that this time she would be the one to control the setting and inflict the shocks. The observer had to register how very painful it was to lose an established relationship which she had expected to continue for some time. She was also, of course, faced with pondering what part she had played in undermining the viability of the observation by her earlier actions. Unlike in the clinical setting, she had no possibility of recourse to interpretive comment about infantile reactions to changes, separations and loss, which might have enabled some working-out to take place, but instead she had simply to swallow the rejection, blame and guilt.

On a smaller scale, observers have to prepare carefully for holiday breaks in visiting, to take opportunities for several reminders, and also to note the upset which so often greets their return. Post-holiday visits are the ones where the observer finds herself met by a note of cancellation on the door, by a baby who fails to recognise her or turns away or seems cross, or a mother who is out-of-sorts or distant. Living through the time it takes to recover from separations when there is a real baby involved whose face registers puzzlement, hurt, anger, rediscovery and forgiveness, is a tremendously powerful lesson.

I shall now present some unprocessed observational material brought to an infant observation seminar, which I think illustrates well some of the primitive anxieties and defences characteristic of the early weeks and months of the mother-infant dyad's life together. I shall then comment on some aspects of the interaction and on the function of the observer in the family. Finally, I shall return to the question of what the observer may learn from this experience.

Observation of Michael, aged 5 weeks

The setting

Michael is the first baby of a young working-class couple (20 and 23 years old), married for a couple of years, living in a working-class suburb of London. They had decided to buy a new house, and this meant that while waiting for it to become available they arranged to move in with the mother's parents. Thus the last part of the pregnancy and the first weeks of Michael's life were spent in the mother's family home. The observer had visited the couple before the birth to discuss the possibility of regular weekly observations, to which they agreed. She saw the mother and baby very briefly in the hospital where Michael was born, and then at more length at home when he was ten days old. This is the fourth regular observation. The father's work is in servicing electrical equipment; the mother had worked as a clerk in the office of a large local hospital. Both grandparents are at work.

*Observation**

The mother let me in, smiling. 'All the action was last night,' she said, 'he's asleep now.' And in fact Michael was in his pram by the front door, the first time he's been in this. He was lying on his front, head to one side, moving his legs under the blanket. Mother asked me to sit down and immediately started to tell me that Michael had been awake until 2 a.m. that morning and had woken again at 5 a.m. 'I could murder him,' she said. 'He seems to be awake all night and asleep all day.' It was actually quite difficult to talk because the TV was on loudly, and she got up to turn it down a fraction. 'It's all Dad's fault,' she said. 'He picks him up and starts rocking him as soon as he cries, and he's got used to it.'

She went on to say that it was difficult at night-time when Michael was awake – she tended to doze off as she was feeding him. He needs feeding every two hours or so – 'Well, at least,' she corrected herself, 'it seems to be like that. At night he can go for six hours or so. The time seems to pass so quickly – feeding him takes half an hour, and in an hour and a half it's time to feed him again.' Someone she worked with was a health visitor, and she had said you could get drugs to help babies sleep. She supposed this wasn't a very good idea. I commented on how tired she must get, and she agreed, saying that she felt very tied to Michael. On Friday evening she had gone out to a friend's who was giving a make-up party, and she had only been able to go out for two hours.

At this point there was a ring at the doorbell ... And I then noticed that father was looking through the window. Mother said 'Oh' in some surprise, and went to let him in. He came in and said 'Hello,' and looked at Michael. 'He's asleep,' he said. Mother shushed him warningly and he said, 'Oh, I give up.' This seemed to be to do with mother's feeling that he might disturb Michael and that he would not do the right thing in relation to the baby. Father gave his wife some papers to sign concerning their new mortgage. 'Here you are, sign your life away,' he joked. Mother signed, and asked him how much the repayment would be. He replied and then mother asked if he could stay. He said no, he had to get back, and went out saying goodbye in a friendly way.

Michael stirred and whimpered at this point, and his mother checked to see if he was asleep. He settled down again and there was a short silence. Mother looked tired, then seemed to rouse herself and said that her husband and his father were starting a new business (some details of this followed) ... she then said ruefully that she and

*I should like to thank Liv Darling for her generous permission to use material drawn from her work as an observer for the purposes of writing this chapter.

her husband had agreed that during the week she would get up to the baby at nights, and at weekends he would. Now he was working Saturdays and Sundays trying to get the business started, this wasn't happening. Another thing which was upsetting her was the fact that the new house would become theirs on Friday, and that they were not intending to move into it for two weeks so that father could decorate it. 'He's gone off decorating now,' she said, 'and we've got to get carpets for the house from somewhere.' She added that if her husband wasn't going to decorate, they might as well move to the house straightaway.

As if to distract herself from these thoughts, she went and picked Michael up, although he was only just beginning to whimper and still looked very sleepy. She held him up and said, 'He always cries just before he has a feed.' She sat Michael on her knee, waiting to see what would happen. He blinked sleepily, making sucking movements with his lips and tongue, moving the sweater he was wearing towards his mouth with his fists with random movements. Then he put his fist accidentally – or on purpose – to his mouth. His face puckered and he gave a low wail. 'Now what's the matter?' said mother in reproachful tones. 'You can wait longer than this – you've done that before.' She got up, put Michael over her shoulder, and went to change the TV channel. 'You can wait while I change the TV.'

Then she fetched a towel and settled herself down with Michael. He had stopped crying when she got up, and connected with her breast hungrily when she offered it to him. He sucked busily, limpet-like, for several minutes. Mother gazed at him in silence for a while and then said it was lucky they had a video – TV stopped at 12 o'clock, and then there was nothing. With the video, she could watch TV at night, and during the day she could watch children's TV. I said it must be quite different now that everyone was out at work (in contrast to the Christmas holiday period). She agreed and said it was nice when they all got home, because they all wanted to hold Michael and she could have her bath, and go to her room and shut the door. The place got into such a chaotic state and needed to be tidied up – this morning she had taken Michael out for a walk in the pram because he'd been crying and had simply left everything, dirty nappies and all, on the floor. Sometimes the breakfast things needed to be washed up too. There was another short silence and she watched the TV. The children's programme had given way to an old film, set in Vienna; a glamorous young girl was being courted by an American musician. They got married and the heroine said, 'What I want is a baby.' Mother did not react, staring in rather a glazed fashion at the screen. Then she roused herself again, sat Michael on her knee and started patting his back. His head lolled to one side, and he dozed. She put him on her shoulder and he hiccoughed. Putting him back on her legs, she said, 'We'll change you in a minute. So do you want more?' She decided to put him back to the breast and he sucked eagerly. She said Michael sleeps very well in the car. A couple of nights ago, father had suggested taking him out in the car when he couldn't sleep – but she didn't want to get dressed herself, and get Michael dressed, to go out into the cold. Even if he did go to sleep, he would wake again when it was time to undress him. One day when he had been crying in the daytime she had simply gone upstairs and left him for a while. When she came back down again he was still crying.

She decided to change Michael's nappy. She laid him on a mat on the coffee table and undressed him. 'If you're good, we'll let you kick for a little while,' she said. She took off his leggings and nappy and proceeded to wash him. He had been gurgling and breathing heavily, and now quietened down. 'He likes this bit,' she said. Michael regurgitated a bit of his feed. As she was wiping his face, he produced a pool of yellow coloured goo from his bottom. 'That's it,' she said, 'get both ends going at once.' She was somewhat testy about this but she carefully lifted his heels clear of the mess on the mat. Then she saw that his vest had got dirty too, so she wiped him clean and took it off. 'It's your fault,' she said, as she lifted the vest over his head while Michael protested.

Once Michael was cleaned up, there was a contented moment. Mother cooed at him and tried to get him to give her a smile. Michael looked intently at her and waved his arms and legs. 'He only smiles at 4 in the morning,' she said.

It was time for the observation to end – I asked mother if this time was all right for her. She said it was fine, except for next week when a different time would be better. She was going to have a coil fitted, and the last time this had been done she had passed out. 'I ought to have an epidural,' she said. We arranged a different time. She accompanied me to the door with Michael in her arms. 'Say bye-bye,' she said. He did not respond, and she laughed and said, 'He's not interested.'

Commentary on observation of Michael

We see here a rather depressed and overwhelmed young woman. She complains about her father (who she feels spoils the baby), about her husband (who is not helping her at nights and who has gone off on a business project of his own in preference to getting their new home ready), and about the baby (who is wearing her out by his demands and who, she feels, cannot wait). She seems to see herself and the baby as in competition for satisfaction (her TV or his feed, her sleep or his night-life). Her own mother is strikingly absent from her conversation, and she seems to feel herself as an uncared-for little girl who has lost touch with an internal image of a loving mother who could support her in caring for her own baby.

The reliance on the TV might be viewed as an attempt to fill herself up with some sense of life, and hold at bay feelings of fragility and emptiness, and also to allay anxieties about being filled with murderous hatred of the baby. She is quite conscious of her hostile feelings and is able to share very straightforwardly with the observer her sense of being under pressure. The problem of the new baby as a rival for attention is particularly striking. The transition has been one from being the favourite daughter, perhaps still viewed somewhat as a child, rather than as an independent adult, to feeling displaced in her parents' affections by the baby, the idolised grandchild. She is touchy about her husband's interest in the baby too, possibly for the same reasons. I would speculate that the return to the parental home for the birth of the first baby might signal that it is linked for the mother with a previous painful loss of a secure position in the family, such as occurs when a younger sibling is born. (At this stage of the observation, we did not know whether she in fact had siblings, but this was later confirmed.)

Under the impact of all these disturbing feelings, she turns to pick up Michael as if to comfort herself, a baby to hold onto and thus restore some better feelings about herself as a mother. She is more pushed by her own needs than by responding to Michael's at this point. Later, when changing his nappy, she is feeling persecuted by the baby's mess and is inclined to blame him for all the discomfort involved for him in having his clothes changed and for the work it entails for her.

Michael, meanwhile, seems to be in touch with his own feelings. He sucks strongly on the breast, having communicated effectively to his mother that he wants to be fed. Everything is pulled towards his mouth during the few minutes in which he is waking up, and his focus is clearly located in his oral sensations. When he gets his fist in his mouth, he seems to wake up to a realisation that there is a difference between the imaginary, perhaps dream-like satisfactions of mouthing, and the desire for real food and a real nipple to latch onto. The experience of being held and suckled serves to gather him together and provide coherence, concentrated attention, an integrative response to the baby's search for food and connectedness. The observer notes the contrast between the sleepy, seemingly random movements and the intent calm of Michael feeding. It is while watching him nursing that the mother talks about her need for the TV, as if unconsciously perceiving that as Michael gains focus from her holding and feeding him, so the anxious, distressed and uncertain part of herself is calmed and quietened by feeling held in relation to something else, and in that way protected from potentially overwhelming feelings of chaos and disintegration, which she refers to in describing the disturbing physical muddle to which the room can be reduced.

The observer felt sympathy both for Michael, whose mother is not able easily to be receptive to his needs and feelings, and for the mother, who is struggling with many confusing primitive feelings and out of touch with either internal or external sources of support. One could add that the observer's visit seems to be of some comfort to this mother, relieving her sense of loneliness and isolation. The observer herself experienced the pressure of the mother's need for attention, which made it difficult for her to see as much of the detail of Michael's behaviour as she would have wished.

Discussion

This particular observation illustrates the depressed mood of the post-puerperal period which is so commonly noted – the revived infantile element in the mother's state of mind – and also highlights some of the primitive anxieties shared by mother and baby. The mother feels threatened by the merging of day and night in the care of a young baby, by the chaos and overflowing mess which may be beyond her capacities to contain, and by the demandingness of the baby, which takes away from her the shape of her previous life and turns her into a feeding machine. Her anger and hostility to Michael and her husband and father serve to hold her together and prevent her from falling to pieces. Michael's anxiety about bodily integrity underlies his distressed response to being undressed and changed, but his experience of being pulled together by the feeding is palpable. There are also tiny hints in this narrative of his considerable resilience, and of his mother's happy responsiveness to signs of his strength, which were to become marked features of their development together.

The observer arrived at the seminar rather shattered by the observation experience since the impact of the mother's anger and sense of persecution, particularly when directed at Michael, was difficult to bear. At the same time, she felt amazed by the undefended directness of the communication to her, for example when the mother's feelings about the baby's voracious hunger were expressed through cannibalistic jokes, and the open hostilities in the household featured in talk about the coffins in the cellar. But the really difficult thing for the observer was to see Michael's vulnerability exploited or ignored at times, and to see the degree of the mother's upset. She felt violently pulled in opposite directions, wanting to help and comfort each, but able to see that the unconscious competition for care and attention was a crucial factor on the mother's side, making it hard for others in the family to intervene helpfully. One hour's observation made her feel exhausted – taking some of the brunt of the mother's exhausted state – invaded by contradictory feelings, and stirred by the strength of the life-impulses manifested in Michael.

The impact of these primitive states of mind can, of course, be painfully disturbing to observers. While the seminar provides considerable containment, as does the discipline of writing up notes which calls on the working capacities of the adult part of the observer, some observers do feel severely shaken and come to want the personal analytic help that is a necessary precursor to undertaking clinical work.

Conclusion

Some of the ways in which observation helps to prepare trainees for clinical practice have been noted along the way, but I shall conclude by briefly drawing these points together. Attention has to be paid to the setting, the constancy of timekeeping, the regularity of visits, and the disturbance consequent on changes in the rhythm, including holiday breaks. Distinctions can be made between transference elements elicited by the non-judgmental attentive atmosphere of the observation, and countertransference features. These latter include both the intrusion of the observer's personal unconscious responses (the classical use of the concept of countertransference), but also the exploration of those elements in the observer's feeling-state which seem to be determined by registering projections from family members (the sense of countertransference in current use).

When the feelings involved are often very powerful, and probably communicated on a pre-verbal basis, the work on transference and countertransference is fundamental, and is connected with another valuable aspect of studying infants, namely, the sensitivity to infant modes of communication which can develop. Students can learn to perceive normal projective identification, to understand some of the body language of infants, and to struggle towards a language for describing pre-linguistic experiences which will serve them well in work with patients if the infantile transference is to be tackled. All these features can prove particularly helpful in work with silent patients, where tiny physical shifts may be a major source of evidence as to what is going on, and also in work with psychosomatic patients, as well as more obviously in work with very young children.

The most valuable lessons, however, concern the creation of a psychoanalytic attitude. This needs to include the scientific component of hypothesis formation which can be tested by observation over time. A two-year infant observation serves as an admirable introduction to this aspect of the task. Also vital is a developed sensitivity to emotion which allows feelings to be recognised by a reflective part of the mind. W.R. Bion wrote of the mother's state of reverie in relation to her infant's primitive emotional communications, and something similar is needed both to be a good observer and to become a good clinician. This requires a space in the mind where thoughts can begin to take shape and where confused experiences can be held in an inchoate form until their meaning becomes clearer. This kind of mental functioning requires a capacity to tolerate anxiety, uncertainty, discomfort, helplessness, a sense of bombardment. It is the personal equipment needed by a psychoanalytic psychotherapist.

2

Psychoanalytic Theory
and Infant Development

Judy Shuttleworth

Introduction

The experience of psychoanalytic clinical work with adults has long supported the conviction that adult patients' current ways of functioning have a complex history dating back to early childhood and indeed to infancy. This gave rise to an interest among psychoanalysts in early development. This interest was at first pursued mainly through clinical work with adults and children, but from the beginning there has also been an interest in directly observing childhood and infancy unfolding in its natural setting in order to study early modes of mental functioning and the quality of infantile experiences (Freud 1909, 1920; Klein 1921, 1952a; Winnicott 1941).[1]* In 1948 Esther Bick,[2] with the support of John Bowlby,[3] established Infant Observation as a central part of the training of child psychotherapists at the Tavistock Clinic (Bick 1964).

This chapter gives an outline of one particular psychoanalytic model of mental and emotional development rather than covering the full range of psychoanalytic theories of development. It is a model which derives centrally, though not exclusively, from the work of Klein, Winnicott, Bick and Bion. This account does not give separate descriptions of their work or explore the differences between their positions. Rather, it seeks to outline the view of infant development which has been derived from their work and which is, broadly speaking, part of a shared tradition of thought among those teaching on the Tavistock Clinic Psycho-analytic Observation course.[4] We have tried to give a description of the relevant psychoanalytic ideas in a form which would be useful to readers who are unfamiliar with this approach. At various points, chiefly in the footnotes, we have related this model to some of the issues currently being debated within developmental psychology.[5] (Students attend a separate course reviewing the academic literature on child development.)

Psychoanalytic theory has arisen gradually. It is not an unchanging body of dogma, nor is it a homogeneous entity; rather, it is made up of a

* The notes to this chapter are on pp. 201-11.

number of different and developing strands of related ideas about the
nature of human personality, generated chiefly in response to the
demands of clinical work. Different theoretical concepts have grown or
receded in importance not through refutation or confirmation but as
elements in a continuing train of thought. The model described here is
one that has arisen within the British object relations tradition over the
last fifty years,[6] stemming originally from the work of Klein and her
immediate group of fellow analysts.[7] Research in infant development
during the last fifteen years seems to have produced findings which are
largely consonant with this model.

It may be helpful briefly to set the theoretical preoccupations of this
book within a historical context (since this is not the way in which the
chapter is organised). There are two distinct, and often contradictory,
strands of thought to be found in Freud's work. Over time, Freud's
mechanistic model of emotional life, derived from modes of thought
prevailing in the nineteenth century (for example, that of an organism
dealing with different quantities of excitation), became interwoven
with, but was never wholly superseded by, more *psychological* formulations. These were principally concerned with the relationship
between instinctual life and the capacity for contact with reality and
rational thought (Freud 1911) and with the role of childhood sexuality
and the relationship to the parents in the formation of an adult capacity
for emotion. His focus was on the formation within the child's mind of
representations of this intimate relationship and the feelings it generated (Freud 1909). Subsequently Abraham (1924), Klein (1928), Fairbairn (1952) and Winnicott (1945) among others took this strand of
Freud's work and developed it as a theory of 'object relations'. In doing so
they looked at the earliest relationships of infancy and the processes
these set up within the developing mind. This model of the mind had
ceased to be one in which the past *caused* the present and had become
one in which experience accumulates and develops within the individual, affecting the present in complicated and indirect ways. The
model had become one in which the *phenomenology* of the mind – the
mind's experience of itself and the world – had become the centre of
interest. This line of development was taken further in the work of
Winnicott (1949), Bick (1968) and Bion (1962a) in their attempts to find
ways of describing how the mind first develops the capacity to
experience bodily and emotional states and, from this base, a mental
apparatus for thinking thoughts and generating meanings.[8]

The different states of being in the newborn

In Klein's model of development, the newborn infant's complex
instinctual equipment led *both* to the development of a primitive
mental world within the infant and to a contact with external reality

(Isaacs 1952).[9] We will consider the 'internal world' below and concentrate first on the infant's contact with external reality. Klein writes in 'On Observing the Behaviour of Young Infants':

> I have seen babies as young as three weeks interrupt their sucking for a short time to play with the mother's breast or look towards her face. I have also observed that young infants – even as early as in the second month – would, in wakeful periods after feeding, lie on mother's lap, look up at her, listen to her voice and respond to it by their facial expression; it was like a loving conversation between mother and baby. (Klein 1952a, p. 96)

Since the early 1970s developmental psychology has demonstrated, through a mass of research, the innate capacities of the newborn and how they add up to an urgent need for, and ways of seeking out and making use of, precisely those aspects of the environment which in ordinary circumstances are most available to the human newborn – namely the various characteristics of a human caretaker. The baby is 'pre-programmed', so to speak, to prefer the human face and voice above other visual and auditory stimuli, to feel comforted by rhythmic rocking and the sound of the mother's heart and the familiar smell of her body as he is held against her. The nipple uniquely meets the needs of the baby both for food and for the physical comfort of rhythmic sucking. Yet the nature of this fit between what the baby is reaching out for and what the mother can provide is not a static phenomenon; it is intrinsically dynamic, providing the basis for a subtle reciprocal interaction between mother and baby which contains within it the potential for increasingly complex exchanges. For instance, in his work on mother and infant interaction Brazelton refers to one aspect of this dynamic interaction when he describes the transformation brought about in the baby by human contact. The baby's movements become smooth and rhythmic, reaching out with circular arm movements. He contrasts this to the state of a baby confronted with a mere object. Here the baby is jerky and uncoordinated, approaching the object with haphazard snatching movements (Brazelton 1975). Such research has increasingly borne out Klein's hypothesis that the infant is (human) object-related from birth.[10]

Despite this increasing convergence, there remains a difference in emphasis between the psychoanalytic approach we are describing and that of developmental psychology. Developmental research in this area has looked, broadly speaking, at the developing *external social relationship* between mother and infant starting from the moment of birth.[11] The psychoanalytic approach being described here has an additional focus of study – namely, what are the beginnings in the neonate of those processes which, in time, will enable the infant to develop *a sense of his own mind*, i.e. an awareness of complex psychological/emotional states in himself and others?

Klein's view was that the meeting of instinctual needs (within the baby) with an external object (aspects of the mother's care) not only results in a physically satisfying experience, an interest in the external world and a rudimentary social relationship to the mother, but also initiates the beginnings of mental development in the infant. Precisely because of the match between the infant's needs and the object's capacities, the external world can be brought within the infant's mental grasp and thought about as well as being available for sensual contact. Klein regarded the 'thirst for knowledge' for its own sake as a driving force in emotional development (Klein 1921). Bion too saw the meeting of a 'preconception' (the infant's innate readiness for certain kinds of experiences) with a 'realisation' (the corresponding external experiences for which the infant is 'seeking') as a crucial moment at the start of mental life (Bion 1962a).[12]

This picture of the neonate has many points of contact with the vivid account of infantile experience in the first two months of life which Stern constructs out of a mass of discrete research findings (Stern 1985). The infant of Stern's model is able to sense pattern and order in the world and in his own body. Stern gives a compelling picture of the excitement of discovery and the pleasure for the infant in experiencing the match between his innate capacity to apprehend the world and the aspects of the world which unfold before him. The infant is inhabiting a world which is coming to meet him and which the infant feels received by, and at home in, presumably because over millions of years his mind has been evolving into a form which can receive these impressions.

While the Kleinian psychoanalytic model, in common with recent developmental psychology, takes the infant to be capable from birth onwards of having experiences in which he feels himself to be integrated and attending to the world around him, particularly to people, it is also a model in which the newborn moves rapidly and unpredictably between different states. He can seem to his parents to be a very different baby, inhabiting a very different world, from one moment to the next. Because of its different method, psychoanalytic observation has not been restricted to studying the infant in the state of 'alert inactivity' which experimental researchers, on the whole, have studied. 'Alert inactivity' is a state in which the infant is peacefully awake but not engaged in feeding or sucking. He is able to attend to the world around him and is therefore able to 'answer' the researcher's 'questions'.[13] Psychoanalytic observation within a natural setting has given attention to the whole range of actual infant behaviour and the transitions between states – alert, fretful, screaming as well as satiated and withdrawing into sleep.[14] Looked at in this way the infant is seen to gain a sense of integration and a capacity to attend and then to lose it, again and again, as his state shifts from moment to moment. This gives a cognitive and emotional dynamic to infantile experience which psychoanalytic theory has sought to address. It is these achievements and losses of a sense of integration which the kind of observations described here attempt to follow.[15]

It is not only the infant who seems more complex when seen in a natural setting rather than solely in 'alert inactivity' but also the parents. Their role in supporting and interpreting the infant's behaviour in attentive receptive states expands to one of attending to him also in his distressed states and in helping him to gather himself together after them. With this comes an interest in the internal mental states of the parents – a gap in developmental research to which Richards (1979, p. 41) draws attention. It is to the role of the parents that we turn next.[16]

The role of the mother[17]

Winnicott and Bion have both been interested in the early relationship of mothers and infants. They both came to view the mother's state of mind, which Winnicott (1956) calls *primary maternal preoccupation,* as closely related to the state of the newborn and as providing what he needs.

Undoubtedly the hormonal upheavals of pregnancy and the post-partum period as well as the experience of the labour itself and (in our society) often of the post-natal ward, all play their part in creating a state of emotional vulnerability in new mothers. But in a large measure, this maternal state of mind seems to arise directly from the actual experience of caring for a newborn infant and the mother's vulnerability takes on a new dimension when it is seen as *an openness to being stirred up emotionally* by the baby. The outcome of this situation is extremely variable both as between different mothers and for any one mother at different times. When things go well the states of mind which the baby seems to engender in the mother become a basis for intense identification with, and sympathy for, the baby. But, on the other hand, these states of mind may sometimes be felt as unbearable and overwhelming for the mother and the baby's presence may then be experienced as a threat to the mother's sense of her own mind and identity. The mother may then seek to withdraw from such intimate contact.[18]

Why should a situation in which mothers are rendered so vulnerable come about? What purpose could it serve, especially as in some cases it seems itself to pose a threat to the mother-infant relationship? Research on mammal behaviour post-partum seems to indicate that the mobilisation in mothers of various instinctual behaviours towards their newborn during this period is vital to the survival of those species

(Klaus & Kennell 1982). Without implying the rigidities of instinctual behaviours and 'critical periods', one might still hypothesise that, as part of the evolution of the human mind, there has developed a set of needs in human newborns which have to do with the conditions necessary for the development of that mental capacity. One might then argue that it is these needs in the baby that are being met through the mobilisation of states of 'primary maternal preoccupation'.

However, while the position of mothers of newborn infants is indeed special, other adults caring for young babies can, and do, experience a similar intense engagement with the baby and with their own baby-like feelings. It was Bion's thesis that the way in which a mother is able to get in contact with her baby's state of mind, and through her attention and support enable the baby to grow psychologically, constitutes a form of relationship in which the mother's mind acts as a container for the baby. He called this relationship *container-contained* and he used it as a model both for thinking about the development of the mind and also as an analogue for other emotional relationships. In Bion's terms, this kind of receptivity to being stirred up emotionally is the basis of our capacity to be responsive in all those occasions throughout life when we are brought into intimate contact with someone else's state of mind.

Yet a benign process in which we are able to sustain the impact of someone else's state of mind, leading to a deep (often unconscious) contact with them, is not the only, or even the most usual, response to this kind of emotional experience. There is something inherently disturbing about such a contact. This renders us prone to seek ways of avoiding the emotional impact and disrupts the capacity for containment. The 'container' may then itself be in need of containment. The observer often becomes the 'container' for some aspect of the mother's experience during the observations and may be disturbed by the process. The seminar group, when functioning well, may then act as a 'container' for the observer's experiences and help to develop and maintain the observer's capacity to attend as fully as possible to the infant and his parents during the observation visits.

Winnicott stressed the particular needs of the very young infant, as against the sort of relationship which the older baby requires, and he stressed the unique capacity of the mother to experience the required degree of emotional vulnerability. In terms of Bion's ideas, the infant's need for this particular sort of adult emotional receptivity continues for a far greater length of time. Even by the second half of the first year, when, as we shall discuss later, various psychological milestones have been reached, the baby will continue to have periods of greater fragility. The recurrent need for a more infantile relationship to his parents and other adults continues in varying degrees as the child grows up.[19] Indeed, it follows that the need for someone else to perform externally, albeit temporarily, the function of a mental container for unsettling feelings is a situation which can recur throughout adult life.

The mother as a container[20]

In Bion's model, the states of mind which are stirred up in the mother by caring for her baby – a sense of falling apart, for instance – are seen as related to experiences which belong to the baby but which the baby himself is unable to experience, having as yet no mental structure which would allow this.[21] An example might be the baby's acute distress on being undressed or held in an unfamiliar way and the feelings of uncertainty or fragility which the baby may then evoke in the mother. Her response to this may be a more tender concern for her baby's vulnerable state or it may be an urgent need to switch off from the baby and press on mechanically with the undressing and bathing lest this too intimate contact and too clear a glimpse of distress overwhelm them both.

Where there is a real imbalance (whether temporary or more long-lasting) between the mother's capacity to cope and what she has to cope with, a situation arises in which, to defend her own mental state, the mother inevitably seeks to rid herself of her mental discomfort, with the baby felt as the source of, and acting as the receptacle for, the discomfort. In ordinary parlance, the mother 'takes it out on the baby'.[22] A common example of this sort of situation would be where the mother feels overwhelmed by the baby's apparently insatiable need to be held and, unable to keep the actual baby and his point of view – his possible feelings of fragility – separate in her mind from the effects he is having on her, she comes to attribute to him a deliberate wish to tyrannise and exploit her. This may be talked about as if the baby were waging a well-thought-out campaign which she feels she must not 'give in to'. A difficult situation is thus made far worse by the picture she now has of her baby and the spirit in which she seeks to limit his demands. Yet close to the surface may be a sense of panic, which is not recognised as such, stemming from the conviction that the baby's needs, if she attends to them at all, will fill her up completely. One might say that only in so far as the mother can register and digest her own experience will she be able to contain her feelings *as* feelings and not translate them into retributive action.

Where the mother is more able to bear the pain of the original predicament, in this case that of having a clinging unsatisfied baby, then a potentially different situation is set in train. The mother's mental processes enable her to digest what is happening to her (though not necessarily consciously) in a way which strengthens her sense of herself and enables her to offer the baby the comfort of that strength as manifested in her care of him. His mother's solidity in the face of his experience of falling apart seems to be the source of that rudimentary trust in himself and his surroundings which allows the baby to relinquish his mother's external presence and enables him to begin to turn instead to internalised images of her.

The model of 'container-contained' allows us to picture the emotional relationship between mother and baby in a complex and dynamic way and to specify some of the factors in the relationship. A mother's capacity for containment seems to be dependent on at least four conditions. (These have been listed in an order moving outwards from the baby rather than in such a way as to imply a hierarchy of importance).

(i) The existence of a capacity in the baby to arouse feelings in the mother. Much work has been done on the infant's instinctual equipment for locating and fixing on to his mother. It is difficult for mothers to feel close to infants where these impulses have been affected by medication in labour or prematurity or by medical conditions in the infants (Trowell 1982). There are also temperamental differences in babies such as passivity or irritability, which complicate their ability to seek and find the nipple or comforting holding. Such babies can be helped towards a more satisfying engagement with the world but more effort and imagination seems required (Middleton 1941). The degree of 'fit' between mother and baby seems to have something to do with the mother's capacity to cope with the particular constellation of feelings evoked by a particular baby.

(ii) The mother needs a sufficiently strong yet flexible sense of adult identity to enable her to experience the sorts of feelings which the care of the newborn infant arouses without feeling endangered by them.[23] With his sometimes extreme vulnerability to external stimuli; his capacity for relating only to parts of his mother's care at any one time rather than to the mother as a whole person; with the intensity and fragility of his contact with these parts of his mother and the tendency for his attention to fragment in discomfort, the baby seems to be prey to states of feeling which are inherently uncomfortable. Much of our mental development and the arrangement of our external lives as we grow up can be seen as attempts to protect ourselves from the possibility of re-experiencing these infantile states. Artists, such as Samuel Beckett, who deal with these primitive aspects of emotional life, tend to get an understandably cautious reception. Yet these are the sorts of emotional experiences which touch so acutely those caring for newborn infants and which can easily make them feel threatened. The experience of parenthood changes as infancy and childhood progress and each stage makes its own demands. Yet what may single out the first stage as particularly stressful is the imagination and resourcefulness required to relate to an infant who is not yet able to relate to a whole person.[24]

(iii) It follows from this that a third condition for the kind of receptive, maternal contact with the baby which we are describing is the existence of sufficient external supports in the shape of partner, family and friends. Through these relationships the mother's sense of her adult identity, and her sense of her adequacy as a container, can be nourished and strengthened. Anxiety and distress which is beyond the mother's capacity to contain can be communicated to others for them to deal with. At times the mother requires other adults to perform for her a similar containing function to that which she performs for the baby.

(iv) There is a limit to the number of other demands (e.g. domestic and financial) which can be borne without reducing to a critical extent the amount of physical energy and mental space available to the baby.

Where the mother has sufficient external support and internal resources, caring for her baby holds many joys and the disturbing experiences she has in the course of caring for the baby contribute to getting to know both the baby and herself rather than being solely a source of persecution. This benign situation within the mother's mind seems to affect her treatment of the baby in at least three ways.

(i) Because of her awareness of the baby's potential distress, the mother is likely to take care in her handling of the baby to minimise sensations which are overwhelming to him.

(ii) When the baby is distressed, she is more likely to be able to keep him in mind and/or in physical contact, rather than to have to turn a deaf ear. This continuity of mental attention is likely to result, for example, in her being more receptive after separations.[25]

(iii) Her experience of the baby's use of her as a receptacle for distress and the conviction this gives rise to that she can understand her baby and that, in so doing, she is performing a vital function for him, seem in turn to strengthen the mother's instinctual capacity to protect her baby from her own anxiety, confusion and panic and allow the baby's needs to take precedence, at least temporarily.

Thus the model is one of a baby undergoing constantly changing psychosomatic states which continuously affect his sense of being more-or-less gathered together/more-or-less fragmented. These changing states continuously affect his capacity to focus on, attend to and be interested in the world around him.[26] Fluctuations in the baby's state stir up corresponding fluctuating cognitive/emotional states within his mother. The mother's capacity to contain and digest what is being stirred up in her is not a static 'given' but varies continuously according to her general personal state at that moment, other moment-to-moment impingements on her, and the particular impact the baby is having at the time.[27] These things, taken together with the underlying factors concerning mother, baby and the environment referred to earlier, make for a constantly shifting, subtle pattern in the flow of cognitive/emotional interaction. It is this level of interaction which seems to hold one of the keys to understanding the nature of the impact of early relationships and it is this level of interaction which Infant Observation is trying to follow and describe.

The infant's experience of containment

We now turn to the outcome within the baby of this kind of experience of maternal attention and sensitivity. We will assume, as Klein did, that the infant is capable of making contact with the external world and registering experience in the mind. The mother's capacity to respond to her baby's experience seems to be felt by the baby at first as a gathering together of his bodily sensations, engendering the beginnings of a sense of bodily integrity.

Winnicott (1960a; 1960b) describes the impact on the baby of the mother's early 'holding' which, if the dimension of time is added, gives the baby an experience of 'continuity of being'. He describes a process of passive integration within the infant ('containment' in Bion's terms), which is made possible by the mother's active adaptation of the environment so that it meets the baby's needs. He distinguishes this from a situation in which the infant is left more unprotected to experience 'environmental impingements' to which *he* must actively react. Bick (1968) writes of the infant's first psychological need as one of being held together physically and describes how this gives rise within the baby to a sense of having a skin. Where the mother's holding is not available, the infant is left to focus itself on non-human aspects of the environment (for example by staring at a light or a moving curtain). Or the baby may endeavour to hold itself together by using its own sensations of muscular tension. While all three modes of being 'held together' are likely to be experienced or invoked by all infants at different times, Bick felt that too great a reliance by the infant on the latter two modes held implications for the development of the infant's sense of self.

If one looks at the whole range and fluctuation in the physical state of the infant (e.g. Dunn 1977; Schaffer & Collis 1986) and his initial inability to regulate his own state, rather than looking solely at the infant in an already achieved state of 'alert inactivity', then the extent of the infant's dependence on his mother becomes apparent.[28] One might broadly characterise the mother's physical impact on the baby as being of two types – holding and focusing. The infant's need for smooth changes of position, for covering, for the firm sensation of mattress or shoulder, and the rhythms of speech and movement are all part of the traditional repertoire of child-care. They seem to calm the infant, creating the smoothness and rhythmic responses described by Brazelton (1975), and give the infant a feeling of being all of a piece within his skin (Bick 1968). But the external world and particularly the human world also has the power not just to lull and soothe the baby but to pull him together into an active focused kind of attention – the mother's eyes and voice have this power to gather the baby into an intensely focused whole, as, most dramatically, does the experience of sucking at the breast or bottle.

These two kinds of containment make their direct impact on the infant largely through physical care, yet the emotional and mental dimension of such physical care is crucial. To soothe a distressed infant involves a complex emotional situation within the mother, which is closely related to the infant's distress and which makes its own impact on him. Similarly, when alert and sociable the infant is engaged, not just by the interesting things that the mother shows him, but by her attentive, receptive mental state when she is with him. The mother's mental qualities make an impact on the baby both indirectly through the effect of her physical care on his psychosomatic state but also directly through the infant's capacity to apprehend emotional states in others.[29] In terms of the theories being described here, the experience of states of being physically held and emotionally contained by the mother not only gives rise to a way of physically experiencing the world which might be conveyed by such terms as 'a sense of bodily integration', 'having a skin' and 'a physical sense of self'; they also bring the baby into intimate, if primitive, contact with mental and emotional processes within the mother. These states within the mother and their impact on him become objects of intense concern and interest to the baby.[30]

This sort of close relationship to the mother provides the setting in which the infant's capacity for mental and emotional experiences can develop. It is argued that in the course of development the sense of being physically gathered together, of having a physical skin, becomes the prototype through which the infant can grasp a sense of a 'mental skin' bounding a 'mental space' within himself. This, in turn, enables him to begin to make sense of his experience of his mother's mind and the communication which takes place between them. The quality of early experience thus has a crucial impact on the beginnings of mental life.

The internalisation of experience

As well as the actual moment-by-moment impact of experiences on the baby, images of experience are being stored in the memory (e.g. MacFarlane 1975) and in the process a world is being created within the baby. The questions raised by this process are three-fold. (i) What is the subjective experience for the infant of this 'taking in'? (ii) What form do these memories take? (iii) What are they the memories of?

(i) The nature of this internal world and the manner of its formation have long been a focus of psychoanalytic investigation. One result of this work has been the hypothesis that the processes of internalisation in infancy have characteristics which distinguish them from later forms of internalisation that are under the aegis of symbolic forms of mental activity. In later life, we have a linguistic and not simply a physical relationship to the world. It seems unlikely that the baby has any such symbolic conception of the relationship of his mental activity to the external world. The implications of this are obviously extremely difficult to assess but, from infant observation and work with patients whose modes of relating to reality are very primitive, it has been hypothesised that when, for example, the baby stores a picture of his mother's face gazing at him, or stores an impression of being cuddled, it is experienced by a baby of under three or four months as a process of actually taking in (introjecting) the perception as if it were itself an object (Isaacs 1952). If this is so, then it lends an important characteristic to early mental life – that of *concreteness* – which distinguishes it radically from later symbolic levels of functioning. This is partly to do with the physical nature of early memory (Stern 1985), but the view described here goes beyond this to say that the 'taking in', 'summoning up' and 'holding in the mind' of these images of physical experience are also concretely-felt processes. Thus the infant feels he contains within himself a world of concrete things of at least as much reality as the material world surrounding him, and his relationships with other people, which can have such an impact on his states of being, seem to him to consist of concrete exchanges.[31]

(ii) What form do these memories/concrete objects in the mind take? There seems a strong case for arguing that early experience must be dominated by (a) the infant's own intense bodily experiences; (b) his perceptions of the external physical world; (c) his rudimentary, but direct, apprehension of his 'human' link to his mother. Memories of experience must somehow encompass all three elements.

(iii) How are these objects in the mind formed? A strong argument exists that they are *just* the images of external reality, no more and no less (Bowlby 1973; Stern 1985). We entirely agree with the view that the infant is in touch with the external world and that the nature of his real encounters with it are of enormous importance.[32] However, when Stern writes that there is no psychodynamic level of experience before language he seems to be suggesting that, before language, the infant cannot make for himself his own subjectively-transformed experience of an external event. This is a position which differs sharply from the one which we are outlining here. We will go on in later sections to outline the Kleinian theory of 'phantasy', operating from the beginning of life in conjunction with the baby's experience of the external world, to create both a human (rather than purely physical) contact with the external world and a world of internal objects.

We hope that in the detailed observations of individual infants which follow, the variety and complexity of the process of internalisation, as well as its content, will become clearer.[33] For the time being we can take the experience of being held together, and the concomitant holding in the mother's mind, as the starting point of this process of internalisation. The baby's dependence on this sort of containment by mother will eventually be replaced by the containment offered by the baby's sense of his own mind. But this development does not come about by a process of physical maturation or, it seems to us, by 'learning to be self-contained', but through repeated opportunities for taking in the experience of being held together by someone else and being kept in *their* mind. Through this process, which as a concretely experienced phantasy Klein called *introjection*, the infant comes to feel the 'containing mother' as a definite presence within him. He is now sometimes able to summon up, in his mother's absence, resources which originated in his contact with her. An external, visible aspect of this process of internalisation has been given wide currency through Winnicott's concept of a transitional object (Winnicott 1951) and the use which the infant may make of a familiar physical object during his mother's absence. However, Winnicott makes it clear that he means this external relationship to a transitional object to be seen as dependent on, and arising out of, the child's relationship to his internalised mother. Later this process within the infant is taken further as he comes to feel *identified* with his 'containing mother', in the sense that this experience becomes a part of himself, part of the hidden internal structure of his personality.[34] At this point, one might say that he has become self-contained and self-confident. The different, characteristic emotional styles of different individuals, and the continuities in this style over time (Dunn & Richards 1977; Dunn 1979) may be seen as arising in part from the different emotional qualities of early relationships which have been internalised and which have become embedded in the self.[35]

Dealing with distress and the development of concrete communication

Understandably, most of the research on mother-baby interaction has focused on the nature of the good experiences which the mother provides for the baby and the ways in which the baby is equipped to elicit these experiences and make use of them. Yet distress is a crucial experience in infancy and one which can by no means be avoided, nor one which necessarily militates against an intimate and creative contact between mother and baby.

What is the emotional quality of the internal representations which the baby is forming? They might, in a state of 'alert inactivity', be envisaged as benign, or at any rate neutral objects, which can be held in the mind. Yet this is not the baby's only state. What happens when the baby is distressed? What happens to the representations of 'bad' experiences – a loud noise, the feed that does not come, stomach aches, an upset or shut-off look on the mother's face? As Hinde (1982) points out, a degree of conflict is inherent in mother-infant relationships.

One characteristic of these 'bad' experiences is that they can arise even in the midst of what would appear to be a 'good' environmental situation and apparently destroy the baby's capacity to use the holding or feeding which is being offered. Thus a common experience for parents of a screaming baby is to feel that, though they are available, the baby is in the grip of a state of mind in which they have become transformed into, or become obscured by, whatever is distressing the baby. Another related aspect of these bad experiences is that the infant seems at first unable to apprehend them and attend to them as experiences in the way that he is able to do with pleasurable or more neutral events. It is only when a more robust and enduring sense of connectedness to his good, strengthening experiences has developed that the baby will be able to maintain his sense of himself and so begin to be able to tolerate and make a more coherent cognitive contact with distress.

Bion felt that an infant who was overwhelmed by distress was in a state which could not of itself become a meaningful experience – rather there was a tendency for the baby's physical and psychic state to deteriorate and the baby's rudimentary capacity for a coherent sense of himself to be lost. The infant then requires the intervention of a more mature personality – an adult who could tolerate the feelings which the distressed baby arouses. Looked at in this way, the mother in comforting her baby, in addition to her conscious attempts to think about and remove possible sources of distress, is also (i) allowing the baby's state of mind to make itself felt within her own mind without being overwhelmed and (ii) through the largely unconscious activity of her mind, the distress is given a shape and meaning which renders it more tolerable to the baby. This view of the process of comfort adds something to our ordinary commonsense conception of it. Comforting is not conceived of solely in terms of the removal of the source of the distress or the distraction of the baby's attention. It is conceived in terms of the impulse within the baby to *project* his distress into others and the mother's capacity to receive and tolerate his distress, so that the experience is available for the baby to reintroject in a modified form.[36]

Just as the infant seems to experience internalisation as a concrete process, so his screaming and kicking when distressed may be felt in phantasy as concrete attempts to *split off* and rid himself of his bad experiences (*projection*). The presence of his mother, her mental activity and capacity for response, transforms this situation by providing a receptacle for these bad experiences and so allowing the formation of a primitive process of communication – *projective identification*. Through projective identification the infant is brought into contact with his mother as a *container* – as an object with a space for the distress which he cannot tolerate, at the same time providing him with the opportunity for internalising a mother who has this capacity. The fact that his mother's capacities allow her not simply to register the baby's distress but to *think about it* (consciously or unconsciously) and respond in a *thoughtful* way means that she is in a position to modify the demands made on the baby's psyche by distressing experiences and at the same time give the baby his first contact with the human capacity for bearing pain through thinking. This model would imply that for the baby eventually to develop a structure within himself for dealing with his own distress he requires a sufficient number of experiences of such a containing structure within another person.

Although we have concentrated on distress, the central issue is how the baby comes to perceive *any* of his experiences as mental processes. In Bion's view it was through projective identification that the mother gets to know her baby. What she is getting to know is the nature of the baby's psychosomatic states through their impact on her. As the baby comes to feel himself to be known in this way by mother he becomes able to get to know his own psychic qualities and those of others. Bion used the symbol *K* to stand for this fundamental type of thinking which is at the heart of his model of mental functioning (O'Shaughnessy 1981).[37]

The growth of a sense of self

Through this contact with his mother's capacity for containment of mental states and their transformation into thought, the basis is laid for the development of these same capacities within the infant, by means of internalisation and identification. Where the infant has had sufficient opportunity to communicate his experience through projective identification and to internalise his mother's capacity to tolerate and think about him, a new emotional resource grows within the infant around which his sense of himself can develop. A sense of self based largely on identification with these internalised experiences (*introjective identification*) makes possible a degree of tolerance of, and openness to, experience, both internally and externally. This forms the basis of a capacity to learn from the emotional impact of life. Bion's model of the mind concerns the nature of this capacity to 'learn from experience' (Bion 1962b). Such a capacity will be sorely needed in the course of a lifetime. As Harris puts it,

> Traumatic events throughout life, from whatever source, test the capacity of the personality to hold new experience with its inevitable pain and uncertainty, and to grow from it. This capacity must always, to some extent, be influenced by the nature of the earliest containing objects and in particular with the primary receptive responsive qualities of the mother. Receptive parents help an infant to have an experience of himself. His identification with them helps him manage later the conflicting emotions and impulses that arise in the ordinary course of living, if he is *being* what he *is* and *feeling* what he *feels*. (Harris 1978, pp. 167-8)

However, it is not generally simply a question of the overall presence or absence of maternal/parental containment and the opportunity to be understood. The process is always partial. Ordinary 'good enough' parents are more able to notice, tolerate and digest some aspects of their baby's experience than others. Some aspects of the baby's experience may be accepted by the parents in the way we have described above and so contribute to a helpful internal situation and the growth of the mind. Other aspects of the baby's experience, which have not been tolerable to the parents, do not disappear but neither can they be so easily accepted by the infant as a part of himself and brought into contact with his growing capacity for thought. Those parts of the infant's experience which have not been accepted by his parents may lead a split-off, repudiated existence on the edge of the mind, but with an undiminished, if not actually increased, potential for impact on the life of the individual.[38]

Where there is, for whatever reason, insufficient maternal containment the baby is forced to rely prematurely on his own resources. This gives a very different quality to his self-confidence and self-containment, even if that quality is sometimes difficult to pin down.[39] Much recent psychoanalytic work with children has been devoted to trying to understand these sorts of phenomena in the course of treating children who have been in and out of local authority care (Henry 1974; Boston & Szur 1983). The work referred to earlier by Bick (1968) on the consequences for the personality of inadequate maternal containment proved extremely helpful in finding ways to understand, and make contact with, the very diverse and complicated ways in which these children's needs manifest themselves. Thus Bick felt that some infants came to rely too heavily on an active focusing on, and clinging to the inanimate physical environment as a means of holding their sense of themselves together, rather than depending on human contact.[40] This means of acquiring a sense of identity came to be described as *adhesive identification*. Bick thought that such children tended to develop the social appearances of a personality but without any real sense of an inner mental space and internal resources. She felt that, in a similar predicament, other children tried to develop feelings of being whole largely through using their experience of their own muscular tensions or the experience of motion. This gave a particular quality of hardness, rigidity and sometimes hyperactivity to their ways of dealing with the emotional impact of experience. Bick called this a *second skin formation*. Such a 'skin' is not conducive to the development of a mental experience of a skin/container which can both hold together a sense of identity and yet remain permeable to emotional experience.[41]

These mechanisms for holding the self together may be used by all infants to differing degrees and for a variety of reasons, not all of them to do with deficiencies in the external environment. But to the extent to which the infant has come to rely on gathering *himself* together for whatever reason, then to that extent he will not have had the experience of his parents' capacity to tolerate his distress and will not have had the opportunity to internalise and identify with their capacity.[42] Children in whom this deficiency is severe seem to grow up lacking the conviction that distress can be tolerated or that it is possible for the human mind to digest, and so bear, distress. This phenomenon seems to have something to do with the mechanism which perpetuates the so-called 'cycle of deprivation'.[43]

We have been describing a model of the relationship between the parent and child which is both social *and* psychological. It is social in that everything is seen as developing through the complex and subtle interaction between parent and child. Yet it is psychological in that it is processes internal to each participant that are seen as essential materials in these interactions. The concern is not only with the development of the child's capacity for social experience but also the child's capacity to have mental/emotional experiences.[44]

Such an internal structure for mental 'digestion' starts to be laid down in the early months of the infant's life through internalisation and identification with his immediate caretakers. As development unfolds, internal processes increasingly take on a life and logic of their own. The infant comes to feel that he contains within himself a three-dimensional mental/emotional space which mirrors his sense of his mother containing such a space within her. As this space becomes filled with experience it takes on the configuration of a world within him.

An internal world

In her work with very young children, Klein observed mental and emotional phenomena which she felt were not only the result of disturbances in the child's development but also intrinsically shaped by, and intimately connected with, mental mechanisms and states of mind which occur naturally, from the beginning of post-natal life.[45] Her child-patients' activities in the playroom ranged from primitive and concrete enactments of internal states in relation to very primitive conceptions of another person through to the symbolic representation of them in play and language as part of an intentional communication with another whole person. Klein's theoretical formulations attempted to offer a picture of the earliest mental processes and the sort of mental constructs they give rise to. Clearly there are enormous problems involved in trying to recount in language mental activity which occurs before the formation of language and, indeed, before pre-linguistic symbolic thought.[46]

Despite these difficulties, Klein's formulation of an internal world does have points of convergence with recent experimental research findings. Developmental psychology gives an account of infancy in terms of a largely external, social interaction between the biological 'givens' of the infant and the provisions of the external world. There is now considerable debate as to whether or not the infant's relationship to the external world is a direct one or whether it is mediated by internal representations and, if so, from what age.[47] Klein's view was that *mental life began at birth* and the chief focus of her work was the *process* of internalisation and *the qualities of the internal mental life* so created.

Klein used the term *phantasy* to refer to the earliest forms of mental activity that, from the beginnings of life, start to shape and fill this internal world. It refers to primitive representations which arise in the infant's mind as a result of (a) his own instinctual activity and (b) his contact with the environment (Isaacs 1952). (This spelling – rather than the more usual fantasy – distinguishes it from its use in relation to more conscious symbolic forms of mental activity such as day-dreaming.)

The term *internal object* refers to the unit of internal representation. The term object does not, of course, imply that they are the images of inanimate objects in the external world – the term applies to people and parts of people more than to objects in the ordinary sense. The use of the term *object* as against *representation* distinguishes it from too great an implication of an exact correspondence with the external world: there may or may not be such a correspondence. A second characteristic of these internal objects arises from the view that, for the infant, these images have an actuality which is different from the more mature experience of them as being merely mental representations of the external world. As adults, we often regard the external world as simply being *the* reality which the contents of our minds more or less mirror; whereas Klein felt that one consequence of the fact that our inner world first develops in earliest infancy is that it continues to have a reality of its own and to be forcefully and concretely experienced, albeit largely unconsciously. One of Klein's central ideas and major contributions to psychoanalysis concerned the status of the internal world as a concrete *internal reality* in its own right and not merely an image of external reality – though it is also that to varying degrees. That being so, she felt that it had to be taken seriously as being the site of processes within the individual which could not be directly inferred from an observation of the external world alone and that vicissitudes within the internal world acted on the individual with a force of their own no less than the external circumstances of an individual's life.[48]

This is an important point of difference between this model of infant development and what is usually understood as an interactive model. For, although the external interaction between mother and infant is of continuing vital importance, it does not remain the only dimension of the relationship. The relationship becomes internalised as memory but also as identifications indistinguishable from the self, and in this way *acquires a life of its own within the baby*. The images of the relationship are in a constant state of modification, growth, stagnation or deterioration within the individual, from birth onwards throughout life. As Winnicott (1950) puts it, the individual has the 'life-long task of (the) management of his inner world'. This includes concern for the state of 'vitality' (in Stern's terms) of his internal objects.[49] This view of internal representations is not only, as in Stern's model, one in which memory is continually being added to and updated by experience of the mother in the external world. The representations are also subject to *transformations* (Bion 1965) from within.[50]

Klein's work centred chiefly on the processes within the internal world which lead to (a) the development of a sense of a whole person (both self and other); (b) an awareness of being engaged in a relationship between whole persons; and (c) the capacity for symbol formation which underlies the self-conscious wish to communicate that is at the heart of such a relationship.

Klein's model of these processes of development involved the formulation of two 'ideal types' (rather than realistic descriptions) of emotional experience. She named them the paranoid-schizoid and the depressive positions.[51] They refer to perceptually and emotionally fragmented and to integrated states of mind respectively. They are *positions* rather than *stages* because, from one point of view, she felt that they were fundamental states of being, which alternate throughout life as the individual copes with the internal and external pressures which impinge on him. In terms of infant development, she maintained that while, on the whole, the infant began by experiencing life in the paranoid-schizoid position (0-3 months) and gradually achieved a capacity for experiences in the depressive position (3-6 months), none the less there were moments in the infant's life from birth onwards when he seemed able to grasp something of the nature of his relationship to his mother as a whole person (Klein 1948).

The *paranoid-schizoid position* was characterised by the infant's inability to perceive his mother (or himself) as a whole person; and by the way his experience seemed limited to one set of feelings, one view of his object (part of mother), at a time rather than encompassing the range of feelings engendered by the relationship. Klein described a period in the first three months of infancy when she thought the baby's relationship to himself and his world was often dominated by extremely fragmentary states – his awareness at any one time being apparently entirely concentrated on a part of himself or his world – for example, on his mouth and the nipple; his skin and his mother's hands; or his attention gathered by the sight of his mother's eyes or the sound of her voice. Thus Klein hypothesised that the kind of world the baby relates to in the first few months of life is predominantly a world of *part-objects* i.e. parts only of what will later become an experience of mother as a whole person (whole object) in relation to himself as a whole person. Klein's rather anatomical conception of the nature of part-objects has over the years been modified into something more like the different functions which the mother performs for the baby.[52]

In Klein's model, the first step in the baby's development is the establishment of a satisfying relationship to aspects of his mother's care – her feeding, cleaning, gazing, holding, talking. Without such a sustaining centre, he does not thrive. The mental concomitant of this fundamental achievement is the establishment within the infant's mind of an image (or images) of this relationship, that is *itself* physically and emotionally satisfying and sustaining – what Klein called *a good internal (part-)object*. By this she did *not* mean morally good, nor that the infant is capable, so to speak, of sorting, filing and categorising experience; rather the infant *clings to* these satisfying moments and the objects associated with them because of the pleasurable, vitalising, integrating nature of their physical, emotional and, in terms of Bion's model and in the light of recent developmental research one would have to add, cognitive impact on him.[53]

While Klein's view of the crucial nature of the establishment of a *good object* can now be linked with research findings about the importance of early mother-infant relationships, there is another aspect of her account which goes beyond this. She held that when the infant seeks out and clings to his good experiences, we should not construe the remainder of his experience as just neutral events, a sort of blank time, something like the equivalent of white noise. Some of what remains is physically uncomfortable, even painful, and emotionally distressing; that is to say, there are infantile experiences as powerfully charged negatively as are the positive experiences. Klein gives both positive and negative experiences equal importance in her map of early development. She thought one had to pay detailed attention to the quality of bad experiences, arising both externally and internally, their impact on the baby, their transformation into internal representations and their subsequent vicissitudes in the baby's sense of himself and his world in the face of these (now internal) *bad objects*.

Psychoanalytic work with adults and children led Klein to a view of early development in which the formation of and relationship to good internal objects constitutes the focus of the infant's drive towards the development of deeper emotional and mental contact with his mother. But she felt that the very young infant could only achieve the necessary sense of being in a strong and unambiguous contact with his good external experiences (and their internal representations) if he could approach those experiences in a state of mind in which he was not encumbered with the bad images of other aspects of his experience. The infant must be able to deal with states of distress or discomfort in such a way that the memory of them does not interfere with his capacity to be alert and satisfied at other times. Equally, he must be able to cope with unsatisfactory aspects of good situations in such a way that they do not complicate and interfere with his perception of good experiences. She suggested that bad experiences are mentally split off and isolated in the infant's mind, so that they are held outside his 'good' relationship to his mother. To survive, the infant needs to introject and identify with ideally good experiences, and the internal objects they give rise to, while making use of an inherent capacity of the human mind for *splitting and projection* to rid himself of bad experiences and their internal equivalents.[54]

Such devices do not always succeed – some discomforts seem to defy the infant's attempts to rid himself of them; some bad memories seem to have the power to flood back and suddenly repossess the infant's mind. Where this happens, Klein felt that there was a tendency for the infant to be overwhelmed and his sense of connectedness to his mother to be destroyed. Once gripped by distress, the infant is apparently unable to perceive the interesting and satisfying aspects of his surroundings which are so compelling an attraction at other times. Thus Klein felt that, for the most part, the very young infant was unable to hold in mind simultaneously both his good and bad experiences.

Yet these good and bad experiences, whether they seem to originate in the external world or to arise from within the infant, are not fixed entities. They are not transformed into good or bad internal objects *only* by virtue of their objective qualities, which the infant, and everyone else, can simply come reliably to recognise. It is not only a question of distinguishing objectively bad experiences from objectively good ones. For the ordinarily well cared for infant, it is also a question of how a combination of external and internal states colours the perception of an event: this can be highly unstable from moment to moment. Trying to get a fretful baby to take the breast can seem to the mother to have just this sort of unpredictable quality.

Bowlby and Stern maintain that the infant can only internalise what is actually happening in external reality. In Klein's model, the infant's perceptions are affected by the operation of introjection and projection. Benign or malign cycles of perception (or misperception) can be set in motion. The projection of bad feelings into his mother in one mood may prevent her from being introjected later as a good object. An example of this would be where an infant has cried himself into a very distressed state of mind while waiting for a feed so that his mental image of the breast becomes full of his distressed feelings. It may then be extremely difficult for him to approach the feed when it is offered as being something separate from the 'bad' image created by his distress. Equally the introjection of 'good' experiences may weaken the impact of frustrating or frightening occasions, thus allowing the baby to be more tolerant. For example, this may be why some babies seem more able than others, or more able on some occasions than others, to deal with the difficulties of feeding when they have a cold, without getting the wanted aspects of their feed mixed up with and spoiled by the misery of the cold.

Despite the vast range of stimuli that continuously impinge on him, the research into mother-infant interaction demonstrates that the infant's innate capacities enable him to find and make the maximum physical and cognitive use of the caring offered to him by the mother. The psychoanalytic view that the first need of the infant's psyche is for an unqualifiedly good object (*ideal object*) around which to organise itself implies a similarly high level of innate drive towards making use of his mother's psychological capacities and a capacity within the infant for a complex sifting of perceptions of his experience in order to facilitate this process. In other words splitting and projection are seen as mechanisms essential for life.[55]

These psychological capacities, namely introjection, splitting and projection, with which the infant approaches his environment, differ quite markedly between babies from birth. For example some infants seem able to cry and kick out when distressed in a way which enables them to rid themselves of what is troubling them, making it possible for them to accept comfort or the breast. Other babies seem to cry in a more constricted way as if their misery remains locked inside them, leaving them less free to accept their mother's attention. It seems, therefore, that the distinctive qualities of an individual's internal world are brought about by a complex interaction of the individual's innate physical and psychological constitution and his external experiences. Developmental research has shown the infant as active, within limits, in the creation of his immediate social environment. In Klein's psychoanalytic model he is also an active agent, within the limits of his real external environment and his biological state, in the creation of his internal world.[56]

The awareness of whole persons and a sense of dependence

The strengths and limitations of this first good emotional relationship at the start of life lie in its being an idealised totally good relationship that can give way abruptly to something totally bad. Klein thought that the very young infant could not at first link the different parts of his experience together. Thus she thought that he could not relate the good relationship that existed at one moment between his mouth and the breast or his cheek and mother's shoulder to the bad experiences that these contacts can also be the setting for – the milk that comes too fast or the shoulder which bumps rather than supports his head. She felt that these experiences existed largely as two separate entities within the infant's mind. For Klein, the next issue in development was how the infant comes to integrate his separate experiences of mother and so perceive her as a whole and continuous person. She felt that this was part of a complex process which led to a sustained awareness, on the part of the infant, of his need for her and ultimately to a capacity to miss her when she was absent.[57]

Although there are many different ways of describing the nature of the change, there seems now to be some consensus that around seven months there is a major developmental shift, whereby the infant becomes able to experience himself and his mother as whole persons (Stern 1985; Dunn 1977; Trevarthen 1980). This development seems to have both cognitive and emotional dimensions since what is being 'put together' is not only a physical object but an emotional object – a human being from whom separateness must be experienced in the midst of emotional need. Also, it is not only a matter of what the infant is aware of in a state of 'alert inactivity' that is involved but a more securely rooted knowledge which can pull together the infant's experience in different states. Klein's contribution was in perceiving the emotional dimension of this development and in focusing attention on the precursors of this transformation in infantile experience. Her model of this development is formulated in terms of how the infant comes to integrate his different experiences with mother, through beginning to grasp the range of feelings he has for her. Being able to keep in mind and combine his different perspectives on his relationship to mother forms, for the baby, something like the axes of a graph, enabling him to fix mother's existence in time and space. The more he can grasp the range of his feelings for her, the more they can be perceived as being his feelings, rather than being part of the given state of the external world. Out of these two developments grows a sense of separateness from mother, an awareness of her capacity to transform his experience and a sense of dependence on her. Klein thought that there were moments of a more integrated appreciation of the reality of his relationship to mother from birth but that, in the main, this transformation in the baby's perception, which she termed *the depressive position*, only gathered momentum after the first three months, becoming consolidated by the middle of the first year.[58]

Klein's ideas about these integrative processes and how they might arise out of the earlier need for splitting and an idealised good object, were centred on the notion of mental pain. She thought that for the paranoid-schizoid position to give way to the depressive position the baby was faced with (a) the painful loss of idealised relationships and (b) the problem of what to do with bad experiences and the negative feelings they give rise to. To recognise that bad experiences, such as being left with someone else or being weaned, come from the mother who, in other circumstances, is a loved source of pleasure, renders the relationship more vulnerable and mother a more equivocal figure. To feel rage towards his mother in these circumstances is an anxiety-provoking experience in which the baby must either, in some sense, retain his anger as a feeling within himself or revert, albeit temporarily, to a paranoid-schizoid situation, in order to have a bad object to act as the source and recipient of distress. Although one might say that it is the baby's more realistic perception of his mother which enables him to give up the paranoid-schizoid position, Klein's view was that it is also being able to bear the anxieties and disappointments of a real relationship to his mother which enables the baby to see her more realistically.[59]

These processes within the baby visibly transform his external relationship to his mother, but Klein also felt that they transformed his relationship to his internalised images of her. As the infant begins consciously to depend on and feel the helpfulness of his external mother, a similar, though more mysterious, process is taking place internally in which the infant becomes able to summon up and hold in mind good internal objects during moments of external need. He can begin to feel held together internally during periods of distress and so begin to experience them rather than merely to disintegrate under their impact. As the baby's internal world becomes more integrated, a sense of internal continuity becomes possible. Around the middle of the first year, this process has developed and strengthened to the point where the infant can maintain an internal relationship to his mother in his mind while she is externally absent. It is this internal relationship which allows the mother to be missed. Dunn (1977) writes: 'There is a profound shift that occurs when the child begins to recognise his mother's absence and to miss her presence in a new way.

This indeed qualifies as a developmental milestone.'

This capacity for a relationship to an internalised mother is not the equivalent of a cognitive development in relation to the external world, which once achieved is not easily lost. Psychoanalytic experience leads one to think that emotional learning develops rather differently. The capacity to relate internally to a loved good figure despite its absence, during which the infant may experience strongly felt unmet needs, is a precarious emotional achievement. This internal good relationship, which can sustain the baby in a mood of hope and trust, or at any rate patience, during delays and separations is at the mercy of anxiety, rage and despair with their potential for undermining and destroying the baby's good internal figures. Because the experience of separation is, in varying degrees, painful, there is a constant pressure towards transforming a sense of missing a good absent figure into a feeling of being abandoned by a bad unloving one. It is a struggle for the baby to maintain his bond to his mother and he may not always manage this. The capacity to struggle at all only develops over time as part of emotional maturing. The need to keep hope, love and creativity alive in the face of the feelings stirred up by external losses and disappointment is a continuing problem in adult life.

The development of symbolic thought

It was part of Klein's view that the establishment of the depressive position brought with it the beginning of a new relationship to external reality that was based on symbol formation. Drawing out the implications of these ideas of Klein's about the growth of contact with external reality and the capacity for symbolic thought and play have been important lines of development since her death (Segal 1957; Bion 1962b; Winnicott 1971).

The account of infant development given so far has centred on the establishment of a relationship of psychological dependence on the mother based on her real presence – an external relationship which is internalised as part of the foundations of the personality. There is a second major thread running through the first year of life, and beyond, which concerns the infant's experiences of separateness and separations – weaning in the widest sense of the word. In terms of the model being described here, it is the impact of both these lines of development on each other which generates the growth of symbol formation within the mind. What follows is a highly schematic account of development, artificially separating different aspects of experience, in order to describe a model of the early stages of symbol formation.

(i) Face-to-face encounters between mother and infant

Both psychoanalysis and developmental psychology have, from their different points of view, described the delicate and complicated ways in which the newborn and his human environment potentially fit together and how this potential needs to be realised, to a certain extent, if the baby is to thrive. The baby needs an environment which matches up to and nurtures his capacity to make contact with it. In so far as this happens, (a) the infant is emotionally supported in his capacity for contact with the external world; and (b) he is given experiences which his rudimentary (but developing) mental apparatus can receive and begin to elaborate. In the work of Bion and Winnicott it is this matching of a need within the infant with an external object which enables the infant to endow such encounters with' significance and which distinguishes them from external impingements which the infant can perceive but cannot render meaningful.

Freud (1911) wrote an account of mental development whereby unrealistic forms of mental activity (fantasy and hallucination) give way in the course of development to contact with reality and to a capacity for conscious thought. As redefined by Klein, the capacity for phantasy ceased to be seen as a barrier to contact with reality and became, through the infant's phantasy of concretely introjecting and projecting emotional states, the *means* by which the infant can enter into human relationships. Phantasy also became viewed as a continuing part of mental life with a reality of its own, with which the mind needed to maintain contact, and was not to be opposed to or superseded by a capacity for contact with external reality alone. In the work of those who subsequently developed Klein's ideas, phantasy became increasingly seen as the aspect of mental life concerned with the apprehension and generation of meaning in its most fundamental forms and the means by which the external world can be imbued with human significance.

(ii) The experience of separateness in the presence of the mother

From the beginning, the experience of being held, fed, looked at and talked to by his mother is being internalised by the baby, enabling him to maintain a sense of being gathered together, attending to the world around, for increasing lengths of time. Internalisation also enables the baby to feel he contains the vitality and intimacy of the first immediate relationship within himself. He comes to regard the space between himself and his mother when they are together as a place in which these aspects of their first relationship can be recreated by him. Thus, in close proximity to the breast, the baby begins to use the pauses in his sucking to look at his mother, to stroke her clothing and hands and to vocalise to her. By calling this a *re-creation* we are drawing attention to the possibility that this second kind of relationship is not *only* the continuing of an immediate relationship conducted in the present tense. Through internalisation, the baby seems to be beginning to have some conception in his mind of an intimate contact with his mother which he is then able actively to invoke and externalise. In calling it re-creation we also wish to distinguish this process from symbolic representation. One might hypothesise that what the baby feels he is doing in his stroking and vocalising is concretely re-creating, rather than symbolically representing, his first experience of being with his mother. (Segal (1957) calls attention to this stage in the development of symbol formation when she distinguishes a *symbolic equation* where meaning has, in phantasy, been concretely put into an external object, from a *symbol* where an external object has been endowed with meaning but where the object retains its external character and its significance is felt by the subject to be part of a mental relationship to it.)

In the description above, the infant seems able to create an external manifestation of his internal psychic situation when he feels held within the intimacy of an external relationship to his mother. Winnicott (1971) took such activity to be the beginning of play. By three to six months the infant is also beginning to play with objects, as well as with his mother, and one might see his interest in objects, while undoubtedly driven by immediate sensor-motor impulses, as also being part of a manifestation of his mental life and an attempt to recreate and explore the parameters of his first relationship to his mother. Thus he mouths and bangs objects where once he sucked and patted the breast or bottle. Looked at in this way, it is not only that the baby learns from external events and receives meaning from the culture around him, but that the external world is increasingly filled with significance by him and can then be apprehended as meaningful and so explored further.

(iii) The experiences which take place within the baby during actual separations[60]

In the first few months of life separations seem to be a class of events which the baby cannot experience as such. This should not be equated with the view that early separations have no impact. Since babies under six months are only in the process of developing an idea of mother as a whole person, what seems likely at this stage is that they are particularly sensitive to styles of care – to the characteristics of the part-objects they come into contact with. It seems likely that it is precisely the predictability and continuity of the infant's part-object experiences of the world that provide the precondition which enables him to start to recognise and anticipate events and so begin to integrate a sense of himself and his mother. Constant changes are likely to disrupt this process. If the infant under six months cannot hold his mother or parts of his mother in mind for long during separations he may be said not to 'miss' her, but he may suffer her absences in other ways.[61]

Yet some degree of separation and 'failure' on the part of the external environment is inevitable. Initially, the baby's fleeting sense of the external world allows him the possibility of withdrawing into his own sensuality and phantasy, as a means of summoning up the illusion of an experience which is not, in fact, present. The most obvious example is thumb-sucking, but some babies seem to have more elaborate and idiosyncratic means of creating a wished-for experience such as by crooning or holding their own hands in a particular way. Other babies use sleep or a loss of attention to unmet needs as a means of staving off the distress of having to wait. Again, some infants, experienced by parents as 'demanding', appear unable to find within themselves the means to exist psychologically without the actual presence of mother and are unable to 'switch off'. What underlies these different ways of dealing with separations is the baby's inability, until about the middle of the first year, to hold in mind an *absent good object* – i.e. an object that is known to be absent, whose goodness is held on to and whose return is waited for. The baby experiencing separation either 'hallucinates' the object, as if it were actually present, loses interest in it, or is overtaken by the presence of a bad object.[62] In that sense the baby is unable to experience separations.

For the purposes of this argument we need to distinguish, somewhat artificially, the implications for development of what one might call inevitable manageable separations and failures of the environment from the implications of more serious and overwhelming separations.[63] Where ordinary manageable separations are a relatively minor part of the infant's life, these 'failures' in his environment allow him a space in which to struggle on his own for brief periods. Infants have the means to evade contact with the impact of such separations, but they also have a growing ability to make something of them.

In Bion's model, it is because of the absences of the external object (at first the breast, but later the mother as a whole person) that the infant is driven to generate mental images which can hold the impact of the experience of absence (thoughts), rather than continuing to be absorbed in the immediacy and sensuousness afforded by the presence of the object. In Winnicott's terms, when the mother is 'good enough', some degree of environmental failure stimulates the baby to make up the deficit imaginatively. The model is one in which *both* the presence of a containing mother *and*, on that foundation, a manageable amount of separation from her, are needed for the baby to develop. Manageable absences help to generate an awareness of separateness. Where the infant is able to cope with the feelings which this arouses he will begin to develop a sense of dependence on his internal resources and on their utilisation in thinking. His thoughts and feelings can now begin to be experienced as separate from the external world and in a symbolic relationship to it. His capacity to communicate can also begin to be felt as a symbolic activity.

For separations to be experienced by the infant, rather than suffered in a way that severely disrupts his sense of being held together, they need to fall within his capacity to digest them. In practice, this is usually determined on a trial-and-error basis, the way weaning is often undertaken when there are not too many extraneous pressures on mother and infant. Being weaned at a time, and at a pace, at which the infant can keep his good sustaining experiences in mind, to some extent, in the face of loss is a very different matter from being weaned, for whatever reason, at a stage or speed at which this is not possible. In the former situation the infant has the possibility of making something of the weaning in his memory and imagination; in the latter situation, there is a danger that it remains something indigestible, unknowable, beyond the compass of his mental world.

(iv) Play as an expression of internal object relations

By the middle of the first year, weaning, in the sense of a growing physical and mental separation from the mother, is an important part of the baby's life. It is part of a long process which will take the rest of childhood to achieve. We have described the way in which the stages of an external process of growing independence can be seen as based on developments in the internal world of the baby, so that dependence on an external figure can gradually be partially replaced by a dependence on internal objects.

The sense of separateness in relation to his mother as a whole person which develops around the middle of the first year allows the infant to gain a sense of his own mind as something distinct from the external world. At this point, his capacity to externalise and recreate internal preoccupations takes on symbolic characteristics and a new relationship with the external world becomes possible. It becomes a place to fill with meaning. This in turn brings it within his mental grasp.

The external world can be used to recreate (for example through play with a blanket) the joys of mother's presence, and somewhat later in the first year, when the impact is more digested, it can also be an arena to explore her absences. However, the fragility of the enterprise is more apparent than in his earlier play (stage 2). The infant can be overwhelmed by his own play, distressed by the configurations or collapses of his toys. The infant could not sustain for long the kind of relationship to his mother externally, or internally in his mind, which fosters this sort of symbolic play – i.e. a relationship based on a sense of separateness and dependence – were it not for the pleasures inherent in the external world itself. The world which held such delights for the newborn continues to be an entrancing place. It holds the sensual and intellectual pleasures of encounters with physical objects. In addition, the activity of play itself also enables the infant to create new containers for his feelings, as well as a widening set of relationships. This assists the infant by lessening somewhat the intensity of the burden borne by his mother as at first the only container and mediator with the external world. But such a widening horizon is only possible and satisfying if his internal relationship to his mother (and increasingly to his parents as a couple) is, on the whole, loving and rich enough to bear its re-creation as the underlying meaning with which he invests his encounters with the external world.

Conclusion

For the newborn only the actual presence of his mother (or committed regular care giver) can provide the continuity, attention and sensuous pleasure needed to call up the infant's rudimentary capacity to integrate his perceptions and set in motion the processes of mental development. When these needs are sufficiently met, and when the infant is able to make use of what is offered, this absolute dependence on an external person diminishes during the first year. The familiarity and pattern derived from a few dependable care-givers will have begun to develop into the infant's sense of having pattern and continuity within himself: he will have a sense of being himself. His mother's attention to him will have enabled him to develop a capacity to attend to what is going on and to be increasingly curious about it. From his experience of being thought about by his mother he will have become able to begin to reflect on his own experience. The legacy of his pleasure in being cared for seems to be found in his expectation of, and capacity for, enjoyment in an increasing range of relationships and activities which he is able to invest with meaning.

3

Observing Infants: Reflections on Methods
Michael Rustin

In this chapter we outline the methods of psychoanalytic infant observation as they are represented in this book. The intention is to explain their relation on the one hand to more behavioural and explicitly 'scientific' modes of study of infancy and, on the other, to psychoanalytic clinical practice. We hope to demonstrate the usefulness of this method of study as a source of understanding complementary to each of these contrasting ways of studying child development.

The basic setting of these observations has been described in Chapter 1. Observers are encouraged to adopt a literal and factual method of presenting their observations. The aim of infant observation is to provide material from personal experience which can be thought about in terms of its emotional significance. It is therefore important that the experience and evidence is made directly available to the supervisory seminar in which the observations are discussed and not prematurely 'coded' into theoretical interpretations and categories. The most useful observation reports are those which provide detailed accounts of the baby's activity, records of conversation and other transactions in the home, and a sensitive and accurate description of the feelings of participants (including the observer) during the time of the observation. The learning process depends on observations being made and recorded in everyday language, close to the immediate realities of the situation. Making and writing up observations is separated as far as possible from the later consideration of how they might be interpreted in more abstract terms. It is important to this method to keep the gathering of evidence and the making of theoretical inferences fairly distinct from one another. It has been found that encouraging the recording of observations rather than interpretations helps to free observers' perceptions, and it often turns out in discussion that they have seen more than they first remembered or realised, or that the situation looks different from how it did in the uncertainty of the moment. Theorising at too early a stage by observer or seminar group is more likely to be a defence against the pain of emotional experience or ignorance than a means of real understanding. Each student at the end of the two-year observation course is required to write a paper about it. This usually presents some of the aspects of the observation most significant to the observer, a review of the whole sequence of development, and substantial extracts from observational material. In this way the observer is encouraged to integrate in her mind the process to which she has been exposed, including both the experience of observation and her own, the supervisor's and the seminar group's reflections upon it.

This procedure of weekly observation, written record-keeping, and regular presentation and discussion, enables each observer to think about the development of the baby and its mother over the period of two years. This allows the development of knowledge in depth of a particular mother and baby couple. The regularity of the observations in the same place, and often at the same time of the week provides a constant setting, and helps understanding of them to be tested and modified over time. The aim of consistency in the framework of observations owes something to the psychoanalytic preference for a neutral and reliable setting for clinical practice, but regular times for observations also provide a kind of sampling procedure, since the same activities of bathing or feeding will be seen frequently. The selection of families for observation was not designed to provide a random scientific sample. The network through which families are found (often making use of Health Visitors, GPs, neighbourhood acquaintances, or the National Childbirth Trust), does provide a reasonable social range of families, but the haphazard nature of this procedure, and the element of self-selection which influences which mothers agree to be visited each week by an initially unknown observer precludes any claim that the families concerned are statistically representative of a larger population.

The observations which follow are presented descriptively, and report selected observations of mother and infant within the first year of the two-year observation period, often in considerable detail. The individual observations are presented as narratives of what occurred during the hour-long visits, and the observations selected in each chapter are reported in chronological sequence. Sometimes reports focus on a particular event which takes place within the hour's observation (for example, the description of a baby's feed). The intention of adopting a narrative structure for the whole period of observation is to explore continuity and connectedness in the development of the infant over the first year.

The natural setting of the observations, in the homes of the families concerned, has already been described. Mothers are encouraged to make as little alteration to their normal routine as possible, though it is not imagined that the presence of an observer has no significance for a family. Indeed, feelings that are evoked in families by the presence of the observer can become significant, and are reported and discussed in some chapters. Nevertheless, the observations seek to follow the natural development of an infant over time, and in its normal domestic surroundings. They do not aim to select specific attributes of behaviour (perceptual or cognitive skills, recognition or memory, for example) for discrete study, as happens in the more rigorous conditions of the child study laboratory, with its technical resources of video-recording, one-way screens, meticulous time measurement, etc.

These observations are also naturalistic in the further sense of being recorded and presented in the form of everyday descriptive language. The intention is in the first instance to study the interaction of mother and baby as a whole, around the normal occasions and circumstances in which it occurs, not to abstract from this whole relationship and approach it from a pre-defined scientific point of view. Once the choice is made to study families in natural conditions, the decision to focus on and report the interaction as a whole follows logically. Just as, by contrast, once a choice is made to concentrate on narrowly specified aspects of behaviour, it follows that an observational or experimental situation has to be set up which will make attributes available for study separate from the hurly-burly of daily life.

The case-study method employed in this observational programme is thus somewhat different from the methodologies evolved during the recent period of growth of child development studies.[1] Psychoanalytic observation methods are closely related to, and have been developed from, the clinical method of psychoanalysis. Hence the central tool is an intimate, one-to-one personal contact whose transactions are subjected to self-reflective thought of as meticulous a nature as possible. Developmental psychological methods aspire by contrast to the methods of hard empirical science. They isolate specific attributes of behaviour for study; they set up procedures which can be routinised and which are thus less dependent on subjective interpretation; they devise experimental designs which aim to allow causal hypotheses to be tested; they aim for relatively public methods of observation, in contrast to the notably private and observer-dependent settings of the methods derived from psychoanalysis.

As we show elsewhere, there has nevertheless been some convergence between the findings of these two schools of thought in recent years, and between both of these and a third important research programme, that of the attachment theorists, notably John Bowlby and his collaborators.[2] The most important area of convergence concerns the new consensus among all these schools of research that specific bonds of recognition, feeling, and attachment (these three terms correspond roughly to the main focus of interest of each school) begin to be established between mother and baby at birth, or from certain points of view even before this.[3] While there is still controversy about what capacities and dispositions it is justifiable to attribute to infants at what ages, it now seems firmly established that the mother's special significance for the baby begins at birth, with his proven capacity to distinguish and prefer his mother's presence to all others, and his rapidly evolving entry into a multi-dimensional (or in Daniel Stern's (1985) term 'multi-modal') relationship with her. Since at an early stage the special significance of the mother or primary caregiver for children as old as one or two years was a topic of bitter controversy between John Bowlby and many empirical psychologists, and since the hypotheses of psychoanalysts such as Melanie Klein regarding the emotional experiences of infants were widely regarded as baseless and dogmatic speculations, this new agreement on the early foundations of the mother-infant relationship is welcome. This better understanding of the needs of infants, and of the demands they make of their mothers or caregivers, is also making a contribution to child-care policy and practice.[4]

The methods of experimental and other behavioural forms of observational study have been able to produce firm evidence of phenomena occurring within carefully specified time-frames. For example, knowledge of what competencies babies have at how many days, weeks and months, and what kinds of perceptual and emotional response babies make to their mothers, over measured, short intervals of interactions and separation. The role of intense and frequent interactions with the mother (or equivalent) in the early years in the development of the babies' various capacities, including that of speech, and the centrality to the baby of his understanding and response to his mother as a whole person, special to him, has been established by these empirical studies. (One might say that this merely brings psychology into line with most ordinary human understanding, but the development is none the less important, for example in the care of newborns, where it has been shown that early separation from the mother through illness or other causes can interfere with emotional bonds between mother and infant, or in the care of infants in hospital.) From this work it can be conjectured what kinds of developmental failures are liable to follow from the absence of an intimate relationship in the early life of an infant, although the mechanisms remain elusive. On the one hand psychoanalytic theories go a great deal further than this in the complexity of their model of the states of mind and feeling of infants in the first two years of life, as we show elsewhere. On the other hand, this emerging consensus of child development studies on the significance of the intensity of care provided in the first months of life has at least established some common basis of understanding. It opens the way to a productive dialogue between researchers in these different traditions.

Empirical research methods in child development psychology are 'analytical' in the more usual non-psychoanalytical sense of that term.

That is, they seek to analyse complex forms of behaviour and interaction by identifying and separately studying their distinct elements or components.[5] The observational methods reported here are, by contrast, synthesising or synthetic in their aim. That is to say, they seek to identify a holistic coherence and recurrent patterns in the evolution of the relationship of mother and baby, and in the emergence through this of the individual character of the baby. The coherence and consistency of individual character and relationship is an important theme, though their inherent conflicts and tensions are also an important topic of study. Whereas in the larger-scale studies of the developmental psychologists, individual identities and differences of character are subordinated to an atomistic and aggregative method, seeking definite findings about specifiable aspects or units of behaviour, not unified accounts of more loosely representative individual cases.

A similar contrast can be made between alternative methods of research in other social sciences, in particular sociology and anthropology. On the one hand, ethnographic, life-history, and case-study methods are used by single observers to study specific communities, individuals or groups as they go about their normal lives.[6] On the other hand, social scientists use quantitative and atomistic methods of data collection, such as social surveys or experimental designs, to study specified attributes or variables of behaviour and their causal relations. The former methods aim to achieve closeness to the subjective experience of those studied (the 'subjective meanings' constituting a social relationship),[7] to represent the whole social context of behaviour, and to be sensitive to the particularity of a group or situation. The latter methods aim to establish valid generalisations or causal laws, by isolating and correlating discrete attributes or factors. Ethnographic or case-study methods can be the original sources of insights which are subsequently formulated as concepts and hypotheses, and tested in more empirically rigorous ways. Alternatively, case-study methods can be used to investigate social processes and mechanisms whose existence can be inferred from large-scale statistical studies, which may demonstrate causal connections without offering much explanatory account of them.[8] For example, broad evidence from large-scale longtitudinal studies of child development of the effects of continuing relationship between infant and primary caregiver or its breakdown can be grounds for investigating such relationships in more fine-grained ways, through case-study or other descriptive observational methods.[9] Our contention is that these different methodologies are complementary.

While the observational studies reported here are 'naturalistic' in the ways described above, they are not undertaken without theories or preconceptions in the minds of the observers, nor is this seen as a possible or desirable precondition for investigation. These observers brought to their families a disposition to focus on particular aspects of behaviour, and some latent but definite theoretical assumptions about what was likely to be significant. Just as anthropologists going into 'the field' will take with them a whole inventory of ideas concerning the kinds of meanings, practices, and values that might be found, derived from previous field reports or writings about village or tribal societies, so psychoanalytically-informed observers also go into their field with certain preconceptions and orientations in mind.

Psychoanalytical observation methods, like those of the field anthropologist or ethnographic sociologist, require observers both to have in mind a range of conceptions and latent expectations, by which they can give coherence and shape to their experience, and to remain open-minded and receptive to the particular situations and events to which they are exposed. They cannot know in advance which of the conceptions of which they are already aware will turn out to have a useful application. Nor can they be sure that any of their preconceptions will fit. They may well be confronted with experiences that, initially at least, fall altogether outside the bounds of their ability to understand them. What this method requires of its practitioners is the ability to hold in mind a loose cluster of expectations and conceptions, while remaining open to the experiences of the observation as it develops. They also have to be prepared to respond to and think about new experiences, both of the families observed and of themselves, which may not easily or immediately relate to their preconceptions at all. This is not altogether different from the situation of field observers doing anthropology or sociology.[10]

One of the main reasons for requiring observers to note and report their observations in everyday, non-theoretical language, is to discourage the imposition of preconceptions on to a situation. There needs to be a space in which the phenomena of the observations can register themselves in all their complexity in the mind before the attempt is made to encode them in theoretical terms. The task of relating the particular and descriptive level of observation to the more abstract conceptual and theoretical terms of psychoanalysis is mostly left, in the practice described here, to the seminar and its experienced leader, in order that the observational material itself may be fully explored and digested. Even by the conclusion of this process, when an individual observation has been fully discussed, or a whole two-year programme of observation has been given the shape of a final paper, no very abstract level of theory is deemed necessary. Up till recently in the development of this observational method, what has been generally aimed for is to explore the application of certain conceptions derived from psychoanalysis to the direct understanding of infant development, not the elaboration or modification of such theories themselves. More recent psychoanalytic thinking has however been influenced by baby observation.[11] A certain theoretical minimalism thus characterises this work, in contrast to Kleinian clinical practice. This is in part because of the many kinds of professional work with children with which student observers are engaged, and with which many of them will continue when the Infant Observation course is completed. Students make use of the experience in different ways, and only about a half of them go on to train as clinical child psychotherapists.

The focus of observation

The observations which follow will be seen to be loosely structured around a cluster of shared preoccupations. These include the following:

Interest in the baby's bodily sensations and experiences, which are seen as the basis of its emerging emotional and mental state.

The nature of the baby's relationship with its mother in the first months of life, especially in relation to feeding, but including the whole range of infant care and comfort.

The process of weaning and its meanings for mothers and babies.

The development of the infant's capacities to express and explore its states of mind symbolically, through play, especially in relation to weaning and tolerance of mother's absence; and to the growing awareness of the wider family context (e.g. competition with siblings, feelings about father).

The mother's (and other adults') reaction to the impact of a new baby and its demands, including the ways in which the mother may experience her baby as dissatisfied, distressed, enraged, or rejecting.

The states of mind and feelings of siblings, especially young siblings, and how they impinge on the experience of baby and mother.

The mother's relationships with other significant adults around her, especially the baby's father, and sometimes her own parents, and ways in which they may provide a supportive context for the early months of child-care.

The observation reports are shaped around these linked preoccupations, which in turn arise from a model of the needs of infants and those who care for them which is broadly shared by participants in this professional training programme. But the emphasis on these various issues differs between observations, depending on their salience in a particular family, or on the observer's imaginative breadth. In some instances, the observer's presence seems to have had some discernible effects on the evolution of the relationship of mother and baby, and these have been described. In other instances, the observer was only able to take full note of her possible significance for the mother long after she had ceased visiting the family. In some of the observations, the role of young siblings in a family is of great significance for the experience of the mother and baby. This is seen most clearly to be the case in the chapter about identical twins, where the emerging difference of character between the two babies, and the parents' response to this, is a principal theme of the report. In another observation, the different feelings directed towards the baby boy and his elder sister by parents are very significant in the dynamics of the family, and reflect the very sharply defined gender identities and attitudes of the parents. Only one observation is of a first-born child – here the full impact of the arrival of a first baby can be described, whereas the other parents are all able to place some reliance on their past experience of having a child in coping with a new baby, even if their earlier experience had been painfully difficult.

Observers have to be free to take up whatever seems most important in their experience of the family, and a degree of variation in the range of issues discussed by them is unavoidable. It would be possible, as we suggest later, to 'match' and compare studies more closely than we have here been able to do. One could in principle, for example, select samples of first babies, twins, or babies born to single parents, and focus on developmental issues specific to them. It might also be possible to develop an observational framework or protocol which would ensure at least some explicit attention being given to every one of a number of pre-defined aspects of the infant's development. But even with more closely-matched samples, a method of naturalistic observation which seeks to be responsive to a family's particular experience, would still be likely to lead to marked variation in the experiences and issues found to be most important by observers. And there is severely limited scope for 'standardising' a procedure of observation whose essence is the observer's receptiveness to recording and thinking about whatever happens in a natural setting.

The cluster of observational interests or topics summarised above has been developed in large part from psychoanalytic conceptions of infancy. The theoretical context of this work is discussed in Chapter 2, but it may be helpful to indicate more briefly some of our underlying assumptions. They include:

The large emotional impact of a baby on its parents and those surrounding it; the intensity of the feelings this induces; and the anxieties that can arise from this experience.

The existence of negative as well as positive feelings in the relationship of mother and baby, and the role of the containment of negative emotions in the sustaining of an intimate relationship.

The importance for the development of the infant of the mother (or other primary caregiver) being able to respond to the infant's needs, both practical and emotional, and to be able to sustain a relationship of intimacy with the infant over a long period.

The pain and distress which can be experienced by infants when faced with loss of the total availability or seeming control of mother, and the challenge which is posed to the infant by this experience, significantly for example in the process of weaning from breast or bottle.

The significance of support being available for the mother from persons close to her (usually partners, but also mothers, sisters, etc.) in helping her to meet the physical and emotional demands of an infant in the first two years; the risks of suffering for both mother and infant if this support is absent.[12]

The jealousy and pain liable to be evoked in families by the arrival of a baby (e.g. among siblings, but also in fathers and others); the need to meet the needs of siblings displaced from the role of baby or youngest child; and the burden this places on caregivers of keeping more than one person's needs in mind at the same time.

The linkage of physical, emotional, and mental experiences in the process of integration of the personality; how the experiences of the baby are brought together into a coherent experience of self and other in part through the physical, emotional, and mental mediation of caregivers; the mother's roles in physically holding her baby, responding to his emotional states, and becoming an indispensable partner in the development of his capacities to think and begin to use language.

The relation of symbol formation, through play and later language, to the experience of absence of the breast and the mother; the relation of transitional or symbolic objects (thumb, blanket, dummy, specific toys) to an image of the absent mother.

The development of the baby's earliest identity through a process of interaction with his mother; the baby's identity, internal world, and position in his parents' minds being the main object of study; the relations between the development of the normal range of personality differences in infants, and early relationships.

These assumptions about the normal development of mothers and infants provide some explanation of the areas on which these observational methods mainly focus. While observers and seminar groups are aware of the potentially catastrophic effects on the development of infants of gross failure in early relationships, these are not usually major concerns in the observation of normal families. They have of course been crucial preoccupations of those engaged in clinical and preventive health practice and research.[13]

Observation and understanding

The main areas of interest of infant observation, and its underlying theoretical assumptions, have been described above. How are these phenomena of observation, and these theoretical preoccupations connected to one another? How does a process which is not in the observer's control, and in which it is often far from clear what should be the main object of attention and thought at a given moment, give rise to descriptions of the relationship of a mother and baby which seem accurate and trustworthy to an observer and her colleagues?

The problems of understanding how 'sense' is made of unstructured observations, recorded as narratives of events and conversations, are not unique to psychoanalytic observation. Field study methods in sociology and anthropology raise many similar issues.[14] The choice to observe in natural settings, in situations shaped mainly by the subject of study, not by the researcher or student, means that material does not come pre-coded or pre-sorted. All that one can do to clarify and refine methodology in these conditions is to be as explicit and self-aware as possible about the point of view of observations, and about the ideas through which they are given meaning. Making available for scrutiny both literal observation reports, and the interpretive descriptions and commentaries constructed from them allows the procedure of interpretation to be as open to inspection as possible. The weekly frequency and two year duration of these observations, and their firm technique, aiming for maximum consistency and minimum obtrusiveness, are intended to provide the best conditions possible in the circumstances for disciplined thought. The facility for repeated observation at close intervals, and for joint reflection on findings, is by no means always achieved in social scientific field-studies, where situations may be too fluid and rapidly changing to be easily returned to in this way.

Another characteristic which psychoanalytic infant observation shares with other ethnographic methods in the social sciences is that observers are unavoidably *participant* observers to a certain degree, however passive and non-interventionist a role they try to take.[15] There is no doubt that observers may have a role of some significance in the lives of the families they visit, and some of the following observations make reference to this. Often it is a quietly helpful role, in that the reliable presence of an observer who merely wants to be present to see a baby with his mother enables the mother to give herself time to think about the baby, rather than be continually carried along by the infant's practical and emotional demands. Mothers sometimes seem to gain from identification with an observer's sympathetic interest, being helped to find an emotional equilibrium between being engulfed by a baby's insistent feelings and needs, and defensively banishing these to a safe distance, sometimes to the baby's cost. The presence of sympathetic adults who support the mother's devotion to the baby, but who are themselves less overwhelmed by its impact, is often extremely important in the care of infants. The tacit emotional use made of observers by some mothers both reveals how important this need is for the mothers of infants, and also to a small degree may help to provide it. There are of course instances where observers are fairly peripheral to the concerns of a mother whose life is already very densely and satisfyingly interwoven with her family or friends. There are yet others too where an observer's difficulty in establishing a rapport with a mother was an indicator of a mother's deeper difficulties in coping with her situation in lonely conditions. (And of course the observer's difficulties in personal relations may emerge in the context of sustaining a regular observation.)

In the case-studies that follow, observations are shaped by theoretical concerns through a number of specific conceptions or 'ways of seeing'. For example, the physical sensations and experiences of a baby are seen as part of a unified continuum of physical and mental states. The significance for observers of a baby's sense of physical togetherness, or panic, or attachment through sucking (or biting) to the mother, is that it is expressive of a baby's whole state of mind/body, not a physical action alone. The assumption displayed in these observations is that babies not only acquire greater physical competence and motor skills as they grow, but also the ability to use these to focus their attention (by glance or movement), follow intentions, express states of mind. The interest of the observers in minute details of physical movement is not to be understood as an unsystematic attempt to mimic the work of a physical development laboratory, but reflects a different and more holistic view of the inseparable links between mental and physical development from an early age. Tenderness or aggressiveness towards the mother during feeding, physical robustness, propensity to illness, are each central issues in the emerging identity of a baby, and in the parents' specific response to it, whether facilitating or otherwise. At extremes of difficulty not reported in these observations, failures of physical development, or their diversion into the ritualistic and self-tormenting routines found in autism, may be the central mode of expression of a damaged identity, whose blocked development has not allowed a clearer differentiation of mind and body to emerge.

A second assumption made in these observations is that the interactions of mother and baby are to be understood as aspects of a developing relationship. It is this which is the central object of study of the observations, especially in their early stages. The observer's first approach to the new baby is usually through the mother's talking about him. We often learn initially, like the observer, about how the mother perceives and experiences the baby as well as directly from observation of the baby himself. We see how the mother meets the baby's needs and wishes, how the baby elicits care and devotion from her, and specific areas of delight or disappointment in their relationship. We find babies displaying attention or liveliness, or inattention and blankness, in relation to the mother's perceived availability and attentiveness to them. These studies describe mothers and babies taking ecstatic pleasure in each other, but also in some instances report serious battles of will between them. One observer describes a baby (at five months) 'negotiating compromises with his mother in the daily minor disagreements of ordinary infancy'. Such processes of mutual adjustment are reported in every observation.

The fact that the subjects of the observations are relationships rather than separate individuals[16] requires description to be particularly subtle and complex. What is described is not merely what the baby can do, or how the baby is, at each point, but how mother and baby are each developing in their relation to the other. Interactions between mother and baby are also of course the subject of much current research in developmental psychology, which even in contrived laboratory conditions has been able to describe some of their richness and complexity.[17] However, there is a difference between describing patterns of interaction in set conditions at specified ages, and attempting to follow sequentially their evolving pattern over two years. While these case-studies undertaken in home settings are unavoidably much less precise in the specific patterns of interaction which they can reveal, they have the advantage of revealing a connected process of development in each mother-baby couple.

The narrative, holistic approach of these observations is linked to a view of the continuity of the developmental process. The psychoanalytic tradition from Freud onwards has upheld the idea that the roots of identity lie in early experience, and (following the earlier development of child analysis) infant observation offers the possibility of exploring such connections even from birth. Clinical and research interest in psychoanalysis has tended to focus on catastrophic developmental failure and its possible causes. Here, in this sample of infants developing fairly normally through their first year, this is not the main issue. Instead the observations explore the more delicate and subtle question of how the identity of one-year-olds within a normal range of character differences take shape. The observational reports explore these issues mainly through the baby's relationship with the mother, and explore ways in which aspects of the baby's innate disposition are encouraged to develop or are rejected or turned aside. In one family (Steven's), a liking (probably partly cultural) for physical forms of expression seems to give rise to a particular emphasis of character. In another family (Harry's), a mother's difficulties in coping with a baby's aggressive feelings seem to store up serious potential conflicts for the future. The family of twins seems to show particularly clearly the meaning and effect which parental feelings for different children can have on their respective personalities. In each case, it is out of the dense and subtle matrix of interaction between the internal and external experiences of both mother and baby (and often other family members too) that one can see the beginnings of well-formed dispositions emerging. It would be of great interest to follow the development of these babies to the end of their second year of life, when these regular observations ended. The development of speech and the relative independence of a toddler will provide considerably fuller evidence of character which it would be illuminating to relate to the earlier experiences described here.

Although they are deeply informed by psychoanalytic thinking, the descriptions of infants given in these studies are not for the most part presented in a theoretically detailed or explicit way. There are various reasons for this. In the first place, the observations were undertaken in the context of training, not as part of a research programme. It is usually found best in this learning process to encourage as far as possible the use of natural rather than theoretical language, to encourage direct observation and clear reflection on the complexity and impact of the experience itself. Attempts to use theoretical language, and to decide between competing theoretical formulations at too early a stage of learning can inhibit rather than assist close attention to the situation itself. Students are first enabled to have some intense experience of the mental and emotional phenomena to which psychoanalytic ideas correspond. Then psychoanalytic concepts – e.g. the ideas of unconscious meaning, transference, counter-transference, splitting and projective identification – can be demonstrated in a specific application, where they meet a descriptive need. One of the main purposes of infant observation as an educational method is in fact to show the 'fit' in emotional experience of psychoanalytic ideas. It is felt that learning about psychoanalytic ideas in purely abstract terms is of little use, if this is separated from thinking about their relation to emotional experience. This corresponds to Bion's influential distinction between 'knowing' and 'knowing about'.[18]

A second reason for the relatively untheoretical form of these reports however relates to the nature of the evidence which observation studies most readily generate. Psychoanalytic theories have evolved mainly through clinical analytic practice, through the analysis of patients' dreams, associations, and verbal and other material. Though the analysis of small children pioneered by Melanie Klein extended this technique to make use of children's play and drawings, these also usually became topics of analytic conversation with her child patients, out of which she was able to infer the existence and dynamics of relatively complex mental structures. Most psychoanalytic theories about infancy were thus developed retrospectively, from the evidence of the persistence or recurrence of infantile states of mind in childhood or adulthood. They have presupposed the existence of complex mental structures, and assumed that understanding of these can be won through the analysis of multi-layered forms of symbolic communication (as dreams are classically interpreted to be, for example). This analytic work takes place through interactive dialogue, the continuous testing of understanding through interpretations, whose meaning for and effects on the patient are an essential criterion of their truthfulness. Clearly the symbolic capabilities of babies of a year or less do not readily give rise to material interpretable in these classical ways, nor is the relatively passive method of baby observation at all similar to that of clinical analysis.

Later analytic work, described in Chapter 2, has become more concerned with understanding non-verbal and somatic forms of expression, and has intuited from these, in the analysis of extreme mental states both in children and adults, many important ideas both about the states of mind of infancy, and about the consequences of the early mother-baby relationship for mental life. These ideas have deeply informed the development of baby observation, whose preoccupations with the links of mental and physical experience, and the intimate transactions of thought and feeling of mother and baby would hardly have arisen without them. Even so, these concerns lead to an initial focus on the mother's and baby's relationship, rather than on the separate mind of the infant as the central topic for study. A mental structure has first to evolve in intimate relationship with the mother, before separate mental functioning really becomes possible.

Thus the learning context in which the observations were made, the nature of the observation process, and the early stage of development of the infants being observed, have all led to a style of presentation which is restrained in its use of elaborated theoretical models. The reference of the observations to psychoanalytic theory, though fundamental to their purpose, is also mostly indirect and implicit. Those familiar with child analysis will recognise in the observations many instances of application of key analytic models and ideas. For example, Andrew, the baby described as alternating between extreme tenderness and being 'a pitiless little plunderer', sometimes to the bewilderment of his mother, shows divisions of his state of mind – between love and hate, good and bad objects – which have been a central topic of the Kleinian theory of mental development. In this same baby, we see too the development of an internal world, modelled on what the baby has taken in and been able to make of his first months, which he then has to test against the external reality of his mother's absence, competition with his brother, and strange out-of-doors places. His gathering realisation that his mother is not completely available to and part of him at first makes him inconsolably distressed, especially at night. But the observation shows how his mother is able to stay in touch with his feelings and help him surmount his frustration through enjoyment of his developing mental and physical capacities.

The particular qualities required of observers using these methods are sensitivity to and capacity to think about feelings. They can only understand the central relationship between mother and baby if they are able to experience some of the impact of baby on mother. Various processes of identification are involved in this, from feeling anxiety and distress in response to the baby, to identification with the mother's different responses to the baby's needs. Being able to remain receptive and calm while with a baby and mother, so as to be able to take in their different states of mind, is the key to this. Descriptions of a mother-baby couple's delight in each other, of a baby's distress, or a mother's emotional withdrawal, though they may seem straightforward are only possible because the observers were able to take in feelings and subsequently remember and reflect on them. The observer has to be a receptive register of emotions in others and herself.

These capacities in observers are a foundation for those required in psychoanalytic clinical practice. As we have already stated, these observations have been undertaken as part of a course which for about half the members is a pre-clinical preparation for psychotherapy training. But as these observation reports are sparing in their use of technical psychoanalytic concepts, so during their observations, observers are encouraged to be tentative in their use of psychoanalytic methods of understanding. An awareness of unintended and unconscious communications from mothers will be noted in the studies. Observers learn to listen for what is not explicitly said, as well as what is, and to think about the meaning of such silences. For example, while giving the impression of being wholly competent, Harry's mother reveals a good deal of distress about her previous experience of childbirth, and her lack of support in coping with her new baby. Observers may notice a marked difference between what mothers say about their babies, and what seems to be in reality true of them. When Andrew's mother describes how 'old' and 'tired of life' her new baby seems, the observer seems justified in pondering the possible meaning of this, and in seeing in these remarks a reflection of the mother's own inner state of mind rather than an accurate perception of the baby at that moment. Observers have to bring an awareness of the implicit and the metaphorical to the situation, if they are to be sensitive to the less conscious aspects of the mother's communications to them.

Observers are encouraged to be sensitive to the mother's feelings about them, which because of the intensity of the situation of early infancy and the mother's own possible need for sympathetic attention, may involve quite strong though perhaps unrecognised attachments. Again in the case of Andrew, the observer noted a correspondence between her comings and goings, which imposed changes of routine and rhythm on the mother, and the moments at which baby was himself pushed to be more independent. Such attachments to observers can be understood as analogous to the transference[19] aroused in analytic relationships, though of course in this case there is no intention or practice of interpretation or therapeutic intervention. The passive, sympathetic presence of the observer is quite distinct in its purposes from a therapeutic role, even though observers can begin to learn in these situations receptive and reflective habits of thought about states of mind and feeling that are usually helpful in their later development.

Clearly a great deal of self-scrutiny is needed by observers in order to clarify the source of particular states of mind evoked by mother and baby. Overwhelming feelings are often aroused by the experience of baby-observation, and it is sometimes far from easy to think about these and make them usable indicators of the actual states of mind of others. Intense feelings may be projected *into* the observation from the needs and vulnerabilities of the observer, rather than receptively taken in *from* it, and may distort rather than add to understanding. While the evidence of feelings is central to understanding the transactions of mothers and infants, it is no easy matter to learn how to respond to it.

Observers gain help in thinking about these emotional transactions, and their potentially positive and negative contributions to under-standing, from their seminar supervisor and colleagues. In thinking about subjective states of mind as possible registers of states of feeling in an observed relationship, discussion in the seminar should be viewed as an extension of the process of observation, not merely as a teaching method. These discussions often also lead to the recall and understanding of unnoticed aspects of a situation, whose significance has previously escaped observers, or which have been suppressed from consciousness completely.

Just as a comparison can be drawn between the transference, and some of the experiences of baby observation, so the concept of counter-transference in psychoanalysis also has an implicit relevance in this situation. Technically, in psychoanalytic theory, the positive use for purposes of understanding of unconscious communications from patients is known as 'counter-transference'.[20] What was at first regarded mainly as a potential distortion of analytic work, came later to be seen as a positive resource especially for understanding very early and basic mental states, for example the processes of projective identification described in Chapter 2. Primitive unconscious communications in analysis were understood in this work as analogous in certain respects to the flow of feeling between baby and mother in the earliest months of life. The mother's mental function was understood in terms of the absorption and mediation of these passionate states. These ideas on early mental function and on modes of apprehending it in analytic therapy have had especial influence on those concerned with infant observation.

Just as with the concept of transference, however, there is little explicit reference to counter-transference in these observation studies. These terms have their origin in clinical psychoanalysis, and relate to central questions of analytic technique. Their application to observation settings is a less precise one, and this distinction is recognised in the sparing use of these terms in this context. There are however many indications given of the observer's awareness of her own feelings as one aspect of the situation which needs to be reflected on for what they can reveal both about herself and about those she is observing. The largely passive role of observers, in which even unwelcome feelings cannot be discharged readily through activities or talk, gives observers a great deal to digest and think about. As has been described in the first chapter, it is because observations provide this richness of material for reflection that they are found so useful a preparation for later clinical training.

The broader problems of understanding the unwitting contribution made by observers to situations being observed, and by the specific perspective of their role within a group, have been widely discussed in connection with anthropological and sociological research. The methods adopted here to minimise distortion from this source (minimum activity, abstention from intervention, a stance of receptivity and neutrality, meticulous recording of everything observed) are similar to those employed in other field settings. It is the focus on the emotional dimensions of experience which is distinctive to the psychoanalytic approach. It requires a particular training in self-awareness and in sensitivity to implicit and unconscious communication if it is to be a fruitful source of understanding. Observers often find that some experience of a personal psychoanalysis is helpful for thinking reflectively and clearly about these experiences.

Remembering and recording observations

Other forms of research into infancy have made extensive use of mechanical systems of recording, including video and observation through one-way screens, as these technologies have become more widely available. Some of the recent advances in behavioural studies of infancy would not have taken place without the opportunities for precise and structured observation provided by these laboratory methods. On the whole, psychoanalytically based observers have been reluctant to make much use of these techniques, though there are significant exceptions.

This reluctance mainly arises from the focus of this method of observation on emotions and interactions of feeling as the main object of study. The kinds of detachment and self-distancing which are appropriate in behaviourally-minded research are viewed here as more likely to create a barrier against sensitive observation than to be a positive aid to it. Since the intensity of the feelings evoked by babies is an essential aspect of the situations in which they are cared for (this may be the case even if these feelings are overtly denied) a form of study which tends to minimise or blot out the emotional dimension has serious disadvantages. Impersonal distance has its potential benefits too – it is acknowledged that systems of recording which depend on a single observer's subsequent recollections and capacities to report them accurately in writing are also likely to involve distortion and information-loss of a different kind. But the evolving relationships which are here the focus of study are themselves so delicate and transitory that they can only be apprehended by methods which involve an element of subjectivity. Another important factor in the preference for reliance on personal recall and writing-up of sessions over mechanical record, is the training function which has hitherto shaped the practice of baby observation. Working at remembering and rendering accurately in words what has been seen, heard and felt, is an important part of learning to observe, an integral part of the development of the observer herself as a sensitive recording instrument.

The primary subject of investigation – the feelings and states of mind of the baby and his mother – requires the choice of specific methods if it is to be adequately registered. These procedures are unavoidably selective; methods of observation which are designed for one purpose may not be appropriate for others. Just as in studying very small or very distant objects one needs the appropriate instruments of microscope or telescope, so to study flows of emotion between persons, one must find a human perceptual instrument which can take in and record the essential phenomena. Even apart from the special problems of studying transactions of feeling, the commitment to the study of mothers and infants in their natural household setting, while going about their normal lives, would make more impersonal or intrusive forms of study or record difficult to use.

Researchers trained in psychoanalysis may sometimes, however, be unduly negative or defensive about the possible uses of mechanical methods of data collection and recording. The primary reliance of psychoanalysis on the method of the clinical case-study, and the counterposed commitment of most academic psychologists to behavioural methods, have at times led to closed minds on research methodology on both sides. There might well be benefit in audio-visual recording of observation sessions of this kind, as there have been valuable (and influential) filmed studies of children in hospital and day care.[21] This would be especially be so if this observational method were to be used more formally for research purposes, as we discuss below, when some independent measure of the accuracy of written recording by observers, and an opportunity to give repeated scrutiny to sequences of interaction, could be useful.

Infant observation as a method of research

The observational studies reported in this book were, as we have said, carried out not as a research programme, but as integral elements of a course of training in work with children. This has been the case for virtually all the baby observations so far undertaken in the Infant Observation course at the Tavistock Clinic since this programme began on a small scale forty years ago. There are significant differences between studies conducted for purposes of professional education, however carefully carried out and supervised, and a research programme with pre-specified scientific aims. Case-studies like these produced in the conditions of an intensive and well-supervised training programme may be rich and suggestive, but they were not designed for purposes of comparative study, nor to focus on precisely determined topics using standard measures. For these reasons, it is not possible to make ambitious scientific claims for this material.

It should however in future be possible to make more use of the particular strengths of these observational methods for purposes of research. In their own ways these techniques of observation are both searching and revealing. They are intensive – much time is required to observe a few cases using weekly observation visits to each family over two years. They demand and make use of high levels of skill (observers, though already experienced with children, need specialised training and supervision to be able to become accurate recorders and interpreters of emotional interactions over a long period). Research in these settings is difficult to pre-structure – conditions in which observations take place cannot be fully controlled, and an observer's interests will shift as a mother-baby relationship evolves. On the other hand, this method brings observers very close to the evolving life-situation of mothers and babies, far more so than laboratory studies seem likely to do.

Case-study research is most likely to be fertile in producing descriptions of new phenomena, in finding hitherto unrecognised links between their different aspects, and in generating new hypotheses. This method is not on the other hand well adapted to the testing of causal hypotheses, to large-scale descriptive studies, or to the exact replication of studies. Its strength is intensive not extensive, and lies in its depth and not its quantitative breadth. Like psychoanalytic clinical research, this work belongs in the context of discovery more comfortably than in the context of validation.[22] Partly for reasons of methodology, and partly because of an increasing preference for models based on conceptions of subjective meaning and coherence rather than models of causal relationship, psychoanalytic theory has also recently tended to move in a phenomenological and idealist direction, away from Freud's strong commitment to scientific method.

Nevertheless, there is scope for adapting this observational method for more focussed studies of infancy. It would be possible, for example, to pre-select for observational study samples of infants or families sharing characteristics which make their investigation particularly interesting from a scientific or preventive health point of view. For example, mothers and babies who have had an experience of early separation, babies adopted or fostered, twins, babies cared for by single mothers, or handicapped babies. If observations were concurrently and collaboratively undertaken on the basis of a shared research interest, with samples selected to fit these aims, one could expect a much greater comparability of findings and cross-fertilisation of ideas to take place than where (with training purposes uppermost) no such pre-selection is attempted. The supervision seminar could then become something more like a workshop on research-in-progress. There would be great advantages in such observations being conducted by very experienced observers.

There would also be a need to use more standardised reporting formats, if observations were undertaken for research purposes. Routine recording of key developmental steps, more standardarised data on social circumstances, focussed recording of particular issues of importance, even periodically more formal testing, could possibly be incorporated into the existing pattern of observation without much disruption or loss. There is a reluctance in the Infant Observation course to inhibit in any way the receptiveness of observers to the emotional impact of the experience of a family, and fears that any more abstract or pre-coded approaches to the situation might do this. But in the context of a research programme somewhat different priorities might be appropriate. In this way a greater measure of cross-reference with more behavioural forms of study might be achieved. This may be particularly useful when published behavioural studies, as is expected, begin to take a more longitidunal form, more parallel to this observational method.[23] Most urgent is the need to follow up these studies of the first year of infants' lives with studies of the infants' second year. The relation between character-development and relationship with the mother and other caregivers seems likely to be greatly illuminated by case-studies reported into the second year of life. The greater independence of the one- to two-year-old, the beginnings of language use, and the toddler's greater capacity for play and multiple relationships, considerably extends the field of study, and may make possible a closer fit with the findings and conclusions of clinical analysis and assessment of young children. It would be desirable to undertake this work both using already-completed observations (as a follow-up to the present volume), and as a specific research programme, focussed for example on the origins and development of character-differences. Follow-up studies later in the childhood of such infants, conducted by means of briefer observations in school or home, would also be illuminating from this point of view.

Psychoanalytic clinical research, at the Tavistock Clinic and elsewhere, has been fruitfully conducted on this pattern, where cases selected for their specific similarities (e.g. children suffering from autistic or psychotic disorders, children in institutional care, or children fostered or adopted) have been treated by child psychotherapists working together as a research group to explore their findings.[24] Such collaborative work by small research teams has allowed the sharing of experience gained from the intensive methods of clinical study, and the exploration of the application of new ideas to comparable case-material. The use of the supervisory group as a locus of research also permits a small number of clinicians with specialist expertise in an area to guide and synthesise the work of less experienced psychotherapists. Findings from research conducted by case-study methods have a different status from those of large-scale behavioural studies. Nevertheless, they may prove complementary. For example, hypotheses derived from case-studies of the painful and damaging effects on development of the hospitalisation of children have been given support by the evidence of longitudinal studies which have shown up developmental ill-effects arising from separation in large random samples. Such case-study research has frequently been a means of advancing clinical and diagnostic techniques, or improved means of institutional or preventive care.[25] Research on the experience of mothers and babies conducted on this intensive scale should also be able to complement research using aggregative experimental or survey techniques.

Small-scale collaborative research work seems a more feasible method of testing and extending the explanatory scope of psychoanalytic theories than more conventionally-designed large-scale studies of the outcomes of analytic treatment. There are great difficulties in achieving the requisite standardisation of sample, clinical method, or presentation of findings, while using the intensive clinical or observational methods of psychoanalysis. It has to be accepted that psychoanalytic study lies near one pole of the dichotomy of qualitative/quantitative, interpretative/generalising, intensive/ extensive methods in social science. It is for these reasons, and because of the non-standardised, open-ended conditions in which psychoanalytic research takes place, that its findings usually have the form of ideal-typical models exemplified by particular case-studies. Both clinical and observational studies provide highly suggestive models and examples of emotional and mental development, which can then be used to recognise and illuminate new phenomena and experiences as they occur. In these respects the products of psychoanalytic researches are not unlike those of historical research (also mostly committed to narrative studies of continuities in development), anthropology, and the more ethnographic forms of sociology. In these too, the presentation of theoretical models, ideal-types, exemplary instances, and descriptive accounts of more-or-less unique cases predominate over universal generalisations, or causal theories whose scope of application can be exactly specified and tested.[26]

We have sought to relate the methods of infant observation to the larger field of the human sciences, which is more diverse in its methods than empiricist critics of psychoanalysis usually recognise. But there are also some attributes which this work shares with imaginative literature. The immersion of the observer in study of a single relationship over two years, the narrative description of this, and the mediation of this experience through the observer's own sensitivity, has something in common with the ways in which writers of fiction or biographers represent the experiences of families, as well as with abstract and impersonal scientific analysis. Understanding the relationship of a mother and baby requires the ability to discriminate subtle forms of expression, and to respond to and understand feelings, in both observer and reader. With infant observation as with fiction, readers are implicitly invited to assess the truthfulness of representations by reference to their own personal experience, and not only by reference to the published findings of psychology. But while these case-studies make use of skills necessary for response to imaginative writing, they are not fictions. Those concerned with this programme are committed to reaching as high a standard of literal accuracy and correspondence with observed fact as possible, even though their specific interest is in aspects of experience defined from a psychoanalytic perspective. All human sciences depend on a point of view, a defined frame which picks out selected aspects of the world for systematic study.[27] This selectiveness of interest is fully consistent with norms of logical consistency and empirical accuracy in the application of theories and concepts to experience. The subtlety and delicacy of representations of emotional and mental states which are found in good imaginative writing are necessary for certain kinds of research in the human sciences, not contradictory to them. The case-study method, as Freud showed, requires researchers to be able to understand and represent the state of mind of a complex individual much as a writer might do.

We have also attempted to demonstrate how the methods of infant observation can complement and support the insights obtained from clinical psychoanalytic practice. The clinical researches undertaken by analysts and psychotherapists in the consulting room lead to descriptions and theories of a greater complexity than those of infant observation. The evidence of dreams, free association, and therapeutic play with children provides a richer source of access to unconscious process than any other, and the therapeutic dialogue with its process of interpretation and response is a more searching method of research than the relatively passive forms of observation described here. The psychoanalytic method, on the other hand, has disadvantages which have impeded the wider take-up of psychoanalytic ideas. The activity of analysis continuously modifies its human subject; its theories about the mental structure and process of subjects are derived from study of a continually changing transference relationship with an analyst. Analytic dialogue is extremely difficult to report in ways which convey the texture and delicacy of communications. It sometimes seems very difficult for readers who do not already have personal experience of the techniques of analysis, to find much meaning in psychoanalytic reports.

While infant observational methods will probably never have the theoretical fertility of clinical studies,[28] they have some different virtues. Because the observer is expected to take a passive, non-intrusive role, her situation is not so dissimilar from that of any observant visitor to a family. The subjects of infant observation seem to be only to a small degree affected by the presence of an observer. The encouragement of reporting in literal, everyday, un-theorised language makes for an ease of communication of findings with people with normal sensitivities but not specially versed in psychoanalytical thinking. Such findings and the inferences drawn from them, though less theoretically elaborate, may also be more accessible and easier to replicate than the complex constructions of clinical reports. Even the transference-feelings sometimes observed in the mother's relationship to the observer, and the observer's counter-transference relations to mother and baby, are in most instances states of mind readily recognisable from everyday life. Psychoanalytic infant observation may thus provide some fresh and independent evidence of the emotional processes postulated by psychoanalysis. Not least, observers of infants are encouraged to describe their subjects as real multi-dimensional people, responding to the experience of one of the most important events in human life. This aim of rendering the reality of the whole person ought to be one virtue in the human sciences.

The methods of observation developed in relation to infants have also been adapted to the study of young children, for example in day nurseries, hospitals and play-groups. The educational value of these programmes is discussed in Chapter 1. The methods of non-intrusive, receptive observation and reporting have proved fruitful in this wider work, and learning them requires a less intensive training than is needed to learn clinical therapeutic skills. They have also provided a method for investigating the qualities and effects of institutional and care-giving arrangements, focussed on the emotional needs and experiences of children.[29] The central point in this is that the quality of the environment experienced by young children can only be properly assessed if observers are in touch with their emotions and inner states of mind. (Several recent reports on tragic cases of child abuse have shown how difficult it has been for weakly-supported or unsupervised social workers to sustain the close attention necessary to stressful and dangerous family situations.[30]) The primary contribution of psycho-analytic observation to the understanding of children lies in its sensitivity to this dimension of experience, on which so much else depends. The methods of close psychoanalytically-informed observa-tion have many actual and potential applications, in settings of health, education and social care concerned with the well-being of adults as well as of children of different ages. But the core of this approach and its most intense value as a learning experience lies in the methods of infant observation presented in the case-studies which follow.

Part Two

Observations

The chapters in this section were written by Mary Barker, Susan Coulson, Ricky Emmanuel, Trudy Klauber, Jeanne Magagna, Ann Parr, Emanuela Quagliata and Gabriella Spanó.

4

Eric*

The impact of the first-born baby on his parents is immense. This chapter describes how the arrival of a first baby affects a young couple. It also shows how the relationship between the parents influences the way in which the mother is able to help the newborn baby come to terms with the experience of being outside her body. The various changes that take place in the relationships in the family are shown through detailed observations of the first three months of the baby's life.

Through an introduction from a health visitor, I met the mother on one occasion and asked her to consult her husband to discuss if they would both agree to my visiting the family. I then met the mother again a few days after the baby was born and she said that they had agreed for me to visit them weekly to observe the baby's development in his family.

The parents were Irish and in their late 20s. They had the traditional notion of getting married with a view to having children. They were in London for two years while the husband was completing some medical research. His wife was working with much satisfaction in a local library. They were well-endowed with attractive features, intelligence and personal charm. This is an account of my first observation.

Observation at 12 days

Father greets me at the door and takes me into the sitting room. After exchanging greetings, mother, an articulate, quiet-spoken women explains that the first two days at home have been terrible, but today the baby has settled. She says that they had felt like two proud parents going through the park with a new pram and a new baby. She adds, 'We felt conspicuous and a bit silly because everything was so new.' In a friendly way, father asks questions as to why I am coming, and then gives a detailed account of the time before and after the baby's birth. He

---

* This observation was supervised by Esther Bick, whose contribution to the development of infant observation is described elsewhere.

describes how four weeks before the birth everything was okay, then the baby ended up in a breech position. He adds that he argued with the doctor as he wanted to see the delivery, a Caesarian, but that was not allowed.

When he saw the baby, his face was all squashed and he had jaundice. 'It was a terrible mess.' Father says he is terribly worried that the baby might not be all right. He might have difficulty feeding or talking because he has a very high palate. He adds that the Caesarian and anaesthetic prevented mother from seeing the baby. As a result his wife felt that she was in hospital because she had had an automobile accident, rather than because she was having a baby. Mother did not see the baby for the first two days as the baby was in intensive care.

Meanwhile mother is feeding the baby. When she sits him up to burp him, he raises his arms slowly and gazes towards the window, lifting his legs slightly. Back at the breast, the baby's hands are clenched while his arm rests along his side. His knees are drawn up, his toes slightly curled up. Mother's hand is wrapped around his leg, but the baby isn't held very closely to her. Mother says the nurse told her to wrap the baby tightly in a blanket when feeding, but she didn't do this because she felt that some babies might like to move about and not feel cramped.

Mother says she is anaemic, and doesn't have much milk and is worried that the baby is getting too little. She has hired some scales to weigh him before and after feeds to see if he is feeding. Mother supplements her milk with bottlefeeding at this point. While waiting for father to get the bottle, she burps the baby again. Then she sits him on her knee and faces him outwards in my direction. He arches his neck with his head bent backwards so that his eyes look up in the direction of mother's face. She rubs his back, pats it slightly, and comments that babies arch their heads like that when they have wind.

Father returns with the bottle saying how he'd become an 'old hand at it'. He is worried about the baby gulping down the milk from the bottle. When father later touches the teat, which the baby has sucked into a flat position, mother makes him get a new one. As the baby waits for the bottle, he arches his neck, looks in the direction of mother's face and begins sucking noisily on his clenched fist.

When mother moves him slightly, his hand falls and he appears to be poised motionless in an interrupted movement. His body is tense. As he makes a few mouthing movements in the air, he seems more relaxed. He rolls his eyes in a backward direction, arches his neck, scowls and begins a muffled cry. Then he arches his head back several times while barely moving the rest of his body. As soon as the baby resumes a light cry, mother rubs his tummy. When the intensity of crying continues, mother gives him her breast saying, 'Probably nothing there.' The baby sucks at the breast, while waiting a few minutes until father returns with the new clean teat. Sounding relieved, mother says that when the baby drinks from the bottle, she can see how much he drinks.

The couple joke about how indecisive they are about the baby's name, saying they have six weeks to name him. Father refers to baby as 'Algie' and recites a poem about the name given to the 'bump on mother'. Mother says he's number three in the family. (It took the couple two weeks to name the baby. Because of his squashed face, he was not as perfectly formed as his parents, and this may have wounded their hopes.)

Mother changes the baby, preparing him for sleep. She argues slightly with father who wants the baby dressed differently. While changing him, mother says, 'You're looking at the new visitor, aren't you? You can't get your eyes off her.'

As I prepare to leave, mother tells me that she doesn't think she wants me to return. She is worried about my coming. She doesn't know why. I tell her that I appreciate how difficult it is to have so many new experiences with the baby and to have me present as well. Mother says she'd like more time to adjust to the baby first. She feels nervous about my being there. Father touches her arm and says, 'By next week it will be okay, things will have settled more.' He tells me to phone and come again. Mother seems to accept father's reassurance and my saying that I will phone next week to see what she thinks about my continuing. Thanking the couple for the visit, I leave.

I feel quite shocked to hear mother's unwillingness to have me visit, but I am relieved when father reassures mother. She is feeling very insecure. Not knowing what she should do to soothe the baby seems to be unbearable. She worries about whether or not she has enough milk for her baby and weighs him before and after his feed. Underneath all this concern about the milk, might she be worried about whether or not the baby will survive, and about whether or not she has the common sense to help him to live and develop?

Mother seems very anxious and yet she has the strength to respond to the advice both of father and the nurse initially by rebelling. She could be feeling that this advice was a criticism of her for not knowing what to do. Also, the advice seems to be experienced as a hindrance to finding her own way of mothering. She seems to protect herself from feeling impinged on by the nurse by doing the opposite of what is advised, for instead of wrapping and holding the baby tightly, she wraps and holds him loosely. When the baby is being dressed for bed, she lightly argues with father about what the baby should wear. The minute father touches the teat, mother shows her feelings about his contaminating it, by having father wash it. Mother seems to be persecuted by worries about not being 'a good enough mother'. My observing her becomes the focus of her worry about being seen to be inadequate and she tells me at the end of my first visit not to come back.

At times father is also enabling to mother through his comforting touch and reassurance that the new task will not always be overwhelming to her. In these moments father's confidence enables him to be a good supportive husband. At other times, father's competence seems based on identification with a 'super-parent' who has had experience. This seems to involve his projecting his anxieties into mother and the baby while having a feeling of being an expert, an old hand at mothering. On these occasions being a good parent is in competition with mother. This competition seems to be a defence against being left out by mother's pairing with baby.

Father's anxiety seems related to his own problem in finding his feet as a support to mother financially, physically and emotionally. He seems to be aware that in order to facilitate mother's gaining confidence in mothering the baby, it is necessary to support her being the primary caretaker for the baby. This requires him to relinquish some of the pleasure of being the baby's main caretaker and to let go of the joys of being the focus of most of mother's attention.

There seems to be a sense of crisis as mother, father and baby establish a way of facing their new experiences together. In the first two weeks, mother feels the baby is crying 'all the time'. Later she says that she was so overwhelmed by the baby the first week that she wanted me to go away and not come back to observe how 'absolutely chaotic' things were. She says that for the first two days when she was at home, she was left with the crying baby not knowing what to do. He was crying all the time before and after his feeds. The feeds were difficult because she was certain that she did not have enough milk initially.

Father took a week off work. Mother later said if father hadn't helped her to persevere in her attempts to breastfeed, she would have just given up. She found it so confusing to breastfeed and supplement with bottlefeeding. She also found support from a woman at the National Childbirth Trust who had encouraged her to struggle to breastfeed the baby and supplement with the bottle if necessary.

Mother says that because she helped to bring up her two sisters she cannot understand why it is so difficult at first for her to take care of the baby. In desperation she invites a neighbourhood friend who has several children. This women is a tremendous support in allaying mother's anxiety. While the baby feeds, her friend sits with her ear near the breast trying to ascertain whether or not he is getting milk. Her friend also helps her to organise some sort of routine in her life. Mother says that just to be home with a crying baby is such a switch from being at work.

The baby's birth has precipitated in mother a sudden loss of identity. She is no longer the capable adult, the slim-figured woman, the competent librarian that she was before the baby's birth. She does not know who she is, having little confidence in her new identity as a mother. She needs to find her own way of doing things and this contributes to her ignoring the advice of her husband and the nurse. Perhaps her bewilderment and aching sense of the loss of her old identity are joined to a realisation of her total responsibility for this baby who depends so much on her. She feels utterly incompetent to perform the task. She is apparently unaware that she needs time to adjust to the newness of the baby. Like her baby, mother seems to feel suddenly vulnerable, exposed and unheld.

Finding comfort for distress

During baby's second week at home, father stays at home and helps mother get adjusted to her new life. When I phone mother at the end of this week to see if I may continue to visit she seems very willing for me to return. During this visit mother tells me with great pleasure that she is no longer giving supplementary bottles to the baby. She mentions that she has visited the doctor who said that baby had gained slightly over a pound since he was born and that was fine. Mother adds, 'So I have enough milk after all!'

In this observation mother and father spend a lot of time telling me their experiences during the previous week with their baby and their impressions of how the baby is feeling. Mother and baby seem to have established a very satisfying feeding routine, with three-hourly feeding times interspersed with giving baby a little time at the breast when he is crying. The paediatrician has suggested feeding on demand since the baby is crying so much.

Observation at 18 days

Father answers the door for me while mother is giving the baby his feed. Mother greets me while the baby is sucking vigorously from her breast. The baby's toes are curled tightly, his legs slightly drawn up to his chest, his hands resting in a cuplike position near his waist. His eyes are closed and I have the impression of baby and mother intently involved in the feeding process. Mother is holding the nipple in position for the baby. She explains that he is nearly finished now.

Shortly afterwards mother lifts baby from the breast and places him sitting sideways on her lap. She pats his back gently while he moves his head backwards and raises his arms and hands upwards towards his face. He can see mother's face momentarily as he lurches backwards, but each time he lurches back, mother gently moves his head to an upright position. The backward thrust of his head and the forward movement of her hand continue five or six times giving the sensation of a slow-motion rocking movement. Mother says he always seems to be pushing his head back like that. As she rubs his back the baby becomes more sedate in his movements. He is continually searching around with his eyes.

Mother returns the baby to her right breast. She is holding him more firmly now into her side. Her right arm is extended the length of baby's body with the palm of her hand making a quite definite seat for him. On two occasions the baby raises his arm while making slight movements with his legs. The rest of the time his body is resting tranquilly while he makes strong sucking movements.

While mother is speaking to me, she begins rubbing the baby's back again. He holds his fingers tightly clenched with his arms placed vertically along his sides. His toes are now extended tautly as his face becomes slightly flushed. He looks as though he is defaecating. He is continuously looking around, but his head moves only slightly. After he burps a little, mother decides to change him.

Mother places baby on the mat and leaves to get some plastic pants. The baby remains looking at me. He extends his arms in front of his face and kicks, moving his legs in a slow circular fashion. He keeps his eyes facing mother when she returns to change him, but his eyes are constantly scanning a great portion of the surrounding area. His fingers are extended as he fans his hands outwards and up and down. This rhythmic movement of baby's legs is interrupted when mother takes off his nappy. He clenches his fingers. His legs immediately curl up into his stomach.

When mother extends his legs, he jerks slightly. Mother then cleans the baby's bottom and genitals. He responds by moving his arms in the vicinity of his face and kicking very tentatively. He remain poised, barely moving as he briefly smiles. His body then begins moving a little. His arms and legs extend in mid-air and he sneezes just as mother is cleaning his scrotum.

Having fastened the nappy, mother places the baby in his carry-cot. She tucks the blanket tightly around him, while he begins moving both arms and legs. Mother says the baby will have wriggled free of all the covers by the time he awakens after his sleep. The baby makes rather muffled crying sounds as though he is approaching a cry. Mother says she is going to leave him rather than rock him as she had recently been doing. As mother leaves, the light cries gradually become piercing screams. I am standing out of the baby's sight. He is now in continual motion with every limb agitated. His head keeps pushing back. When the screams become stronger, mother returns and brings the carrycot into the living room.

As mother rocks the cot on the floor, father bends over him and says the baby really works himself up sometimes. He remarks that mother seems more bothered by the crying than the baby. The couple discuss how bored the baby must be. They don't understand why he shouldn't stay up a bit rather than just go to sleep. They list a group of items which they have used without finding them of interest to him: a baby bouncer, some bright toys, a mobile. They don't know whether or not they should play with him very much.

When baby begins to kick and flail his arms, father asks mother if she would like him to pick up baby. Mother says that if he'd like to, he could. Father tenderly lifts the baby onto his chest. Father is sitting in a semi-reclining position on the chair, with the baby's head nestled near his neck and baby's body nestled into his chest. When father says 'There, there', baby immediately becomes quieter. His body, with knees tucked under his stomach is still. His hands are near his head, with fingers wrapped under his thumbs.

Father explains that because baby can't smell the milk on him, it isn't so tantalising for him to be held by father. He says baby sometimes pulls at his shirt as though there is milk. Now, as father is talking, the baby moves his head upwards so that his face brushes in several slow movements against father's neck. Father responds, saying, 'There, there old boy. We're two men together against the tyranny of women.' Then father tells me, 'Oh, by the way, we forgot to tell you ... we've named him Eric.'

Father starts rubbing baby's back, arms and legs and then, after a few moments, the baby starts hiccoughing. His whole body quivers as the hiccoughs become more forceful. At one point he begins whimpering briefly. Father links the hiccoughing with colicky spasms. After a few minutes, mother takes Eric and places him in the cot.

Eric begins sucking his fingers as mother rocks the carry cot. Father suggests that he sleep on his stomach, but both parents simultaneously say he doesn't like that. Mother says if he did sleep on his stomach, he couldn't look at things as she walked through the park. The parents express worry about his having his fingers in his mouth. Father moves his hand away saying he shouldn't be hungry. Baby falls asleep next to a small teddy placed at his side.

In this observation mother and father are working together to comfort their baby and understand his needs. The baby is easily comforted when held and sucks heartily at the breast. Apart from nourishment, the baby's primary needs seem to be to feel firmly, securely and closely held. When he is held more distant from mother's body, on her lap, he needs to see her and hold on to her face and gaze. While in father's arms, baby is searching for skin to skin contact with his neck. Father says when baby is hungry he searches for a breast on father.

While experiencing the security of mother's presence, baby smiles briefly, looks around and relaxes his body. The baby makes it clear that it is the emotional and physical presence of the parents rather than toys which are of major importance to him. When left by mother on the changing mat, baby fastens on the observer's face to continue to feel 'held together' emotionally. When he is left completely alone he emits piercing screams, flailing his arms and legs in non-stop movement. He seems absolutely terrified at being left alone.

Mother wants him to develop the capacity to be alone and wait. She is perhaps worried that he will take too much of her. Because of this, she delays picking up the baby until his distress feels overwhelming. Eric is very responsive to her approach and through his cessation of crying shows mother that he wants to be with her. He is able to fall asleep with the help of his fingers in his mouth. He holds onto them not for food, but as something to hold onto as he falls asleep.

When Eric is twenty-one days old, father returns to work. A few days afterwards, mother says it is strange and difficult to be at home on her own. She realises that she has worked all her life until just before she had the baby. She wonders about what she can do with her days, she doesn't know what to do. When a friend invites her for tea, she doesn't know if she dares to accept. She is worried that feeding the baby outside his home might upset his routine. After some consideration, she decides to invite her mother to come and visit. She says she had not encouraged her mother to come until she herself felt more settled with the baby.

When the grandmother does come, mother indicates that, although he is usually a whimpering baby in the morning, he is very placid during the few days of her mother's visit. Mother seems to be acknowledging that the presence of a supportive person enables her and Eric to feel more settled. On my subsequent visit, mother notices that when grandmother left, the baby returned to his restless state.

Observation at 24 days

Mother serves me coffee and tells me a little about her family. Eric can be heard whimpering. We listen quietly. Mother says several times that she wants to wait until he is really wailing. She explains that father had fed the baby at 11 the previous evening because she was so tired. She feels that it is good for the baby to have bottles occasionally so that he can get used to it in case they go out. Mother again emphasises that she now has enough milk.

Eric begins to cry more loudly. Mother clears away the coffee cups and then goes to his room. Eric is lying on his back with his head pushed up into the corner of the cot. His right hand is tightly clenched with his thumb held between his fingers. His left hand is waving about with the fingers extended. His legs are kicking under the covers.

Mother begins telling me about the baby's vivid multicoloured striped jumpsuit hanging on the wall. She says Eric enjoys looking at it. As she is speaking Eric makes a few faint sounds, opening his mouth, moving his arms in the air. His tongue rests between his lips and then he moves it round in his mouth. At one point he catches hold of his left hand and holds it lightly. When mother peers into the cot he makes a louder sound. He opens his mouth more widely, crinkles his eyes, makes quicker leg movements. Mother leaves the room briefly to fetch nappies and he begins wailing 'ahh...ahh...' in a crescending cry.

The minute mother returns and lifts Eric, resting him on her right shoulder, he ceases his intense crying. Mother gently rubs his back while holding him firmly against her shoulder. She repeats, 'There, there.' Eric burps loudly.

Mother begins to change his nappy. Eric screws up his face, starts kicking his legs in a forceful and agitated manner. He keeps his head turned far into the right hand corner of the mat. His forehead rests against the raised edge of the plastic changing mat. He rubs his head against this slightly soft edge as he becomes more agitated. He stares in my direction.

Mother removes the wet nappy. When she lifts his legs he cries loudly, kicking his legs more rapidly, flailing his extended arms. He lets out some wind and then defaecates a little.

The instant mother wipes under baby's scrotum with cotton wool, he becomes still. He stops his crying for a few seconds, and regains a calm facial expression. His arms rest near his body. When mother lifts his legs to put on the nappy, Eric cries sharply. Mother says that he hates having nappies put on. She doesn't know why. Eric continues crying until mother picks him up. When he is lifted onto her shoulder, Eric finds both hands, holds them together and brings one part of his hand into his mouth. His eyes are wide open as he stares stright ahead. Mother sits down and begins feeding Eric on her left breast. He is in a reclining position supported very lightly by mother's left arm under his body. She holds her breasst and rests her hand on the baby at various times. Mother describes how Eric is now lying with his legs curled near his body, his hands held tightly near his waist with his fingers holding the adjoining thumbs. She says he gradually moves into a more relaxed position.

Eric sucks vigorously at first and then more slowly. When mother removes Eric from the breast and rubs his back, she comments on his droopy eyes and drowsiness. After she returns him to the other breast, she holds him more closely with his whole body curled into her side. Eric now relaxes. His fingers are slightly separated. Using his index finger and occasionally the adjoining fingers, he moves along mother's breast in up and down movements. His legs move slightly and his big toe is rubbing with up and down movements along his other leg.

Afterwards mother seats Eric on her lap to burp him. He is like a floppy rag-doll with his head rested on his chest, his hands hanging limply at his sides. He seems to be asleep. Then he opens his eyes, screws up his face as though about to cry and emits a few weak sounds. Soon he moves his arms up towards his face.

Eric burps lightly and then mother returns him to her right breast. He is very still, with his body relaxed and his eyes closed. One hand holds onto his other arm. Mother holds the breast to his mouth. Eric then rests his hands one on top of the other in a cupped position near the breast. Mother is silent during most of this feed. The atmosphere seems very relaxed.

This observation of Eric at 24 days shows how he relates to stressful situations such as being left alone, being hungry, mother going away and being moved from one position to another. Initially when he awakens, Eric frets in a slightly discomforted way. Mother seems worried that she will be worn out by his demands, so she decides that she will only respond when he is deeply distressed and crying loudly.

Alone in his room, the baby acts as though he feels this intensely distressed state will go on forever. He has not yet developed a certainty that there is a mother who is there, a mother who will return to comfort him. Mother wants Eric to 'really cry' before she picks him up.

Left alone to face his fears, he must rely on his own ways of surviving. When mother finds him screaming, Eric is holding his thumb tightly clenched between his fingers. His head is reaching back up into the corner of the crib and rubbing against it. He seems to be holding onto his thumb and rubbing his head into the side of the cot as a means of holding himself together emotionally and physically. He is also kicking his legs under the covers as though this non-stop movement will alleviate the terror of disintegration. The powerful movement holds at bay anxieties of nothingness.

Eric's panic is extreme until mother enters the room. As she approaches he finds mother with his eyes. Then he finds his tongue, resting it between his lips and then moving it round in his mouth. He catches hold of his left hand. Finding mother with his eyes seems to be echoed by his finding a way of holding on to something with his mouth and his hands. His tongue, like a nipple in his mouth, is held between his lips and then used to comfort himself as it rubs inside his mouth. His left hand is also briefly held.

Eric is able to feel connected to his mother while she is present. The second she disappears to get the nappies, he wails. He was holding on to her presence and feeling safe while he had this connection with her. When she leaves he seems not simply disappointed, but frantic. Mother needs to pick him up and hold him firmly and absorb his distress before he can be calm.

Mother then puts Eric away from her body, down on the changing mat, uncovering his body, and moving his legs apart. He cries loudly, kicks his legs more rapidly, flails his arms, lets out some wind and then defaecates slightly. Even though mother is present, in this early stage of infancy, the moment he is unprotected by mother's holding and by his nappy covering his body, Eric seems to be 'spilling out' with a flurry of uncontained emotions. Mother's physical holding is what gathers him together. Eric feels that every change may herald loss of safety.

It is striking that the instant mother wipes under the baby's scrotum, he becomes still, stops his crying for a few seconds and regains a calm facial expression with his arms resting near his body. When mother touches Eric, he feels pleasure. He is held and prevented from 'falling into bits'. His remaining still is more than a reflection of his liking to be touched. Mother's touch derives its power from its significance for Eric as re-establishing a sense of concrete physical attachment.

When mother removes her hand and lifts his leg, Eric emits a piercing cry of distress. The link with mother is broken. When mother holds him, he is able to respond quickly and to use the comfort she provides. Subsequently he is able to recover his own ways of holding himself together: he holds his hands together, puts some fingers in his mouth. It seems that he must feel mother holding him in order to regain his own ways of holding himself together.

During the breastfeeding, Eric is able to relax and depend on mother. At the same time he shows his wish to touch her. Having been fed and held by mother, Eric rests his hands cupped round each other near the breast. The way he holds his hands relaxedly seems very similar to the way he is held by mother. By holding him physically, nurturing him in a pleasurable way, and emotionally responding to his distress, mother enables Eric to internalise capacities to struggle with his anxieties.

It is not only the baby that is affected by this satisfying experience at the breast. It is also mother. Eric accepts the breast, feeds satisfactorily and responds to mother's comforting. This enables mother to take in the experience that the baby feels she is good, and loves her. Because this is her first child and mother feels uncertain of her identity as mother, she needs frequent reassurance from Eric that she is a good mother.

Between feeds, mother generally leaves Eric in his bedroom. She is reluctant to feed him upon demand, fearing that then she'd be doing it every 2½ hours. She is also worried that if she responds to his crying he will never settle into a pattern. Gradually mother realises that Eric is grizzly each morning because he doesn't really want to go back to his bedroom after his morning feeds. She says that he'd much prefer simply to stay up in the sitting room watching what she is doing. Mother says he is keen to look around and often fastens on the colourful striped jumpsuit in his bedroom. She also notices that he looks at me particularly upon my arrival. Eric seems to be intensely curious, exploring his new world and new faces.

As well as using his eyes for exploring, he also needs to 'hold on to mother' with his eyes, for he does not yet have a mother internally who would leave him feeling safe when he is awake and apart from his external mother. Similarly, in mother's absence he focusses on the familiar jumpsuit near his bed for security. Having the same object around serves as some indicator that all is not frighteningly new and different.

Several patterns have emerged in Eric's ways of relating to his world. When he is extremely frightened, he seems to attempt to expel his panic. This is done through various ways such as rapidly flailing his arms, kicking violently as if to kick out unpleasant sensations, screaming or crying out, defaecating and passing wind. When mother helps him to bear some of his distress, Eric is able to remain more integrated and use some of his own protective devices to 'hold himself together'. For example, with his eyes Eric fastens on to his vividly coloured jumpsuit; he puts his fingers in his mouth, clenches his thumb between his fingers and holds his legs curled into his body. These are Eric's attempts to prevent their collapse. This rigidity involved in 'holding on' in an adhesive way, means that no change is tolerated, so Eric cries when mother makes a move.

At other times, when Eric is held, comforted and nourished at mother's breast, he seems to introject some kind of internal holding mother. This enables him to relax his entire bodily defences – the characteristic stiffening of his hand, foot and neck muscles. Relaxing his bodily defences enables him to take in mother and to explore and learn about his world. After some time spent in being firmly held and fed at the breast, Eric begins to move his fingers in up and down movements feeling the texture of the breast that feeds him. Likewise, he moves his toe along his leg, feeling the texture of his skin, soft like that of the breast. He has moved from a sense of struggle for survival into having a relationship with mother which enables him to get to know her.

Ways of developing a dialogue

The couple have managed to leave their usual routine at home and spend a weekend with friends. They find that it is possible to have a restful time even with baby around. They notice that Eric has begun to discover what he can do with his hands and to laugh a lot. As well as giving me a detailed commentary on baby's activities during the week, mother mentions that every day when her husband returns from work she tells him about what Eric has been doing. This observation shows various ways in which the baby shows what he is feeling and the parents try to understand his requests and respond through touching, talking, holding and feeding him.

Observation at 6 weeks

When I arrive mother greets me vivaciously. Father is serving tea. They describe how refreshed they feel after their weekend away. During this time the baby is lying on a plastic changing mat on the floor. He is crying with a light, feeble cry without much intensity or annoyance. He finds his mouth with his thumb and index finger and begins sucking. Mother says he can suck his thumb when he wants to.

Eric begins to cry, moving his head from side to side and kicking his legs. Father asks if mother minds terribly if he picks up the baby. Mother says that's fine and he rests the baby next to his chest, holding him very firmly. Eric's head is near his neck. He rubs his head against father's neck. He becomes motionless, seeming to be completely relaxed. Even the sucking of his thumb ceases. Mother says, 'Look, he feels so comforted.' She adds, 'But really, he's starving, he just wants to eat.'

After a little while mother takes baby to the bathroom for a bath. As she lays Eric on her lap, he begins wailing. His wails become increasingly loud until he is terribly pink. He waves his arms agitatedly, kicks his legs with a quick pushing out movement, knocking his head back in rapid movements. His crying feels very agonised and disturbing. Eric's movements of distress increase in rapidity and forcefulness when his clothes are removed. His face and body become redder. After testing the temperature of the water, mother begins washing Eric in his small bath.

First she puts wet cotton wool on his eyes. He shrieks and jerks both arms and legs. She then rubs his head soothing him with 'There, there, it's all right.' He becomes calm. When she puts his head in the water, he cries loudly and reddens. She rubs his head with soap, dribbling water over the soap afterwards. His arms are wrapped firmly to his side with a towel. One arm finally becomes free and he momentarily stops crying as his hand goes into his mouth.

Next mother puts wet cotton wool around one ear saying, 'There, there,' in a sing-song fashion. Eric's cry is barely perceptible now. As she cleans the other ear, he relaxes his limbs slightly. When mother removes the towel, he kicks frantically. He rapidly waves his hands in the air, rocking his head back repeatedly, and begins shivering near his lower lip. As mother immerses him in the tiny baby bath, he cries as though he were terrified. She starts pouring water on his chest and chanting 'Rub a dub dub'. Then she rubs his chest and both legs and his bottom, describing to him everything that she is doing. By the time the water completely covers his chest, Eric is quiet. He becomes calmer and makes some sounds in a playful, high pitched tone 'Ah...ah...uh'. He seems to be enjoying himself. He begins kicking gently and slowly with his legs in the water. Mother asks him if he is going to smile at her.

At this point father comes in and comments to Eric about how he really seems to be enjoying himself. He brings a picture of himself as a baby and shows his wife. He asks her if she thinks that the baby looks like him when he was little. Father adds that he is six weeks old in the picture, just like Eric. In the picture father's mother is leaning over him and smiling. Mother agrees that Eric looks like father. Father then shows the picture to me. I agree that there is a similarity between the two of them. Father then says, 'Yes, well, maybe all babies are alike.'

When mother removes the baby from the tub, he begins shrieking again. He reddens, kicks in lightning quick movements and his lower lip trembles. He keeps moving his head in a backward thrusting motion. He continues doing this as mother puts on his shirt. The only time that his crying lessens in intensity is when she rubs the back of his head a bit and holds him close to her. When she puts on the long nightdress and carries him into the sitting room to feed him he is crying forcefully.

Then Eric finds his hand and begins sucking on it. He is quiet as mother places him on the floor to fasten his rubber pants securely. When mother lifts him up, he immediately begins crying again, waving his arms in the air, thrusting his head back and kicking. He continues until mother has settled him quite firmly against her left breast. Mother removes Eric's hands which he is sucking. When she puts the nipple in his mouth, he gulps down the milk with vigorous sucking movements and loud swallowing sounds. Mother says with amazement that he is very hungry. She says she doesn't know why: 'Maybe taking him out in the fresh air is responsible.'

At this point, father comes and bends over to observe the feed. He rests his head against mother's head and talks about how Eric is enjoying his feed. He remarks on how beautiful Eric's small hands are. The couple seem very close, calm and pleased to be together at this moment.

In this observation, the dialogue between mother, father and the baby is on many levels. Mother provides Eric with physical holding and nurturing at her breast, communicating that she is reliably present to alleviate some of his distress and comfort him through physical means. Father and she also talk with their baby about his emotional experiences of comfort and discomfort in the bath. Father supports mother in her communication with the baby by being gently but not intrusively affectionate, as he touches her head and shows his appreciation of the new baby.

Throughout this time, Eric continually shows mother how he is feeling about his experiences. He is terribly distressed, shrieking with fear as he begins the bath. However, he is quickly comforted by mother. He becomes calm as she says, 'There, there.' When settled in the bath, he shows her his pleasure as he makes his playful, high-pitched sounds of 'ah...ah...'. Despite his marked frustration during the process of bathing and dressing, Eric is able to approach the breast with intense eagerness once mother removes his hands.

These are dialogues in which mother and baby find a meeting point. Eric's need to be comforted is met and mother's need to be accepted as a good mother is fulfilled. These dialogues in which mother greets the baby and meets his needs provide the basis for the introjection of a good, reliably present mother who knows what he needs and is reliable in providing it.

Interesting also is father's contribution. His touching identification with the baby (in the episode of the photograph) modifies his potential rivalry for attention and signals his capacity for enjoyment of mother and baby's intimacy.

Discovery of new identities

Getting to know her baby seems linked with this mother's feeling of being accepted as a good mother. When mother is persecuted by the baby's cries, she often finds it difficult to think about him. Instead of thinking she simplifies and says he's tired or hungry or colicky. At times this is how Eric feels, but he also has the potential for a whole complexity of feeling which mother is able to know and understand when she feels more confident.

Getting to know her baby and see him as a person whose needs she understands gives mother a sense of security in her mothering role, to feel established in her identity as mother. This sense of being satisfactory in her role gives mother relief. It also frees her to acknowledge how very difficult it was in the beginning when the baby was born. She begins asking me questions about my work with children: Do children develop through my work? Do I get pleasure when I am successful in helping children? These questions about my role with children are being asked concurrently with mother's own experience of helping the baby and of gaining pleasure in being successful in her new role as mother.

Mother begins now to puzzle over the meaning of Eric's less obvious gestures. She begins talking more with him, understanding what he likes and doesn't like. Here is an excerpt from that period:

Observation at 9 weeks

Mother greets me with a cheery hello. From his bedroom Eric can be heard crying momentarily and making sounds. Mother says that he has slept through the night. She says that he woke at 8 a.m., but he did not cry, he just lay in his cot talking to himself.

She describes how much things have changed since Eric was born. She says that he was just 'a lump' when he was first born. Now he has a personality, he is a real baby. He does so many things. Now he has all sorts of different cries. She can distinguish a cry meaning he is hungry, another cry indicating that he wants to be picked up and cuddled. He is beginning to smile frequently. She recounts how one day after he had had one breast and began the second breast he turned away from the breast, looked up at her and smiled.

Mother reflects on the difficulties in the first days of baby's life, saying that if father hadn't supported her in continuing to try to breastfeed, she would have just given up. Today she phoned the National Childbirth Trust helper to thank her for her help.

Lying in his cot in the bedroom, Eric is sleeping. His fingers are slightly curled into his hand. His left hand remains against his chest. After a short while his lips move as though he is sucking. He puts his left hand near his face. Then he rolls from his side on to his back. He puts both hands near his mouth and rubs his face with hands. His eyes are squinting and he kicks slightly.

After a short while Eric puts his left thumb into his mouth and begins sucking. Then he lies on his side and sucks vigorously on his thumb. At the same time his three fingers are fanned out and held in a slightly curved position on his face. With his left hand Eric makes a slight movement of grasping and touching along his babygrow near his chest. Soon all the baby's movements apart from his sucking stop. Then the sucking ceases as his thumb drops from his mouth and he falls into a deep sleep. He lies completely still for about five minutes.

Eric's eyes then open slightly. I am virtually out of his sight as he makes very slight mouthing movements. His thumb goes to his mouth and he begins sucking again. This time his hand is clenched and the index finger is rubbing underneath his nose. The sucking continues for a few minutes. He interrupts the steady sucking and as he releases his thumb he relaxes into sleep. Shortly afterwards, he again begins the grasping movement with his left hand. His arm jerks a bit and his fingers touch his cot coverlet. He smiles again briefly.

For the first time, mother enters Eric's bedroom. She deposits some nappies and then exits. Eric begins moving again. He turns onto his back and lifts his hands near his face. He occasionally rubs his face with his hands. He holds on to his sleeve momentarily and then he lies sideways again.

In this observation, mother acknowledges her enjoyment of Eric. She is aware of his appreciation of her as shown through his smiling with love as he looks up at her in the middle of the breastfeeding. His capacity to be comforted by mother provides her with relief and space to think about the various meanings of his cries. Mother experiences the baby as being transformed from 'a lump' into a real person. She then feels the pleasure of being a mother who loves her baby.

Eric, even though asleep, shows how he has developed from being a baby easily terrified by the slightest change. He no longer seems unintegrated. When disturbed, all his movements are directed towards the mouth. He is no longer tightly 'holding onto' his fingers with his mouth, no longer 'holding on for dear life'. His movements are gentle. His sucking and grasping movements are all tender, light touching movements, like those observed during breastfeeding. He smiles as though at the breast.

When mother enters the room and leaves it again without picking him up, the baby's movements in his sleep change, becoming quicker. He now holds firmly, though briefly, to the sleeve of his babygrow. He does not awaken.

Eric is hovering in and out of sleep, sucking his thumb, resting his fingers on his cheek, then releasing his thumb from his mouth, smiling and falling asleep. This seems very similar to the way mother describes him at the breast, sucking on one breast, then smiling at mother. Perhaps in his sleep he may be re-experiencing a breast present to comfort him, a mother whom he loves, a mother who causes him to smile with joy as he looks at her or touches her. It seems that Eric is enabled to sleep through slight disturbances because he has found a way of being linked to his warm memories of mother and thus able to comfort himself.

Conflicting feelings towards mother

A period of contentment in mother and baby is followed by a rash developing all over Eric's face. Alongside this somatic disturbance is his beginning to turn away from the breast. Initially it is difficult for mother to understand the development of Eric's more complicated relationship to her while she is breastfeeding.

Observation at 13 weeks

Eric is feeding from mother's left breast. After about two minutes he turns away from the breast, rubs near his eyes and then puts his left hand knuckles into his mouth. He sucks them vigorously until mother removes them. She quickly returns the nipple to his mouth. Once again Eric turns away from the breast and sucks his knuckles. Mother says he has been doing this recently. She doesn't know why. She lets him suck his hand for a few moments before returning hiim to the breast. Eric whimpers slightly but begins sucking again on the nipple. His eyes are slightly open. He seems to be falling asleep on her shoulder. Then he burps and whimpers.

A week later his facial rash has disappeared.

Observation at 14 weeks

Eric is undressed, wrapped in a towel with the bath water ready. He is lying on his mother's lap with his face turned to the mirror behind her. Now he is laughing, looking at himself, using his feet to push back his head even further in the direction of the mirror. His entire back is arched tightly. Eric laughs continually except for a few quiet smiles. He stretches his arms back above his head. Mother says that he will push himself off her lap if she isn't careful. She then puts him back into a more secure position, with his head resting on her leg. Eric protests by waving his arms and emitting a loud protest sound.

Mother holds Eric on her lap and begins soaping his entire body. His wriggling backward is interrupted by short moments of restful attention to mother's face. Then mother places him in the bath. His backward head movement ceases as he relaxes his body. He seems pleased. He alternately rubs one foot against the ankle of his left leg and pushes both feet against the edge of the bath. At times he repeats this rubbing action with foot movements on the opposite leg. Eric then turns his head away from the mirror and looks at me standing on the opposite side.

As mother begins speaking to me, Eric looks at mother's face. He curls over on to his right side, getting near to mother. His hand touches mother's rolled-up sleeve. After holding on to it momentarily, he moves his hand downwards along her arm. Several times he uses his hand to repeat this reaching, holding, gliding along mother's arm in a slow, tentative manner. Mother says that Eric likes to feel the different textures of fabric on the cot and his clothes. She doesn't think he likes the toys that she has around, but he does like to reach out for things and repeatedly touch them. He has just discovered her arm this week. Eric is now gently patting the surface of the water. Then he brushes his palm along mother's sleeve.

When mother takes him out of the water, Eric moans, 'Ah, ah.' He waves his arms rapidly above his head. He is protesting. Mother lies him down crosswise on her legs with his head hanging over the edge. In this position Eric firmly makes repeated backward thrusting movements with his head and trunk. When he catches sight of his face in the mirror, he smiles. Occasionally he glances upwards towards my face reflected in the mirror.

Mother turns Eric on to his stomach and he leans forward to reach his clenched knuckles. He sucks them briefly before he lifts his head, jerks it back and turns away from his knuckles and looks at the mirror. His smiling has ceased. As mother pulls his shirt over his head, Eric begins whimpering, kicking, waving his arms and jerking his head in attempts to get away from the shirt. His hand finally finds his mouth and he sucks several knuckles again.

As mother carries Eric to his changing mat in his bedroom, he cries. She immediately speaks to him in a soothing voice and pulls the cord of his music box. As the music plays a lullaby, mother tells him to listen. Eric remains quiet and still. He slowly puts his middle two fingers in his mouth and begins gently sucking. Shortly afterwards the music stops. He stops sucking and remains still with his fingers in his mouth and then turns and looks at my face. Mother says he is just getting to recognise me.

When the breastfeeding begins, Eric cries. He then places his middle two right hand fingers into his mouth. He sucks them vigorously. When mother removes his fingers he again cries. She firmly puts the nipple of her right breast into his mouth. He begins sucking while looking up towards her face.

After about five minutes, Eric turns away from the breast, and cries. Mother tells me that nowadays Eric often turns from the right breast and cries. She doesn't know why. Now he puts his fingers in his mouth and sucks them noisily. Mother kindly asks Eric, 'What is the matter?' She then turns his face towards the breast, removes his hands and places the nipple in his mouth. Eric sucks for a minute before again turning away to his fingers. His left hand touches his head, while his legs kick briefly.

Mother moves Eric to rest him on her shoulder. She rubs his back gently. He burps loudly. Then he returns his fingers to his mouth. Again he moves his head backwards to look at me. Mother then places Eric at her left breast. She cuddles him more than ever. Eric sucks the nipple but mother worries that he is simply mouthing it rather than drinking the milk. Eric's eyes close gradually and mother rubs his cheeks several times to rouse him. He begins to cry. After he has been burped, mother returns him to the right breast which he sucks for a few minutes before dropping off to sleep.

Mother carries him to his bedroom and carefully tucks him into his cot. Eric turns on to his right side. He holds his two right hand fingers in his mouth, while cupping his left hand round them. He sucks his fingers gently while immediately closing his eyes.

In the observation at thirteen weeks, Eric has begun to experience mother as having a more reliable and predictable way of responding to his needs. He seems to be in transition from the breast regardless of what frustration is experienced immediately before he is fed. Now he seems to be expressing displeasure while at the breast. Mother experiences his protest. She bears it and tries to help him to approach the breast again. It is interesting that a week later his facial rash has disappeared. Possibly a psychosomatic expression of irritation had been transformed into a recognised emotion.

In the next observation it is possible to see the strength and pleasure which Eric has. He seems to feel delighted to be able to discover, lose and rediscover himself in the mirror. He does not like his mother to thwart his freedom. When she puts him into a more restricted secure position on her lap he protests. His protest is mitigated by the soothing way in which mother soaps his entire body and he is able to rest while gazing at mother's face.

Having had an experience of his comforting mother, Eric is pleased to relax and then to move around in the bath. He looks around to the mirror, to mother and towards me. He does not have to hold on to one face. As mother talks to me he turns his eyes towards her face. He holds her with his eyes while his hand is directly in contact with her sleeve. He repeats the gliding movement of his hand along his mother's arm several times. His ability to stop and then repeat his action again and again is his repeated claim to intimacy. He seems affectionate as he finds his own tender way of remaining close to mother. He is able to explore, touch the water and then return to touching his mother's arm. This all appears to be an expression of his feeling. 'I am safe – I can touch the water – I can explore and mother is still there. I am safe.' There is a continuous discovery that he does not have to 'hang on' constantly because mother is there. His sense of security has to be continually renewed and confirmed by mother meeting his needs.

In the past Eric was easily soothed simply by having mother hold him in her lap. Now he can show her that he is very displeased when she does not fit in with exactly what he wants. When he feels something is not right he protests. For example, when mother restricts his movements, takes him out of the bath and dries him, he complains and stops smiling. When his head is covered and he can no longer see mother he begins whimpering, kicking and waving his arms. Concurrently with his increase in protesting sounds is his distress when his head is covered by his shirt. When he can no longer see his mother, perhaps he feels she may disappear. Having his head covered is felt as exposure to a bad experience with a mother who doesn't do what he wants. His cry, which sounds stronger with that protest in it, suggests that he is feeling more than fear at this point. Eric recovers when he finds his knuckles to suck.

He cries during the disruption mother causes by returning him to his bedroom. However, he is easily comforted by mother's soothing voice and the music.

Later, at the beginning of the breast feed, Eric cries when he loses hold of his fingers. He turns away from the breast and regains his finger. There is a growing sense that now Eric loves mother more. His pain of separation from her is more acute. It is not simply fear of 'falling apart' which he is experiencing, but also the pain of not always having the mother he feels understands him, the mother he loves.

At this point in his psychological development, his distress seems to move from some of the somatic irritations which he has been experiencing on his face and bottom. One sees his protest, his rage towards the mother who becomes bad when she is different from the mother who behaves as he likes her to. Mother sees a pattern emerging in which his protest seems directed to something not quite right about his feeding experience at the right breast. Mother is puzzled by the changes in her baby. In the past he was generally forgiving, readily accepting her after a frustrating experience of waiting for her or not being held firmly enough by her. Eric is how psychologically stronger for he feels free to protest rather than simply use his physical methods of 'holding himself together' to protect himself against distress.

Tolerating frustration

There gradually seems to be a new development in Eric which prompts
mother to describe him as being able to be 'so good', remaining so
contented, 'so absolutely perfect' with them when the couple spent the
weekend away. At this time mother says Eric has begun 'to stop his
moaning' and referred to a two-hour feast at which he just sat in his
baby bouncer and watched everyone. The observation below describes
some of the changes in Eric.

Observation at 15 weeks

Lying very contentedly in his cot in the bedroom, Eric is sucking his
middle two fingers. When I approach him, he looks at me and continues
sucking. Then he takes his hand out of his mouth, smiles and makes an
'aah' sound. He then moves his arms about his head and becomes a little
excited. With both hands he grasps the soft, white angora blanket. He
pulls it up near his head. Then he moves his hands about until his left
hand again grabs onto the blanket and his right fingers are in his mouth.
The blanket is then covering the fingers in his mouth. He continues to
look at me until mother arrives.

As mother talks about how lovely Eric has been over the weekend, he
kicks and lets his fingers out of his mouth. He uses both hands once
again to grab onto the blanket and pull it upwards towards his face. The
he lets it go and grabs hold of it again. He looks at mother as she bends
over him and picks him up.

When mother lays Eric on his changing mat, he sucks on his middle
fingers for a few seconds. Then he remains motionless as he looks at me.
When mother removes his nappy his legs move slowly, giving the
impression of a kind of slow bicycling movement where the foot of one leg
brushes against the other. The bicycling movement is then repeated with
the other foot and leg. The brushing part of this experience seems to
predominate over the bicycling movement. Eric occasionally grabs onto
the cloth of his babygrow and touches mother's hand. He then releases
his fingers from his mouth. Soon he breaks into a smile and then a laugh
with a kind of 'goo-aah-hi' series of sounds. The sounds become more
excited as he waves his hands in a flapping motion near his shoulders.
Very much in response to mother's talking to him, he makes more
sounds. He seems very pleased as he sometimes mouths his fingers and
releases them. He kicks his legs very slightly as he moves his fingers in
and out of his mouth.

When mother puts the nappy on and begins fastening it, Eric tightly
holds onto her right index finger. Mother says he should let go, but he
doesn't. She releases her finger, but he grabs it once again. When she
releases her finger this time by picking up his hand with her own, Eric
starts laughing. When mother tells him not to hold on, Eric rubs his hand
alongside the sleeve of her blouse, and alongside her hand. He is looking
at her face with the fingers of his other hand in his mouth. He extends his
other hand towards her. He alternates his movement towards mother

with his looking at me. He becomes increasingly excited. Eric begins laughing. He again holds onto her index finger very tightly. Slowly he rubs his hand along the sleeve of her blouse, near her hand. He is looking at her face. While continuing to look at mother, Eric extends both his hands towards her. This rocking towards mother alternates with his looking at me, with his fingers of his right hand in his mouth.

Mother pulls the neck of his jumpsuit over his head and Eric bursts out laughing. Mother says to him, 'It's like a game of hide and seek. Now you're hidden and there you are.' Eric is waving his left arm with delight. He utters some 'aa aah' and 'ee eeeh' sounds. He enjoys the sounds and continues to make them with pleasure. The sounds vary in pitch, intensity and form. Tickled by this, mother says that Eric enjoys it when she talks to him.

After bringing him into the sitting room, mother feeds Eric at her left breast. While he is sucking the nipple, he keeps touching mother's arm and putting the thumb of his right hand in his mouth. Eric then holds onto her shirt. Eric is sucking without intensity, suggesting that he is not very hungry. Still sucking, he looks first into mother's face, but then at the large green leaves of a plant behind mother.

As soon as mother begins speaking to me, Eric turns away from the nipple and looks at her face. When she looks down at him, he makes 'aah' sounds and smiles. Mother turns his head back towards the nipple and he begins sucking again while continuing to look at her. The rest of his body is very still, with his arm resting against his waist. He moves his hand along mother's blouse, holding onto it momentarily. He continues to glide along the breast with his fingers. He lifts his hand again and repeats the tender gliding movement continuing from mother's blouse onto her breast. The rest of his body is very still.

After a while he stops sucking. He looks up at mother's eyes in a more attentive way than before. Afterwards he puts his two fingers in his mouth. Mother then plays with Eric on her lap for a few minutes. He looks at her and then he looks at me. He smiles and makes a variety of 'ooh, aah' sounds. Subsequently, he looks around the room on either side of mother, but then he rests his eyes on her and smiles. Mother says that he enjoys staying awake for much longer periods now.

Later she decides to place Eric in his cot, telling him not to get too disappointed because she will let him rest in the sitting room. As the blanket is tucked around him, he begins pulling on it with his right hand. He then uses both hands to lift it to his face. Mother asks him what he is doing. Eric puts his right middle fingers in his mouth and covers them with his left hand and then he covers his nose. His fingers are extended in a relaxed way. Eric very slowly moves his hand downwards along his face until his hand rests on his other hand. He releases both hands from his mouth. Slowly Eric repeats this whole repertoire of movement of his hands on to his face and on to each other.

Eric's panic when his face was under his shirt has changed into a hide-and-seek game with mother. It seems he is beginning to develop an internal picture of mother feeding him, her silky breast touching his face, her physical holding and her voice all intent in his mind. When mother is present Eric affectionately tries to make contact with all the aspects of her. Being close to her in every way is very important to him.

Accompanying his search for emotional and physical closeness to mother is Eric's new response to mother's going away. He is now able to tolerate mother's departure through 'recreating' the situation of being held and fed by mother at her breast. He does this through sucking his fingers, resting his hand on his face and cupping his hand around his fingers in his mouth. Eric's new inner strength seems to be derived from his dialogue with the good mother he has inside himself.

Conclusion

This chapter highlights some of the baby's central preoccupations during his early experiences, in particular his lack of integration and fear of disintegration. The stressful task of taking care of a new unknown baby creates in a new mother a sense of loss of identity. The observations show how the impact of the baby's infantile terrors initially unsettles mother, preventing her from being able to understand his needs and feel emotionally close to him. Through the support of her husband and friends and a baby who welcomes her presence and can be easily comforted, mother is enabled to develop her sense of confidence in her mothering. Because father is able to assist mother in her many ways of caring for the baby, Eric is able to count on two caretakers. Thus Eric is enabled to develop and hold inside himself an experience of caring parents whom he loves.

5

Kathy and Suzanne: Twin Sisters

The observation reported on here arose from an interest in questions about heredity and environment. The observer also hoped that observation of the development of twins would allow her to explore the complexities of identifications and identity formation, and to understand some of the special at-risk factors in twinship. A pair of monozygotic twins could not be found at the time and the twins eventually observed were girls, dizygotic, born nine weeks premature, with a caesarian delivery. One of the two, Suzanne, was at one point in great danger, for she was squashed on one side of the womb by the other baby. An urgent operation was required when only one heart-beat could be detected and Suzanne seemed to be beyond hope. So the situation at birth was much more complex than had been anticipated by the observer. Reflection on the importance of pre-natal experience, both for the baby's subsequent development and for the parents' psychological state, was a significant part of the observer's experience. The interest in differentiating between innate and acquired aspects of the twins' personalities gave way to involvement in the painful drama of their early months of life; in a situation of so much real anxiety about survival, the observer was drawn into a vortex of emotion and distress.

The parents

I was introduced to the parents by a nursing sister in the hospital five days after the birth of their twin daughters.

Mother, a dark lady in her thirties, was in bed, looking sleepy and in pain. She seemed to have forgotten what the nurse had told her the previous day about my wish to observe the development of the babies; she explained that she was still taking a lot of drugs which made her feel very drowsy all the time. Father then came into the room and spoke rather loudly and enthusiastically almost as if to compensate for the weakness and pain audible in mother's voice. He told me that they both have twins in their families, and were thus not surprised to have twins themselves. I was surprised that the parents did not ask me any questions about my request to observe regularly. They seemed very keen on the idea of having a weekly visitor; this made me wonder if they might be a lonely couple.

Mother told me about the birth which had been very painful, 'a terrible experience'. The intra-uterine development of the babies was apparently normal for the first months. Around the sixth month a scan was taken. Mother said one baby looked 'like a monkey'; she felt terrified at the idea that this baby might be 'subnormal'. She told me that she had said to her husband, 'I do not want the baby if it is not normal'. A subsequent X-ray showed that one baby was in a very dangerous position, squashed by the other, and only one heart-beat could be heard. At this point mother had an urgent caesarian delivery; the babies were thought to be nine weeks premature. But one of them, mother told me, the one who had been squashed, had in fact been conceived five weeks later, so she was 14 weeks premature. When I first visited, mother had not yet seen the babies since she could not stand up, and the babies were in the incubator. She had been convinced that one baby was dead until her husband showed her some pictures of them in order to reassure her.* Mother said she was probably going to be able to see the twins for the first time the next day.

Mother's account of the pregnancy and delivery was unclear at several points; she spoke as if she had learned it by heart. There was no space for questions and this habit of not questioning later appeared to be a characteristic of her personality.

I shall give a brief description of the parents here, utilising the material gathered over time.

Mother looks in her late thirties but is probably younger. She comes from a small village in East Africa where the rest of her family still live, apart from a younger sister who lives with them in London.

Her body and posture are characteristically African, but her face has marked Asian features. Her father's family, in fact, came from Sri Lanka. I never saw her wearing woollen clothes even when the weather was very cold; the babies too were were hardly ever warmly dressed although their health was not very good.

Mother is rather overweight and gives the impression of a woman who is physically strong. Her hands are as large as a man's. She has a very sweet face and looks much younger when she smiles. Her tone of voice is always very soft and her English is still rather poor, both in grammar and in pronunciation. She came to live in London with her younger sister about ten years ago and worked at London airport until she got married. At work she met her husband, who appeared to be exactly the opposite of her.

He presented himself as being very efficient, educated and

* I think in retrospect that the deep anxiety mother felt in relation to Suzanne's health during the later stages of pregnancy, and especially during the five days after birth before she was able to see the babies, had a powerful influence on her expectations.

charming, and tended to use his qualities to draw attention to his wife's deficiencies. He is a short, rather plump man in his early forties. He works nights at the airport and was therefore often around during the observations. He is extremely good at making things and ambitious to improve their home. He was always busy while at home, possibly this served as an escape from family involvement at times, but it was probably also his way of contributing to family life.

Mother had very little education, and father used to react to her lack of knowledge with impatience and arrogance. She never seemed to resent this, as if she was almost expecting to be treated in this way. Their relationship appeared to be based on an expectation that mother would undertake all the hard work of child-care, and father would have the fun of playing with his daughters.

From the beginning of my observations mother wanted to establish an informal affectionate relationship with me. She asked me to call her by her Christian name, showed me pictures of her family and wanted to give me clothes that she could not wear any more. I came gradually to think that mother was worried about being 'too much' for me; she seemed afraid that I would feel as emptied as she did, and her gifts were intended to replenish my resources. Related to this was her habit of changing the position of the furniture in the sitting room: once a month, or more, there were changes in the room and the babies' clothes seemed to be always different. Possibly these continual changes expressed some of her dissatisfaction.

Despite her basic trust in me, mother was very embarrassed by dirt and untidiness. She never allowed me to watch her changing the babies and did not like me to go into the bedroom to watch them sleeping if the room was not tidy. At first I thought this was just an attitude of reticence towards the private parts of the house, but it continued. Perhaps it arose from some discomfort of hers about the intimate care of the babies which she wanted to keep private.

Father, when present, was always trying to attract my attention. He liked to 'explain' things he assumed that only he knew about; I felt rather patronised. Perhaps all women were felt to need educating. However, he became gradually less pressing and more eager to know my opinion rather than to impose his own, and as time went by he began to sit and watch the babies playing and show interest instead of falling asleep as he often used to do.

In the hospital

Observation at 18 days

My first observation was when the babies were 18 days old. Both were being tube-fed. Once a day mother fed them by bottle. She told me she

did not have enough milk to breastfeed them, but once later on she said
that she had found it extremely difficult when she tried.

> She seemed very pleased to see me and apologised for not being able to
> offer me a cup of coffee. She talked about the hospital, saying that she
> felt relieved that the babies were going to stay there for a few more
> weeks, because she did not feel ready yet to have them at home. She also
> spoke about the work she and her husband were doing in their home.
> After about ten minutes of this conversation, she introduced me to the
> babies. Kathy was sleeping in the cot and Suzanne was held on mother's
> lap and had just finished being fed; I remember I thought they were very
> similar and that it would take me time to be able to tell them apart. In
> that first meeting, mother showed clearly how she needed the observer
> for herself and that only after she received some attention did she want
> me to turn towards the babies. This became a pattern in many
> subsequent observations. Mother soon moved on to talk about the
> differences she had already noticed between the twins and it seemed
> very important for her to have the differences clearly in her mind.
> Suzanne weighed more and was more advanced than Kathy in taking
> milk; she was also more wakeful. Their birth weights had been identical,
> 1.67 kg.
>
> Suzanne fell asleep soon after having been put in the cot. Mother went
> to prepare the bottle for Kathy who had just woken up. After a while
> Kathy had a short cry and mother, picking her up, commented on the fact
> that Kathy never cries whereas Suzanne does very often and very loudly.
> Mother said in a tone of complaint, 'You can hear her crying from the
> other end of the ward.' While mother was changing Kathy she said that
> she can feed at any time, while Suzanne will feed only if her nappies
> have been changed. A noise in the corridor was heard and mother said
> that Kathy was very sensitive towards every noise. 'Suzanne' she added,
> 'recognises only her father's kisses.' Kathy was looking at mother while
> she fed and finished the whole bottle; mother congratulated her and
> mentioned this to the nurses very proudly. Kathy looked very
> comfortable and relaxed with mother. I had the impression of having
> done only half an observation, because although I stayed for an hour, I
> had only watched one baby. I decided then to come back another day to
> observe Suzanne.

This feeling of 'having left something out' which I had during the
first observation, became almost a pattern not only in my personal
experience but also for the seminar, where my colleagues always felt
frustrated at the end, not having had enough time for both babies.

Observation at 4 weeks

When I went to see Suzanne, she was four weeks old; mother was not
there, as she had changed the time of her visit to fit in with her
husband's shifts.

> Suzanne had just finished being fed and changed by a nurse and was

lying in her cot; nobody else was in the room except me. She seemed to be trying to fall asleep and struggling with the fear of doing so. Many times she closed her eyes and opened them suddenly; she also kept moving her fist in and out of her mouth. After more than half an hour, she looked around for a while, then brought her hand in front of her eyes and watched it carefully, until it flopped on her face. She looked surprised. She seemed nearly asleep but suddenly woke up again; she touched her nose for a while then let her arm fall down on the blanket. Again she brought her hand in front of her face and then it flopped down; she pushed her fingers almost into her eyes which were now closed. Eventually she put her thumb into her mouth, then she leaned the other hand under her cheek and fell asleep.

Leaning on her hand seemed to have given Suzanne some feeling of comfort, of holding on to something, which allowed her to overcome the fearful feeling of letting go and falling asleep. It took her about an hour to fall asleep. It seemed to me that Suzanne was attempting to establish a link with a comforting external object, first with her hand movement then by pressing her fingers into her eyes and eventually by putting her thumb in her mouth. The baby seemed to be using her hand to fill the gap left by the end of the feed. It was when Suzanne felt she had something to hold and suck in her mouth that she could also enjoy the support of her hand for her face.

At home: initial interactions between mother and babies

The parents live in a rather remote area of London, which has few amenities. The closest shops are at about half an hour's walking distance. Their flat is very small and simply furnished; the babies did not have a room of their own and their cot was at the bottom of the parents' bed.

Observation at 6½ weeks

The first observation at home was when the babies were 44 days old. They had remained in the hospital for 37 days, but mother cancelled our first appointment at home the week before saying they were not properly settled yet. I think she may have meant not only that the work they were doing at home was not yet finished but also that she herself felt unsettled and disorganised and did not want visitors.

Mother was in the bedroom, feeding Suzanne; Kathy was sleeping in the cot. Mother seemed pleased to see me but rather embarrassed. Suzanne fell asleep while mother was giving her the bottle and she commented wearily that it always takes a long time to feed Suzanne because she so often falls asleep ... Suzanne cried when father put her in the cot and went on crying although he changed her position and then put her on their bed. Both parents said to me that Suzanne was a real problem for them. She was really bad; she cried too much and took so long to feed. She also did not want her nappies to be changed after Kathy. Mother said pointedly that Suzanne gets everything she wants.

... I noticed that mother did not hold or touch Suzanne's body while she was feeding her but she just lay her on her arm; Suzanne kept her arms alongside her body and her eyes were closed most of the time – as if she was not interested at all and was not getting any pleasure out of it. Mother then fed Kathy who sucked the whole bottle straight away. Kathy was looking at mother intensely and holding mother's blouse with one hand and the bottle with the other one. Kathy appeared much more connected with mother, who commented on her being very nice and quiet. Kathy searched for anchorage with her eyes, mouth and hands, and found it.

Mother asked me to hold Suzanne while she went to the kitchen with Kathy to make some coffee. The atmosphere became very chaotic:

... Mother was describing their previous house; then father wanted to show me the new video-recorder and put a film on; the radio was also on and later father introduced me to their three cats.

... It felt to me as though they were distracting me by showing me new and exciting objects, perhaps thinking that being an observer was boring. Father certainly could not find anything interesting at this point in the babies and said he was 'looking forward to them growing' so that they would respond to him more.

In retrospect, that first observation at home contained some significant elements which characterised the relationship between the babies and their parents. The problem of finding a place for two distinct babies in their minds was temporarily solved on the basis of there being one 'good' and one 'bad' baby. Mother seemed capable of holding and giving attention to only one baby at a time. The observer was asked to hold the other. Father's excited conversation served to distract and seemed intended to enliven. Perhaps it was his way of covering up whatever he felt to be depressing, boring or empty. When mother leaves the room, he wants to turn on the video. When she is occupied with the babies, he introduces the family cats.

Observation at 8 weeks

I was left alone with Suzanne during this observation.

Mother went to change Kathy in the bathroom. Suzanne suddenly woke up and started crying very loudly. I was surprised by the power of her cry and by the fact that mother did not come but remained in the bathroom with Kathy. When eventually mother came in, Suzanne was still crying. Mother picked her up and took her into the bathroom without any attempt to soothe her. Suzanne cried even more and Kathy started crying as soon as mother came in with Suzanne. Mother left Suzanne on the divan and picked Kathy up, saying that she had some tummy problems and she may have difficulties in digesting milk. Mother asked me to hold Suzanne on my lap since she was still crying. I noticed her rigid posture; her head was turned back towards the wall and she was watching it intensely.

It seemed to me that mother could cope with only one baby at a time; that is to say, if one baby got something the other manifestly did not. She did not seem to have enough inside her for both twins, and I felt she needed my attention quite urgently herself. Mother's own need for attention at times made me feel that she herself felt like a child.

Observation at 10 weeks

I noticed that the babies were fed with two different types of bottle. Mother explained to me that 'Feeding Suzanne is much more complicated as she continuously spills milk, so I use a larger and shorter bottle, which is easier to hold.'
... Mother was holding Suzanne a bit distant from her body; Suzanne was keeping her eyes closed and her arms hanging loose. She seemed to be supported just by her head against mother's shoulder. Suzanne cried briefly and distractedly looked around. Mother was talking to me non-stop. When she fell asleep, mother woke her up by bouncing her on her knees and distracting her with toys, but Suzanne clearly did not like this at all.

Mother's relationship with Suzanne

Observation at 11 weeks

I heard from mother that Suzanne had a very bad cold and the night before had been hardly able to breathe. Mother had called her husband at work and he came home. After a few hours Suzanne was a bit better and so they did not call the doctor. She told me she had been extremely frightened that Suzanne might die. She looked very tired and tense. Suzanne was in bed and cried frequently. Mother said she was doing it for attention. Father was also present and he commented on Suzanne's habit of 'pretending' to cry. 'Suzanne always cries when my wife's sister comes back from work because she knows that she will cuddle her until midnight.' It seemed possible that Suzanne was finding in this aunt some warmth that she could not evoke in her parents.

Observation at 13 weeks

Mother was holding Suzanne against her shoulder for burping. Suzanne was watching the wall intensely with her arms alongside her body. Mother was not touching Suzanne's body but just kept it against her. She then lay the baby on her knees, her feet pointing at her stomach. Suzanne was laid completely horizontal and she was watching the ceiling. Mother tried to give her the bottle again but she would not suck.

There were repeated observations of Suzanne being held at a distance and holding herself together by tensed muscles and intense gazing at walls or ceiling. She did not have the experience during my observations of having her cry responded to as a communication of her needs, or of being held physically close and secure.

Observation at 14 weeks

Mother talked to me about how much Suzanne was still a problem although her digestion had improved. The doctor had prescribed some tablets and she was now crying much less but nevertheless she was still very often awake at night and this was a problem for her and father. Mother, however, continued to deny the baby's need for special caring.

... While mother was telling me this she was holding Suzanne on her knees. When she cried mother commented on her being a naughty child and changed her position. She put Suzanne across her knees and upside down so that she was facing the floor, with her arms and legs weightless. Mother then patted her back with regular movements but Suzanne continued to cry. She was holding mother's dress in her fist and lifted her head giving me a very distressed look from that uncomfortable position. Mother pulled Suzanne up after a while and told her to stop crying, looking at her hard. Suzanne calmed down. Immediately afterwards mother passed her on to me saying she wanted to make a cup of coffee. The baby burst into tears again as soon as mother disappeared behind the door.

... In the same observation mother talked to me about one of her sisters who had been breastfed regularly until she was three years old and occasionally until she was five. Mother, looking disgusted, said that she did not envy her sister because ' ... it is revolting to see a child being breastfed.' Immediately after saying this mother pulled Suzanne up and made her bounce on her knees saying: 'We can dance, we can dance.'

By not holding Suzanne and hardly touching her, mother held at bay the impact of the baby's needs and demands. The discomfort that Suzanne had to bear seemed to be linked with disturbing memories of her sister being fed. The disgust that mother showed, followed by her play with the baby, seemed to me to express mother's defences against feelings aroused by images of breastfeeding. Suzanne's neediness sparked off memories of her greedy little sister and possibly also inflamed a greedy part of mother herself. Mother did not seem to have a hopeful conviction in the natural processes of growth, through which dependency can be met and lead on to separation and independence.

On the other hand mother seemed able to understand the different needs of the two babies, providing, for example, two different bottles and feeding techniques. Yet it was striking how she never attempted to consider whether Suzanne's distress was due to anger, discomfort or wind, for example; she always responded in the same way, diverting the baby's feelings away from herself, making them vanish in excited play instead of offering to absorb distress within herself.

Mother seemed to experience Suzanne as difficult to be with, not enlivening but instead boring or depressing, rather fat and slow. This also seemed to echo the way in which father frequently made mother feel. Possibly Suzanne reminded mother of her own dependent feelings. When she felt inadequate as a mother, the baby was experienced as a big burden.

Mother's relationship with Kathy

The observations of Kathy were strikingly different and although they took place at the same time, it seemed at times as if she lived in a different environment, with different people.

At 9 weeks mother showed concern about Kathy's health. Kathy had a bad tummy.

Observation at 10 weeks

Mother gave the bottle to Kathy, holding her on her lap, close to her body. Kathy sucked regularly, watching mother's face, and touching the bottle with both hands. She stopped sucking after a while and closed her eyes. Mother caressed her cheeks gently and told her not to sleep. Kathy sucked again and finished the whole bottle in about twenty minutes, alternating sucking with pauses. Mother said that Kathy liked that and sounded very tolerant and respectful of her timing. After the feed, mother sat Kathy on her lap and massaged her back gently; the baby was holding mother's skirt tightly in her fist.

Observation at 14 weeks

Kathy had a bad cold. Mother held her on her lap all the time during the observation and justified her continuous crying, saying sympathetically that she was not feeling well. When Kathy refused to take milk mother said she might have difficulty in digesting it and it was better to wait and try later. When Kathy looked distressed, mother pulled her closely towards her body and held her in a foetal position, saying that this was what would calm her down. Kathy in fact relaxed very soon after.

Observation at 16 weeks

Mother played with Kathy, singing the words as she touched her fingers, hands and arms. This was unusual because it was rare for mother to play without using a toy as an invitation to very excited behaviour.

Kathy seemed much more 'real' than Suzanne. Mother was able to live through experiences with Kathy, to allow her to set her own rhythms and to reassure her by offering her physical contact; she also seemed to know well how much she could ask from her. In response to mother's attitude one could see Kathy smiling at her, reaching with all of herself towards her mother and looking absolutely delighted to be surrounded by mother's arms.

Kathy was a 'text-book baby' who sucked vigorously, slept with regular patterns, hardly ever cried and was on the whole healthy. Suzanne, however, required more attention and patience as a predictable consequence of her additional prematurity. One might have expected that precisely because she was relatively backward in her development and more needy, she would receive more care and protection from her parents; but as a matter of fact their reaction was the opposite. They seemed to find Kathy more appealing and attractive and less anxiety-provoking. Overall, Kathy's growth and contentment reassured the parents. Sadly Suzanne, who was already the weaker, was relatively neglected and her development in consequence less vigorous.

The tendency to neglect Suzanne was in contrast with the enormous fear and concern that mother showed each time she was seriously ill. The first time she mentioned this was in relating the details of her dangerous birth. Later she described more than once Suzanne's breathing difficulties in hot weather. On these occasions mother looked very tense and wanted to talk at length about her, to relieve her anxiety. Possibly she felt recurrently persecuted by the experience during the pregnancy, when she felt Suzanne might be dead or damaged. Perhaps in her tendency to reject Suzanne there was an attempt to avoid the pain of a loss she dreaded through limiting her awareness of Suzanne as a live baby. Later on, mother spoke of wanting to work in a hospital to help and support the dying, which seemed a further indication of her deep preoccupations with death.

Later developments

When the twins were 17 weeks old for the first time I saw a brief interaction between them.

Observation at 17 weeks

Kathy was complaining of mother's absence and I put Suzanne close to her on the divan; Kathy's cries increased but Suzanne's immediate reaction was to smile twice at her sister. Mother told me that on a previous occasion when they were sitting very close, Kathy kicked Suzanne and made her cry.

During the fifth and sixth months mother's perspective changed: both babies were described as clever; both could not sleep at night because of their teeth; both responded to her in the same way. Similarities, not differences, were the focus of comment. This important shift seemed to herald a very big spurt in development in Suzanne. When I returned to see the family after the summer holiday, the twins were eight months old. Suzanne looked much grown: taller and plumper. She smiled openly at me, showing two front teeth. Kathy did not have any teeth yet and struck me as shy and withdrawn, as if she did not recognise me.

Observation at 34 weeks

Although Suzanne looked bigger, she was not able to sit straight but tended to slip down to one side. However she looked content and watched what was going on around her. She looked at her feet and then touched them with both hands. She then scrutinised a ribbon on her dress and played with it, pulling it up and down; she enjoyed doing this for about ten minutes.

In observations from this period Suzanne often showed a capacity to be on her own, playing for a long time with a toy, generally a cube or the top of the bottle. Kathy by contrast could sit up straight but she tended to tire of her toys more quickly, occasionally asking Mother for others, using hand movements to indicate what she wanted.

In the observations that followed, Suzanne smiled readily at the observer and made herself understood when she wanted to stand up or jump. She could make sounds like words and occasionally this led to a sort of 'conversation'. Her interest in and capacity for reciprocity with the observer seemed to be more developed than with her parents; she was particularly interested in her clothes and jewellery. By contrast, Kathy was remarkably silent and serious, and when left on the observer's knee she would complain and cry. In fact, Kathy was anxious with strangers around this time, whereas Suzanne's social responsiveness was growing.

Relationship with father

At this time, father's active presence in the observations became a regular feature; mother was busy and often absent, in the kitchen, ironing or washing. From the time of the birth until the summer he had often been asleep during the observations.

He drew constant attention to the differences between the babies; he not only ignored Suzanne but openly rejected her. He used to call her 'fatsy' although he knew she did not like this and would turn away.

Observation at 36 weeks

Suzanne did not turn towards father when he came in but looked at my jumper and at my brooch; she touched them both and tried to take the brooch out but eventually gave up and gently leaned against me while father was still trying to get her attention by calling 'Fatsy'. Father told me then that Suzanne was too fat, she was – he said – like the twins in his wife's family, whereas Kathy was slim like relatives in his family.

Father was very seductive towards Kathy, always trying to get her attention by offering her sweets or chocolates. Kathy would then climb on his knees and put her arms around him; very proudly he would then say to me: 'See what she wants? She wants me!'

Father regularly informed me about Kathy's developmental progress and very seldom acknowledged Suzanne's. I felt at times that it was important for me to mention Suzanne's progress and so I did; in response, father would say that she was far behind Kathy and I would then feel I had to remind him of her greater prematurity. Here I found myself getting drawn into the family conflicts through identification with the rejected twin.

Suzanne often looked for father and was visibly jealous when Kathy was getting something from him and she was not. Possibly to evade this painful situation, she started to stare fixedly at the window and thus remove herself from the rivalry for father and everything else.

Observation at 38 weeks

Father was lying on the armchair watching TV and holding Suzanne on his lap. She was drinking milk holding the bottle against father's body. As soon as she finished it father gave her to me and left the room. Mother and Kathy were in the kitchen. Suzanne started to complain; I picked her up and sat her in front of me. Suzanne smiled briefly and then turned her look away from me and stared fixedly at the window for about five minutes. Mother came in with Kathy, she left Kathy on father's lap and went to make coffee. Kathy played with a piece of paper and put it in her mouth, showing a sense of disgust. She then looked at father's rather big tummy and watched it for a while. Then she touched his belly and eventually her hands slipped down onto his genitals. Father pulled her up and held her up over his head, saying to Suzanne: 'Look Suzanne, Kathy is a supergirl!' ... Father then gave an envelope to Suzanne and she played with it; he then turned again towards Kathy, who was still on his lap, now playing with father's neckchain. Suzanne made some sounds, which got gradually louder. She then patted my knees with both hands and eventually again fixed her look on the window.

The first three times in which Suzanne cut herself off seemed to be related to father's presence in the room and his attitude towards Kathy; but later on these day-dreamy states seemed to occur without any external stimulus.

Father often increased the competitiveness between the twins by putting Suzanne in the position of wanting to do what Kathy could already do:

> Father walked into the room and lifted Kathy up; Suzanne looked visibly angry at that. Father went to sit by the table and offered Kathy a biscuit. He then called Suzanne and told her to go and get one for herself. Mother put Suzanne on the floor although they knew that she could not crawl yet. However, with 'swimming' motions, she managed to get to the middle of the room. At this point father showed the biscuit to Kathy (the one which was supposed to be for Suzanne) and put it in her mouth. Then he said to Suzanne: 'Look Suzanne, Kathy can get it! She is a clever girl!' Suzanne was watching Father intensely, then she turned her eyes towards the door and moved in that direction.

Suzanne's day-dreams seemed to reveal a withdrawal from parental rejection as in this example and a search for something more satisfying elsewhere. At times, the observer provided a focus for her. Kathy continued to be a quiet baby, on the whole less vocally expressive than Suzanne.

At eleven months Kathy could crawl a long distance, whereas Suzanne was still finding it difficult at thirteen months. The pattern of their motor development was nevertheless very regular: Kathy was able to crawl at nine months and she walked at fourteen months; Suzanne crawled at fourteen months and walked at nineteen.

One year old

After the Christmas holiday, Suzanne did not smile at the observer but looked sad and was on the point of crying when she approached her. Kathy smiled briefly. Mother, perceiving the observer's surprise, said that Suzanne had become very dependent on her in the last few weeks (while her husband had been away). In fact she wanted to be with mother all the time and cried as soon as mother tried to leave her with the observer. Mother said she was worried about the degree of Suzanne's dependence and she was thinking of going to see the doctor. Kathy was clearly very jealous of this new closeness between mother and Suzanne and often attempted to join in; mother therefore had to carry both of them. She complained of having tendonitis in her right arm. It seemed that father's absence or other events during the Christmas holiday break which were unknown to the observer may have made mother more available to the babies and in particular to Suzanne. Suzanne had found out that showing her feelings was more gratifying than cutting herself off. Moreover, during father's absence, Kathy was probably under less pressure to compete, as this was something he tended to encourage and this may have helped Suzanne to find a way to come closer to her mother.

This big change indicated how painfully Suzanne felt shut out by father's scorn. Her confidence and hopeful expectations were undermined and this suggests that her need to cut herself off was because he was really 'too much' for her. When this factor was removed, her expressiveness and struggle to gain mother's attention came to the fore.

Immediately after Father's return home (at twelve months and one week), the observation was cancelled because Suzanne had to be admitted to hospital for an asthma attack. This serious asthmatic episode may have registered her distress at the readjustment required by father's reappearance. A week later mother cancelled saying that she was not feeling well and Kathy had been vomiting all night. Kathy had been left at home with mother's sister when mother was with Suzanne in hospital, and the vomiting episode suggests this may have been difficult for her. Was she unable to contain the anxious and turbulent feelings evoked by the absence of mother and twin sister? The vomiting may well have expressed her psychic distress in a somatic form.

During the next observation Suzanne looked very pale and both twins had colds but nevertheless they were wearing the usual thin dresses. Suzanne had one hand bandaged and mother told me that she had got burned the day before. The accident apparently happened in the kitchen when mother was pouring some boiling water into father's cup while holding Suzanne, who suddenly brought her hand forward. They had taken her to hospital for treatment. In spite of this accident, Suzanne looked much as usual, smiling at mother and observer.

The following week Suzanne was attempting to emulate Kathy who could almost walk. There was also a great deal of competition for father and both the babies at one point tried to climb on him.

The week after, Suzanne poured some tea on mother's lap. Mother complained, very annoyed, saying: 'This always happens with this baby, because she never looks at what she does!' Father, for his part, continued to complain about her slow development. Again both babies competed for a place on father's lap.

Observation at 1 year 5 weeks

Mother was holding Suzanne on her lap, by the table; something dropped down and mother leaned to pick it up. Suzanne grabbed onto mother's arms so as not to fall. When Mother sat up again she suddenly screamed because Suzanne had provoked a sharp pain in the arm in which she had tendonitis, by leaning on it. Mother was in tears while father said that it was nothing serious (but clearly being very frightened that it might have been). Mother calmed down after a while and said to Suzanne (whom I had taken on my lap): 'You are a bad baby, you always hurt mummy!'

A few days later Suzanne got burnt again on the same hand and she was again taken to hospital.

All these accidents might be seen as the result of Suzanne wanting to prolong the closeness with mother that she had found while father was away, and that now, because of the many needs around, she could only get this by desperate means. The accidents might be understood as attempts to convey her dread of being forgotten or 'dropped' by mother. This sequence of illnesses and accidents occurring just around the time of her first birthday might also be linked with mother's reawakened anxiety, the birthday recalling to mind the difficult birth and vulnerable beginning. Kathy seemed to represent the other pole, the excitement of growth, particularly in the successful achievement of walking.

Conclusion

One theme of particular interest in this observation was the influence which the twins' pre-natal experiences seem to have had on their physical and behavioural characteristics at birth.

Suzanne's greater immaturity in gestational age was followed by her being more active and wakeful, more irritable and more hungry at birth than her sister. Differences in these traits also appear in studies of monozygotic twins; this would suggest that they are acquired during the intra-uterine life or the process of birth.

The picture that mother gave me of Suzanne's behaviour at birth was of a voracious baby: she was taking more milk than Kathy at ten days when they were still fed by both tube and bottle. At fifteen days, Suzanne weighed 5 g more than Kathy and she continued to be the heavier child. At eighteen days, mother told me that Suzanne had a very loud cry, which was embarrassing; this characteristic also continued and she remained a 'noisy' baby, although this was partly due to her breathing difficulties. Suzanne was also reported to be more often awake than Kathy at eighteen days, and this remained a constant pattern in that she always had problems in falling asleep and tended to wake up at night.

Suzanne's prenatal experience was marked by a real fear for her safety and the frustration of inadequate space for her growth. Perhaps some anxiety about survival was expressed by the desperation of her cry? Her hunger and restlessness at birth were probably signs of her unsatisfactory undernourished life in the womb. All these factors made her a very demanding baby to take care of. Her neediness was manifest both physically and psychically. She had very fragile health, with constant difficulties in digesting first milk and then some solid foods. Asthma attacks led to a number of sudden admissions to hospital. She showed great anxiety about being separated from mother on these occasions.

Having such an anxious and needy baby enormously increased mother's worries about her mothering skills, and made heavy demands on her. Mother seemed to react from the start by seeing the babies as distinctively good or bad. Suzanne was seen as greedy, insatiable and at times almost disgusting. There was evidence that mother herself had felt rejected as a child and stigmatised as clumsy and fat and these memories seem intertwined with her perception of Suzanne. Striking also was the fact that in her marriage she seemed to be repeating the experience of being looked down on.

Mother saw Kathy as the healthy and lovable baby, while Suzanne was an 'insatiable' baby who had to be kept at a distance. She avoided touching, holding or kissing her. When she did come closer, she showed no joy or pleasure in doing so.

Suzanne responded to this by withdrawing from interaction with her mother. She did not look at mother during feeds and hardly ever grasped her clothes when she was held on mother's lap. In the absence of gratifying active interchange between the two, a secure attachment to mother did not develop. Instead, Suzanne turned her attention to inanimate objects and would play for a long time with a toy or the top of the bottle; although she enjoyed being bounced, mother often chose the wrong moment to do this, to which Suzanne responded by becoming very upset.

As a baby, Suzanne dribbled constantly during feeds, to the extent that mother tried a different bottle. This continuous spilling was also an echo of the lack of physical and psychological containment, the 'poor fit' between mouth and teat, baby and mother.

Her illnesses were a source of persecution to mother and every complaint was interpreted as her wanting more attention and being envious of what Kathy was getting. This reaction served to establish a vicious circle in which Suzanne responded with even more desperate crying; the parents would then lose their patience with Suzanne, and feel angry with her.

During father's absence from home over a period of four weeks, mother and Suzanne made a closer relationship. But in the observations which followed father's return, this development came unstuck. When they were closer to each other Suzanne and mother seemed to show some similar features, clumsiness for example: while mother once spilt boiling water on Suzanne's hand, Suzanne poured hot tea into mother's lap. Mother also told me about her own fatness as a child, to the extent that if she ran her legs used to bleed. She seemed to fear that Suzanne was going to be a fat child as she had been and would talk to me about this. In reality, Suzanne appeared an ordinarily plump baby.

Kathy's experience in the womb was also difficult although there had not been the risk of death. She was underweight at birth and her feeding was difficult to establish. But after that (when they were back home) Kathy became an easy baby. She began to have regular feeding and sleeping patterns and her health was always good; this profoundly reassured her parents. She was less needy and demanding than Suzanne and easier to respond to. Her attractiveness and affectionate nature made for benign interactions. The difficulties that Kathy had in feeding during the first month in hospital were reduced at home with the constant care and presence of mother; she became an extremely easy baby to feed, and her responsiveness meant a great deal to her mother who needed to feel appreciated.

These babies had the task particular to twins of finding space for themselves in their relationship with each other and in relation to their parents. It was interesting to see that when they were very close to one another Kathy would immediately show great anxiety. She would burst into tears of tremendous distress and Suzanne would be most astonished to have her play so rudely interrupted. This tendency of Kathy to withdraw and be frightened of any contact with other people did not attract mother's concern. Possibly it echoed some of mother's own sense of shyness and social isolation.

Kathy must have had a very difficult time adjusting herself to the presence of a second foetus after having spent some time on her own in mother's womb. Her sister was perhaps felt as a threat, as someone who intruded on the space that she needed to grow. This fear of damaging competition persisted markedly in post-uterine life. Suzanne's puzzlement at Kathy's reaction at times seemed a distressing repetition of the negative feedback that she already faced so frequently from her parents, and the turning away from interest in her family to preoccupation with playing on her own thus received further reinforcement. The problem of shared space was therefore resolved in the first year of the babies' lives by Kathy usually taking more of the parents' intimate involvement and Suzanne tending to look both beyond, to toys, to the observer (and perhaps other adults) and within, to explore her own resources.

6

Andrew

Andrew is the second of two children; his older brother was two and a half when he was born. His parents, both in their early thirties, are a well-educated, middle-class couple. Father is now self-employed; mother was a teacher before getting married and having children. Mother was not born in England although she has lived in this country since she was a very small child. She has a sister living abroad; both her parents are dead. Father has a brother and both parents alive and well, living in England in a different town. Their first child was a good-looking healthy boy who did not present any particular problems.

Observation at 3 weeks

At the first observation, mother had much to say after our initial exchanges: 'Luckily he sleeps a lot, even at night; my first child was always awake during the night. It was terrible! At the moment he is not sleeping really deeply because of his cold; I have a cold too. Sometimes the baby seems old and tired, and so bored!' With a voice full of concern she continued, 'Sometimes I put him on my bed so that he has something more to look at', and later, 'This baby is luckier than the other because now, with the other child around, there is always noise in the house. His brother often puts his face very, very near to the baby's face, smiling at him. That is wonderful for the baby, and adults never do that.'

What was most striking in this very first meeting, when mother introduced me to the baby, was the impression that she was out of touch with her real baby; there seemed to be a preconception about the baby which led her to a misperception of him. It is quite difficult to think of a newborn baby as being old, tired and bored with life and yet that is how his mother saw him. She found it difficult to get to know her actual baby, and to listen to the baby, tending instead to superimpose on him her thoughts about him. Where had these thoughts come from? Her experience of a 'cold baby' seemed to be connected with her feeling of herself as full of cold; the warmth of feelings the baby needed she felt unable to provide herself. She put him instead on her bed where she could find something nice and attractive to look at, to take in. She felt very pleased that some warmth might come to the baby from his little brother who, unlike her, can get very, very close and smile at him; she felt she could not do that.

She also appeared full of worry about coping with the demands that both children were making on her. In relation to her first child, she was anxious that he could be feeling abandoned and would experience her as a nasty Mummy; she was also worried about his feelings of anger and jealousy in relation to the baby. She tried to compensate for these fears by emphasising how understanding the older child could be and how nice he always was to the baby.

> 'I don't like to fit the baby into a routine; I prefer to follow his needs, but having two children to think of makes it quite difficult. Now I have to consider the different needs of both of them'.

She said she felt much better with the second child, much more self-confident, less anxious. But one might also think that her relief about the baby sleeping a lot was related to the fact that he did not then make demands she felt unable to cope with. Her anxieties about having a demanding baby are put in the past, attributed to her first 'wakeful baby' and 'how terrible' that was.

> She then took the baby out of the pram so that I could see him. 'He is very thin' (again with a very concerned note in her voice) 'look how thin he is: the nappies slip down. Before you could see his veins.' As soon as she took his clothes off the baby started to cry desperately and he cried more and more while his mother cleaned him with some cream. As soon as his skin was again covered by his clothes the baby's crying was completely different: the sound not so intense, the rhythm slower, and soon he calmed down.

He had a reaction of panic and collapse when his clothes were taken off; perhaps one could say he was not yet at home in his own skin. His mental skin was not strong enough to protect him from overwhelming anxieties of disintegration. The experience of being held together was lost when he was put down and undressed. Hearing her baby's cries, the mother felt flooded by her perception of him as a very fragile creature needing her to hold him together, provide a containing experience for him. She tried to put all her anxieties far away in the past experience with her first child because they felt so painfully acute. 'I felt so anxious. When he cried, I was worried I could hurt him, worried about not having enough milk.'

This worry about not having enough milk seemed in the present moment to increase her feeling of being inadequate. She stated that she did not like to make use of food to comfort a child; it was perhaps difficult for her to hold in mind the comforting aspect of food, the picture of herself as a feeding mother sought by her baby. She wanted to rely on other resources; for example talking to her children: 'I prefer the older ones, they can speak, and say what is wrong. With babies we can only guess.'

> At this point in the observation it was feeding time. She put the baby to her right breast. The nipple slipped out of his lips; his mother did not help him because, as she put it, 'He must learn how to find the nipple.' The baby was sucking very gently, and when he did find the nipple he sucked more intensely for a little while, then more slowly again. Sometimes he stopped and seemed to fall asleep. Mother would then push her finger very gently on his cheek and he would begin to suck again. Once when he lost the nipple he put two fingers in his mouth.

One might describe this experience of losing a grasp on the nipple as losing a feeling of oneness or at-oneness. The baby reacted to the threat of differentiating himself from his mother's breast, of feeling the space in between, by recreating the nipple in his own finger.

> Meanwhile mother was talking to me: 'There are babies who only eat a little; they don't want to be completely full; this one is like my first child. They only stop sucking when they are completely full, they suck to the last drop.' She put the baby to the left breast: 'He prefers the right breast. That is why when I started to breastfeed him I gave him the left side first. My first child refused resolutely to suck on the left. This one doesn't seem to have such fixed opinions.'

This account of a very hungry baby doesn't seem to match the actual baby's behaviour. It seems much more connected to mother's anxieties about being faced with feelings of inadequacy or emptiness. She felt quite persecuted by the baby's possible rejection of her. She could not actively offer the nipple because she feared rejection and wanted the baby to be looking for it and thus reassure her. She quoted to me what a demanding idea she had of a good mother: 'A professor was saying that the ideal would be to have the baby at the breast all the time, so he can do whatever he likes: to suck, rest, sleep whenever he wishes.'

The baby's movement of his left foot was rhythmically in tune with his sucking: his closed eyes also suggested that he was completely involved through the feeding in an experience of continuity with mother where the rhythm of mother's beating heart, and of the flowing milk, was being recreated within himself as his own possession. Mother then gave him a bottle: 'With the bottle he doesn't have to work, the milk goes directly to his tummy. When he sucks from the bottle his eyes are open.' It seems as if mother is comparing herself with the bottle; while the bottle provides food, her breast gives and demands something more than that.

Observation at 4 weeks

The following week there was a marked change in mother's attitude to the baby. This might be related to her experience of the observer who offered attention as the holding mothering object she feared she had lost touch with internally, with whom she now felt in touch again. She expressed a fear that the very hungry demanding baby within herself might damage the needed object. The observer as somebody interested in getting to know about 'being a baby' seems to have offered mother an opportunity for getting in touch with the understanding function of mothering. She became much more open to the baby, feeling less anxious about being totally invaded or eaten up by him. The relationship between mother and baby seemed more relaxed and enjoyable. Her breasts were producing more milk and this helped her to think afresh about breast and bottle feeding. She tried to recreate the breast experience when the baby took the bottle and thus to give a feeling of continuity – she said, 'With a big hole in the teat the milk goes straight to his tummy, but with a little hole it is more like the breast.' She also tried to reproduce the temperature of the breast milk. She seemed to enjoy enormously considering the details of the baby's care. She discussed her older child as 'the big one' now coupled with Daddy, and herself and the baby belonging with the observer.

'I have been feeding him for ... (she looks at the time) about three quarters of an hour; in the morning when my other child is out we are not in a hurry, are we? In the evening when I am with the other one' – she says with amusement, looking at the baby and smiling sweetly – 'he seems to know it; he whimpers, he cries as though he is hungry, but he is not hungry, he just wants me, but now ... you are the only child, aren't you? After all it's a pleasant way to spend our day, isn't it?'

Here mother showed a collusive intimacy with the baby which responded to the baby's desire for oneness. The mood was to be exclusive and to shut everybody else out. (But the observer was part of this.)

The baby looked very quiet; he sucked slowly, looking at the observer and at mother. He lightly moved his hands and feet. His perceptions seemed very much turned to his external world, to his mother who constituted this. She said, 'This baby loves to be cradled in my arms.' He seemed indeed to get enormous pleasure from being in mother's arms; with the teat of the bottle in his mouth, he sucked uncertainly; he seemed to be more involved in sucking love, looking at his mother, listening to her voice, being cradled in her arms. Mother seemed in touch with the baby's feelings, lightly putting aside the bottle and waiting for his reaction. As the baby began to get both excited and upset (his tension showing in his body's stiffening, in the movements of his mouth and most of all in the movements of his head which he turned swiftly to right and left), mother offered him more milk from the bottle. She repeated the same thing quite a few times with entire devotion until the baby seemed satisfied. 'My first child too wanted to be in my arms when he was a baby, but what he really loved was to look around while carried in my arms everywhere. This one,' she continued, 'is completely different, what he loves is just to feel my arms around him. He just wants to be cradled. You are a cradly baby, aren't you?'

Mother was sensitive to some of her baby's needs, particularly those which corresponded to her wish for him to be a tiny baby totally dependent on her. At this stage it looked as if she divided the 'grown up' and 'baby' aspects between her two children, so that one was felt to have always been independent of mother's surrounding arms, almost using her just because he could not yet walk, and the other, her actual baby of this moment, entirely dependent on her and not at all interested in growing out of his oneness with mother.

Mother then asked me to hold the baby while she dressed herself. I am facing him, he looks at me with great interest; every single movement suggests he is trying to reach me as if he would like to take me and 'eat' me. When I turn him in mother's direction he looks at her completely absorbed; holding him, I can feel there is no tension in his body, he is completely relaxed. Mother takes him for bathing. She says he doesn't cry so much now when being undressed: 'He is not so frightened, now that he knows what is going on.' The baby starts to cry; she wraps him in a towel; he seems to find comfort very easily. She remarks, 'He doesn't like going out, he feels out of his element.'

The news of the observer leaving for a holiday break a few weeks later brought a further change. Mother reacted to being in touch with a feeling of loss by weaning the baby very quickly. This particular mother formed quite an intense relationship with the observer from the beginning (possibly because of the absence of female relatives of her own family), and changes in the rhythm of visits were correlated with changes in the relation between mother and baby.

She now tried to make her baby a 'big baby' (this was how she now referred to him) and felt quite persecuted by the 'being a baby' aspects of both her children; she talked about her first child being very jealous, asking for a bottle, wanting to lie in the pram and getting cross because he was too big. 'He has been pushing the baby at times and I worry he might hurt him.' The baby was also agitated and tearful in the afternoon and in the evening when little brother and father are at home. Her milk was no longer enough: 'The baby is either very hungry and gets disappointed with the breast or is not hungry and not interested in it. I want to try and have the baby sleeping all through the night (without being fed) but meanwhile I asked his father to give him the bottle at night time. I am going to put myself on a diet; now that I will not be feeding the baby I need to control myself.' The diet and the weaning echo each other and the deprivation of the support and enjoyment of the observer's visits.

Two weeks later, when the observer returned, mother said that many things had changed. She had suspended breastfeeding and the baby now slept in his own room; at night she no longer gave him milk, but calmed him down with the dummy. Her older child had been quite difficult, asking for a bottle at night, at times sucking it by himself, at times asking her to give it to him. Father had been giving the bottle to the baby; at first the baby didn't like this (because father, she says, treats the bottle as food, while she gives it to him as a cuddle) but now it is all right. These changes had produced a completely different attitude in mother towards her two children and her husband. 'When I was breastfeeding the baby, his father had the feeling that the baby belonged to me only; now it is different, he puts him on his lap, he gives him the bottle and plays with him.' The baby, however, has not been enjoying food. 'He begins to feel unhappy,' mother says, but 'He loves music and is getting interested in little toys – but he can't cope with threes' (referring to a three-piece toy she had offered and he didn't like).

Observation at 11 weeks

When I arrive the baby is lying in his new cot; he has his eyes wide open. He is looking at some little toys hanging on his bed, trying to catch them which makes quite a lot of noise; moving his hands, sometimes he catches something while his attention is completely devoted to something else. He is very absorbed in what he is doing; often he opens his mouth and puts out his tongue. At first he doesn't notice me; when he does see me, he looks at me completely absorbed now in his smile, then goes back to his activities. He looks wonderfully lively and excited. This goes on for quite a long time; when the noise that he makes catching the toys is both unexpected and too loud for him, he looks astonished; also he is greatly surprised that sometimes he catches something, other times everything seems to slip out of his hands. He moves both his hands but he catches things with the right one. Then he moves the left hand across to what he has in his right hand. He never catches what is just in front of him: it's a little red toy, which, because it hangs just in the middle of the string, is not within Andrew's reach. Mother comes in to get something for his bath. She smiles, satisfied with the nice atmosphere; without interrupting Andrew's activity, she winds up the chick-shaped music-box hanging on the left side of his bed, telling me that he enjoys listening to it. Andrew seems to respond to the music: he starts to make more and more sounds. He seems to be having a very peaceful time, full of discovery and emotions. Mother comes in again: the bath is now ready and she sweetly interrupts Andrew's play, picking him up from the bed. Andrew seems to be surprised at this: he doesn't cry, he doesn't smile at his mother, he doesn't move; he seems not to understand what is going on. We go into the kitchen for his bath. When mother puts him down on the table to undress him, facing her, he seems to find immediately some continuity with his earlier feelings. She starts to play with him making jokes, talking affectionately to him.

At this point he looks happier than he was before; he is completely involved in the situation, he responds to his mother, expressing his feelings by moving his body towards her, by smiling and with a nice laugh. After a bit, mother starts to clean his face: she cleans his eyes first, very, very gently while talking to him; he watches her enraptured; then she cleans his cheeks, then she goes on for a while caressing and fondling him. When she moves her face away from his face, starting to undress him and silent at this moment, Andrew's reaction is very similar to the reaction he had before when he had the experience of the interruption: he looks suspended, he stops his talking, waiting for what is going to happen; he doesn't look frightened or upset, he seems rather to be deeply disappointed, bewildered or disorientated. Sitting in mother's lap, facing her while she gives him a shampoo, again he looks at her spellbound, they start to talk; their speech has the quality of music.

Andrew has been faced with the experience of being weaned in the broad sense of being exposed to many different changes all leading to the breakdown of his phantasy of oneness with the breast-mother. He seems to be adapting to his circumstances, making strong efforts to hold himself together in mother's absence. While exposing the baby to feelings of falling apart, the weaning is offering him the opportunity to differentiate himself from his object, the external from the internal. He is expanding the universe he is interested in, becoming more aware of other people and many new things. In his play he is making a kind of exploration; he is getting interested in the idea of 'being two'; he seems to be struggling to make connections, to sort out possible links, thinking about the question 'What comes from whom?' The impression is that from this more advanced level of experience where he is more able to invest the toy with some symbolic meaning, he can easily regress to a state of mind where he loses himself inside the object and there is no longer a sense of 'twoness'. Being wrapped up in the music might have pushed him in this direction so that when mother comes to pick him up he is unprepared for the transition; he cannot immediately connect his internal relationship with his actual mother who arrives in external reality. He gradually becomes more integrated again when held in mother's arms, by his mother's eyes, gaze and voice.

Music seems to be the chosen substitute for mother. The increased 'sound-making' of the baby suggests his attempt to recreate from within the lost object associated with patterns of sound, the music of voice. The loss of mother's gaze while being undressed and mother's voice (her silence at that time) makes him go silent and seem lost. But the liveliness of the external object puts him in touch with life coming also from within. While bathing he looks at the observer and smiles, and while being powdered he looks with interest at the white flowers on the towel. Fortified by the experience of taking in the object, reassured by his perception of the holding object, both externally and internally, he can allow himself to take in other people and other things around him. When it is time for his feed, mother gives him a bottle; sucking on her lap he looks very sleepy, looking at her but almost through sleep. Every now and then he closes and reopens his eyes. For a moment he refuses the bottle but immediately afterwards starts to suck again. He sucks quite a lot and then stops. Mother puts him sitting on her lap facing me. He wakes up completely, smiles, but then starts to cry. Mother says he always cries when his burp is coming up. She puts him over her shoulder, patting his back gently; he burps and immediately stops crying, 'You see?' mother says, looking at me; she offers him some more milk but he refuses firmly. He looks very tired.

The impression is that the baby enjoys being in mother's arms, losing himself inside her (when feeding is associated with a state of sleepiness). The actual feeding is gratifying in more complex ways. Being awake, aware of feeding, confronts the baby with an object that can be both good and wanted, and bad and rejected. The burp and the baby's reaction to it might suggest that he is struggling with a feeling of being persecuted by something nasty inside himself which at this moment he links to something nasty outside (the observer actually felt she was the nasty one, who was making him cry). When he feels the nastiness has been expelled in the burp he feels relieved.

Mother says he doesn't cry if she puts him in bed during the day but in the evening, she says, 'He understands the day is ended and he cries. He loves his brother although at times he gets a bit suspicious about him,' she added. One might suggest that during the day being in bed is not connected with feeling excluded while at night time he feels left out. The notion of the third element coming in between mother and baby seems to be at the moment a focus of his attention. He is struggling with the pangs of jealousy now that he is more aware of the separate members of the family.

There is a striking fluctuation in Andrew's capacity and eagerness to acknowledge fully his separateness from mother when this is linked with having to face feelings of anger, pain or frustration. It seems that Andrew finds it very difficult to take the step of giving up a very idealised relationship with mother, a relationship in which he experiences the gratifying illusion of a complete oneness.

His attitude to vocal exchange is a good example of his way of responding to what he definitely recognises as coming from 'outside'. The observer notices that when Andrew is the one who makes a sound and mother imitates him, he is delighted, almost blissfully throwing himself into the 'conversation'; when mother takes the initiative with her own sound or word he is quite reluctant to respond, and, when he does, the level of his involvement seems to be different; he can be interested and even eventually amused but there is certainly something disturbing, something which makes him wonder before he embraces the game.

At this time of movement between different levels of experience both of himself and of the world around, Andrew is particularly sensitive to the surrounding atmosphere. He is aware of his mother as frustrating him in relation to the fulfilment of the 'at-oneness' phantasy, yet supporting him in approaching the reality of two-ness as something he can enjoy very much in spite of all the difficulties he might have to face. He certainly seems able to follow her lead:

Observation at 20 weeks

Andrew is lying in his room while mother gets the bath ready. He sucks or licks, according to whether he puts his finger or his hand in his mouth; in either case he doesn't seem very satisfied. When he licks his hand he does not get the feeling of holding something firmly, for his hands very easily slip down. When he sucks his finger or thumb, he seems to have a similar feeling of uncertainty: he doesn't hold his thumb away from his fist so he can only grasp the very top of it in his mouth. From time to time mother comes in to take something for his bath; Andrew turns his head and looks at her with great interest. He seems to be agreeably curious about what she is doing, enjoying her presence but not astonished and enraptured as he used to be earlier on. She tells me she has the impression he recognises the sound of his name.

Andrew is becoming more aware of his feelings which are still very much associated with bodily sensations; he seems to be intensely occupied in the experience of sorting out all the different possibilities to express, explore and discover the feelings located in his mouth. Although not yet very skilled in terms of voluntary movements, he does seem to get pleasure in practising to achieve a better mastery of his hand and mouth play. Mother is at a distance but he is taking her in through his eyes and ears; he enjoys her presence which sustains him. But at times of strain and distress Andrew's liveliness tends to disappear suddenly. He would completely withdraw from external reality, either by falling asleep or by sucking his bottle, retreating to his private safe place of being 'the inside baby', in phantasy at one with mother by being inside or part of her.

Observation at 21 weeks

Andrew, who was wide awake when the bottle was given to him, fell into a state of total unawareness of the world around. Even when he opened his eyes he had a blind expression.

Observation at 24 weeks

'I took the children out,' mother says, 'Maybe there was too much noise or maybe it was being in the open air. I don't really know what it was but Andrew fell deeply asleep and slept for more than two hours; his over-sleeping worries me at times.'

The implications of Andrew's having been introduced to solid food at this time (which he takes sitting in his high-chair while he still has his bottle sitting on mother's lap) seem to be quite relevant. The new experience seems to have made him much more aware of his own mouth, actively taking in or having to wait for food, the mouth experienced as a space which can be full or empty in relation to the coming and going of the spoon. The new rhythms of feeding seem to have reinforced the 'at a distance' relationship. The new qualities of food linked with the new sensations aroused in his mouth by the spoon and cup seem to have strengthened and deepened his recognition of all the different qualities mother has. With the growing perception of mother as an external object, separate from him, and so much needed, Andrew increasingly moves towards the attempt to take possession of what he fears he might lose. As mother says: 'He tries so hard to reach things and when he can't he dissolves into tears of frustration and disappointment.' This goes together with a tendency to be greedy about whatever he does reach.

The way he puts things in his mouth – the bib, the towel, the sponge, his toys – has a voracious quality. And yet his hunger seems to have nothing to do with food. When I arrive, mother anxiously tells me, 'He has not been eating. I haven't been able to give him solids which he always liked and even giving him the bottle has been quite difficult.' She refers to the possibility that it might have something to do with his first tooth coming up through the gum. Perhaps the approach of the time for cutting teeth assaults his attempt to live in a world dominated by feelings of softness and smoothness. Once more threats of pain and distress interfere with his sensuously defined sense of ease. Feelings of wanting to bite or attack and wishes and phantasies of eating mother all up are much more into the open and this seems to have a tremendous impact on Andrew's relations to actual eating. Hunger is getting mixed up with anger, devouring mixed up with destroying. This might be the reason why, while feeling so hungry, he finds it so difficult to eat. His biting actions and imaginings fill up his mouth with rage; the chewed up food may seem to be something dangerous, not good to take inside his body. Being active is for Andrew associated with being destructive. What he does allow himself to take in has to enter him while he is passive. 'Andrew has been refusing solids,' says mother, 'but he seems to enjoy the sucking.' One has the impression that he can eat by making himself into a tiny baby just waiting for something nice to come to his mouth. All the nasty cross feelings are a threat.

Observation at 35 weeks

When the observer comes back after the summer break mother reports that Andrew has been having the most terrible time both in relation to feeding and sleeping.

'I have tried everything. One day he seems just to want milk, the day after he will refuse it; one day he seems to want the cup, the following day just seeing the cup makes him cry. At night time,' she continues, 'he is desperate. For him, everything seems to be a disaster; I have to return over and over again to give him his dummy and if after all my attempts this does not work, I offer him the bottle. Eventually that calms him down.'

One can conjecture that Andrew's destructive impulses are felt by him to be the cause of all these disasters; he no longer succeeds in keeping apart the 'dangerous world outside', where he believed all the nastiness could be put away from the 'safe place inside', full of all the goodness into which he retreated to rescue himself. At this time he seemed to be dominated by feelings of persecution; at night when he is so restless and distraught perhaps he fears that the mother he has been attacking in angry phantasy will come in the dark changed by his rage into a horrible creature wanting to hurt him back.

Mother also told me about how things had been developing between Andrew and Martin (his older brother) during the holiday: 'They spent all their time together. They have their bath together now, but a couple of times when Andrew had it all on his own he was so happy!' This picture of Andrew in the bath made her smile but the smile soon faded away, and she told me that Martin had been jealous again over these weeks. 'He wants anything that belongs to Andrew who in turn wants to grab whatever Martin has got. Not at all easy,' she sighs, 'Andrew has become a little vandal, he destroys books, newspapers, everything! He is not like Martin, who used to love books even when he was a very small child.'

One has the impression that mother's difficulties in having both children at home over the holiday are related to what she has been already faced with in relation to each of them separately; what she really finds difficult, especially if she is under strain, is being in touch at the same time with different levels of experience. During the holiday she has been trying to cope with the situation by putting them on the same level, and seeing them both as more grown up; Martin's jealousy on the one hand or on the other Andrew's way of treating the books have been disappointing in this respect. Each reminds her of their more awkward and infantile aspects. What impressed the observer as something new, in the sense of being more evident in Andrew's behaviour, was the fluctuation of his loving feelings with feelings of anger and rage; they seemed to be of the same intensity; the contrast between the pitiless little plunderer and the tenderness he expressed at times, specially in relation to mother, was quite striking. He would touch her hair gently, put his arms around her, his face caressing her face, as if wanting to kiss her. He still adored music, which seemed to have an almost magical effect on him; when it came to his ears, it didn't matter what he was doing, he would just stop and start to move his body in a rhythmic dance.

Observation at 37 weeks

When I arrive Andrew is sitting on the floor in his room surrounded by several toys and books of different sizes; mother is making the bed. 'He woke up with a cold again,' she says, 'and he is cutting his second tooth.' Andrew doesn't raise his eyes towards mother while she speaks to me; I bend down to say hello to him. He looks at me with a dazed glance, quite indifferent; his feelings seem to be far away: he has a little toy in his right hand which he puts in his left hand, then again in his right, then in his mouth, but it doesn't seem to provide him with a feeling of 'having' something of his own, or of recognising emotionally what is around him; the toys and books which he takes up and puts down again or which he just touches do not seem to have meaning for him. Sitting down, I put out my hand to him which he looks at with interest but he doesn't look at my face. After a while, in a very determined way he tries to catch his mother's leg; she kneels down, takes a book and shows him some pictures. Andrew looks at it for a while then picks up a different book, the biggest one, and covers his face with it. He opens his mouth as wide as he can and then tries to put the book in his mouth. The corner of the book does fit in. Still resting on her knees mother stands him up to get him ready to go out: it's time to collect Martin from the nursery. Andrew puts his arms out and plunges towards her but she says to him they are in a hurry and she has to dress him; Andrew cries, very disappointed. At the front door, in mother's arms, Andrew is very excited; he moves his whole body around, babbling happily, but as soon as he is put down in the push-chair his mood changes. At first he refuses to sit, then he doesn't move at all and gives no sign of life: on the way to the nursery he is absolutely silent, with a dull expression. I accompany them on the short walk and nothing interests Andrew.

Once there, a girl wants to pick him up: he doesn't seem to want this but he doesn't object either; he remains totally indifferent. Mother puts him in the child's arms and he stays there, absolutely impassive. He doesn't show any kind of feeling or reaction to his brother when he rather sweetly takes hold of his hand to say hello. On the way back, one of the other mothers offers a biscuit to the children. Andrew takes it. The biscuit is eaten very, very slowly in spite of his attention being completely devoted to it: he puts the biscuit in his mouth, he takes it out, shifts it from one hand to the other, then grips it with both hands; with the biscuit, or sometimes without it, he puts his hands into his mouth sucking them vigorously. Even his wrist seems worth sucking. The only thing that attracts his attention apart from the biscuit is a little dog in the street.

When we arrive at the front door he comes joyfully to life, full of emotion; his excitement increases as we enter the house. Sitting down next to Martin, who is playing with some bricks, Andrew now becomes very busy, touching everything within reach on the floor. Then he picks up a soft brick with a bell inside, and shakes it excitedly. We are in the living-room; when he hears mother's voice calling Martin from the kitchen for lunch he begins to cry; he stops quite soon, looking with a puzzled expression as Martin pulls down his brick construction, but he brightens up when mother comes to pick him up for feeding.

Martin is eating at the table; putting Andrew into his high-chair, mother gives him a cup with some orange juice; he cries furiously. Mother puts on his bib and starts to feed him. Andrew demands his food crossly; he doesn't use his hands to grab anything but cries angrily; he leans forward to get the food, and stamps on the chair with rage. During the meal he throws his cup onto the floor and later also the spoon mother offers him. She then gives him some peaches in syrup; I hold the plate while he uses his hands to eat it: he finds it quite difficult as they are slippery. When he finishes mother comes to offer him more; Andrew dives toward her and pushing himself forward he grabs at her hair. To calm him down she puts some peaches on his plate; Andrew firmly refuses to eat and begins to cry. Mother points out to me that he can eat everything now but doesn't seem to enjoy it at all.

When the observer arrives, although awake in physical terms Andrew is still in a state of sleepiness quite remote from all the things around; he cannot relate in a lively way; something seems to be missing between himself and his toys, and this renders his relationship to them quite empty and meaningless. Throughout the observation Andrew demonstrates repeatedly how his feelings of identity and the possibility of giving meaning to himself in relation to the world around is based on the recognition of his emotional link with his mother. This is true both internally and externally and he is acutely sensitive to any distance between himself and mother which leaves a space within which his anxiety grows. At moments, his overwhelming aggressive impulses – vividly shown during his feed – seem to be dominant and fill his mind with the fear that he may have lost the mother he loves and who loves him. Mother's presence is not enough to reassure him; he desperately needs something concretely proving that their relationship is a loving one; his demand for physical closeness seems to be related to his anxiety that mother will reject him, push him away, keep him at a distance from all her goodness as a result of his being wild and aggressive. Andrew's requests at feeding time seem to be imbued with a sort of furious accusation; her giving seems to be experienced by him in terms of her not wanting to give; there is no feeling of a nice mother feeding him delicious things; rather, he is taking from her in an angry way almost as if he feels that to get what he needs he has to fight with a nasty mother who wishes to withhold the food and keep it either for herself or to give it to somebody else.

The walk to school seems to drive Andrew deep into himself. The outing is dictated not by his rhythm but by his brother's needs, and this perhaps provokes jealousy from which he retreats, as well as frustrating the urgent wish to have all of mother for himself. (The attempt to gobble up the book.) Perhaps it is the hurry which deprives mother and Andrew of time in which to manage this transition with a more manageable degree of distress. His motionless silence seems to show him in a deadened state – being put into a push-chair from the desired position in mother's arms feels like a fearful loss, but he is also perhaps coldly furious with her. In an older child, one would describe his behaviour as a sulk, but Andrew seems in a more desperate plight. He cannot respond to the numerous overtures made, only show by his possessive behaviour with the biscuit something of the relationship he was searching for – a biscuit which can be totally his, in and out of his mouth, confused with parts of his own body (the chewing of hand, wrist and biscuit seem indiscriminate). Without this, he feels truly lost, and out of contact with a continuing sense of himself, manifest in the dull expression in his eyes. It is as if he experiences not being the apple of mother's eye as near-death. The remarkable revival as the familiar house appears betokens the rebirth of hope – the good mother he had left behind there, the lost image of a loved and lively Andrew simultaneously reappear.

Observation at 38 weeks

Andrew is in his walking-chair, he seems lively today and active; he doesn't stop a second from his happy babbling. He is playing with a teddy bear. He touches the bear's nose with his finger, then the mouth, then he puts it to his mouth quite greedily, but he doesn't do it in his usual dramatic way. He is not so much biting it, but rather rubbing faces, a mutual caress even if a bit of a rough one; he seems to enjoy this enormously. When the teddy bear falls down he bends over to pick it up even though this requires an effort. This impresses me as something he has never done before. I help him when he can't quite manage, and at this point Andrew moves towards me, grabbing my nose, my mouth, then my whole face. He pulls my hair and he does it again and again; it is the first time that he clutches me in this way. Mother comes from the kitchen and takes him out of the walking chair; hugging him she tells me that Andrew is very affectionate and loving to her now, he doesn't want just to be cuddled. Andrew cuddles up to his mother, rubbing his face on hers. Closing his eyes, he rests for a second on her shoulder, then straightens up and sweetly holds her hair and touches her face. We move to the kitchen; as soon as mother tries to sit him down in the high-chair he gives out a scream of anger. 'He hates it,' she says.

She tells me that Andrew has not been eating. She doesn't prepare a proper meal for him so that if he doesn't eat she will not be too upset. In the meanwhile she gives him a piece of pear which he starts to eat by himself with pleasure. 'He is almost living on milk. Sometimes at night he might even drink two bottles.' When Andrew finishes his pear he protests; mother looks very happy because he is eating. When he demands more pear she smilingly says: 'Usually he has to share it with Martin.' She watches him eat, sharing his pleasure. She says she wants to take advantage of his wanting to eat today, so offers him a drink and then starts to feed him with a tin of baby-food. Andrew is very active, he wants the spoon which he puts in his mouth. He then plays with it while mother uses a spare one. During the meal she speaks to me a great deal: 'The important thing is that he gets the nutrition he needs. It doesn't matter what he eats or when; sometimes because a child does not eat at lunch time one has the feeling he has not eaten at all, but thinking about all the things he might have had during the day like sweets, chocolates, fruit, one might realise that he had more than enough; one could leave around pieces of cheese and bread so that he could just find it and take it when he likes ... I am thinking of changing the time of his meal; after collecting Martin from the nursery, Andrew is too tired. Maybe it would be better to put him to bed and feed him later. He is not too thin is he?' smiling at him, 'You are a chubby boy, aren't you?' Andrew seems very happy to have her whole attention for himself. Martin today has been invited to a friend's house.

He tosses down the spoon, then he wants it back. I pick it up and give it to him; again and again he drops it, sometimes on his left side, sometimes on the right where I am sitting, and he always expects to get it back; he is not doing it angrily as he did the week before when he was throwing it away; it has much more the quality of a nice game. 'What do they do at the nursery?' mother asks me, referring to the place she knows I visit. 'Do they leave them to eat by themselves? What do they do if they overturn the plate over their head, do they offer them another one?' At this moment she seems very relieved that Andrew has been eating. 'Today,' she says, 'it has been quite different, he got all the attention. But it cannot always be like that.' Mother stands up and takes his bib off; Andrew grabs her hair, she lets him play; with her head in his hands he looks sweetly triumphant; while she cleans his face he plunges into the sponge. He does the same thing even more passionately with the cloth she uses to dry him; she lets him have it and he rubs his face on it with his mouth open. Mother picks him up, saying he is very tired now and she wants to put him to bed. In Andrew's room while changing his nappy, she says that he wakes up many times during the night and that she can sleep quietly for just one hour in the morning when Andrew and Martin play together. 'Well, they do not exactly play together,' she adds, 'Martin very nicely shows him how to play; when he can walk and talk, he won't feel so frustrated; sometimes he does seem to talk, but what does he say?'

Mother is struggling not to be in a panic about the eating and sleeping difficulties but to use her good sense. She holds on to rationality but at a different level she seems to be under a terrible strain. Andrew's difficulties evoke deep anxieties for her. The lack of trust in the goodness of what she has to offer is taking her back to the time of early breastfeeding; Andrew's behaviour now is feeding her fears of not being a good mother, not knowing how to care well for a baby, as we see in the questions about the nursery. She is feeling exposed to rejection, to feeling humiliated if he does not accept what she might have cooked for him hopefully. There seems to be a danger of their getting stuck in a vicious circle where they both feel rejected, rejecting and persecuted and where they feel very dependent on each other to re-establish a sense of trust in the liveliness of the loving life-giving good mother.

Andrew seems more able to experience mother as good when she is his own possession; his playing with the teddy-bear, his approach to the observer and then to mother, when she comes in, seems to be related to his passionate longing to take possession of the object of his desires; he seems almost to want to put his smell all over it, to define it as his property and to keep off everybody else. His waking up at night, taking mother from father, may well be connected to his constant need to check on her availability for him. Interestingly, he seems able to allow his parents to be together when, in the morning, he is together with Martin and feels less excluded and lonely.

Mother attempts to find in Andrew's growing the evidence of the goodness of her giving; to compensate for the painful anxieties she experiences in feeding him, she puts all her energies into offering him different sorts of 'food', completely devoting herself to encouraging him to talk and walk. 'Looking after them is not enough,' she says, 'they need stimulation,' and she spends lots of time showing him all kinds of books, naming for him objects, colours, animals. 'He definitely said "teddy",' she announced one day, very pleased and proud, and another day, 'He is delighted by his feet; he just pretends nothing special is happening but in fact he is trying to stand on them; he will be nearly one when you come back after Christmas.'

Observation at 51 weeks

Martin opens the door when I arrive; Andrew appears from the kitchen
in his walking chair, he rushes towards me along the corridor with a
radiant face; he embraces me then stays quietly resting on my chest.
Martin is sitting on a car; it was while playing on this car that last week
(my first after the holiday) Andrew had recognised me emotionally; he
now suddenly wakes up, and raising his head from my chest very
excitedly starts to push his finger on the horn making a sound very
similar to the one I did the week before, 'Pa...pa...pa...pa...' Martin
points out to me some details of the car which is a milk-van, then he
moves with it to his room while Andrew runs after him. The two brothers
for a while go to and fro in the room, running and pushing one another;
Martin laughs; Andrew seems to enjoy it much more when he is the one
who gives the push; he suddenly breaks off the game and Martin goes out
of the room, leaving the car. Andrew moves himself around with an
extreme quickness and resolution, exploring all the different possibilities
Martin's room has to offer .... Later on in the observation it is lunch time.
As soon as he gets the spoon from mother, Andrew gives it to me; mother
smilingly says that he wants me to feed him, which I do. Andrew eats
with great pleasure; he is now eating and drinking with the same
quickness and resolution he had shown before in play; he then notices my
watch. 'Tic...toc', he says; I put it to his ear; with a thoughtful expression
he seems to look for an answer in my eyes, an explanation, or perhaps
just someone to share the extraordinary experience he is having. 'Where
is the clock?' mother will ask him later, 'Where is Daddy's picture?'
Andrew turns his head to the right place; mother looks very pleased with
him. When it is time for me to go they come with me to the door; for the
first time after a very affectionate bye-bye he bursts into tears as I leave.

Andrew is full of energy, joyfully interacting with his brother,
fascinated by the boyish toys; instead of a 'gone away' milk-van leaving
him close to despair there is a more internalised milk-van available to
sustain his activity in a more constructive way; there is a father in his
mind helping him not to be stuck too close to mother. In the
observation, the observer represented for Andrew the function of the
father as the one who is reminding him of the time, the 'tic-toc' of the
coming and going instead of the timeless way of being together. The
experience of the departure and return of the observer from the holiday
break might have given him an opportunity to work over the
experience of losing something and finding it again. He is much more
able to cope with the feeling of ending. The discovery of his new
capacities is helping him to recover from the pain of the weaning and
at the same time opening up a new area in his relationship with
mother, which is giving great satisfaction to both of them. Two weeks
later mother welcomed the observer with the news of Andrew having
taken his first steps.

7

Rosa

Rosa is the second child born to a young couple. Father is in a skilled working-class job, mother has been at home since the first baby's birth. Their flat is small but cosy and they are hoping to be able to move to a larger house fairly soon. The parents are Moslems, but not part of a traditional community. The first child was Emma, born when mother was 20 years old. At the time of Rosa's birth Emma was 22 months old. As mother had planned, her second baby was born at home in their small bedsitting room. The birth was reported as quick but more painful than the birth of Emma. Rosa weighed eight pounds at birth; she was said to be eight days overdue. On the first observation visit, six days after Rosa's birth, mother expressed disappointment about having another girl; she would have preferred a boy this time although she intended to have more children later. I learned at a subsequent observation that mother was a middle child and that she had an older sister and a younger brother.

Observation at 6 days

The quotations are selected in order to convey an impression of Rosa soon after birth and to show how she expressed herself and made an impact on the people around her.

> After I had been there about fifteen minutes the baby started to make little sounds, at first infrequently and then increasing clucking and muttering. There were rustling sounds as she moved in the crib. It was as if she was responding to the conversation. Emma picked up a small naked baby doll. The baby's 'conversation' developed into a gentle crying. Mother said, 'Is it her feed time? I cannot remember, her cry sounds like it, doesn't it?' She moved over to the crib and Emma threw her doll onto the floor. Mother lifted the baby out of the crib and handed her to me, saying, 'Would you like to hold her?' I held Rosa for a few moments. She had stopped crying when mother picked her up. Her eyes were closed and slightly screwed up. I was surprised that I could get no feeling of her in my arms.
>
> I handed her back to mother who sat on the bed and made a little nest by putting one of her legs underneath the baby. She put Rosa to her

breast and Rosa began to suck vigorously; her body was quite still. After
a few minutes mother said that Rosa had fallen asleep. Mother sat her
up and then placed her over her left arm and gently patted her back.
Rosa's head, which was unsupported, lolled to one side. After a moment
or two in this position mother sat Rosa in the centre of her lap, facing
her. I could not see Rosa's face but shortly afterwards mother said 'She
has been trying to do poos all day and her face goes like this,' imitating
Rosa. Rosa brought up some wind.

Mother carried Rosa over to the crib and laid her down. Rosa's eyes
were wide open; she looked contented and I thought that she was about
to smile. Mother removed the nappy, saying, 'She has done it at last.'
Emma leaned into the crib and put her hand to the baby's face. Rosa's
eyes moved in Emma's direction and then swivelled to look towards
mother. As mother removed the nappy Rosa produced a lot more of the
runny yellow substance on her crib sheet. Mother said, 'More washing: I
have more washing this time than I had with Emma, but that is because
I give Rosa water, it makes it easier to come out.'

Later mother left the room briefly and Emma sat on the double bed
propped up with pillows, holding Rosa. When mother returned from the
kitchen to continue feeding Rosa there were protests from Emma who
hung on to the baby. She let go after mother suggested that she should
show me Dougal (a toy dog from the television programme 'Magic
Roundabout'). I never did see Dougal because Emma was occupied with
Rosa's engagement with mother.

While mother fed Rosa, Emma jumped on and off the bed and several
times she bumped them. Mother calmly fended Emma off in order to
protect the baby but there were some difficult moments.

Mother asked me if I would like to hold Rosa again, handing her to me.
Rosa appeared to be content in my arms, her eyes were closed but I
noticed that she did not snuggle into my body and lay quite still.

After some conversation with mother it was time to go. I prepared to
leave and mother stood up. She said, with her hand on her tummy, 'A few
days ago I felt a kick, and now I look across the room and say to myself,
she is out there now. All I have to do is to bring her up. I feel sad.'

From the outset Rosa impressed me with her capacity to make
herself understood through joining in and making 'conversation' and
then expressing her needs in a manner which left her mother in very
little doubt about what she wanted. I shall try to trace how her
capacity to express herself developed during her first year. Both
methods and content changed as she negotiated the different stages of
development. I shall show how and in what circumstances she used
pre-verbal signals, physical signs, words and symbolic play to express
herself.

The context in which Rosa's own particular way of being and
communicating is taking shape is the close intimacy with her mother
and her sister; Emma's insistent presence is a major feature of the
world into which she has been born. In this first visit, one gets a hint of
mother's sensitive identification with her baby, as she speaks of giving

water to make it easier for her to defaecate, and with Emma she tries to
help her into the big sister role by inviting Emma to be Dougal's mummy
or friend while she is Rosa's. Many subsequent observations charted
mother's struggle to find a place for both children. Her repeated offer to
the observer to hold the baby might be evidence of a strong wish to keep
everyone happy and included, and hold at bay any sense of exclusion
which could cause pain. Emma's difficulty in allowing mother and baby
to be peaceful together is, however, considerable. Rosa's slightly inert
physical state might be part of the not-fully-in-the-world state of some
babies in the first days of life outside the womb or possibly (as it
contrasts with her communicative waking and her strong sucking)
might be expressive of some degree of caution about the world outside
which includes Emma's unpredictable intrusions.

Observation at 21 days

A pregnant girlfriend and her fifteen-month-old daughter were present
throughout this observation. Mother invited Emma to hold Rosa soon
after I arrived. After a while and in response to the adults'
preoccupation with their own conversation, Emma was overcome by
her feelings and began to push the baby away.

> Rosa began to whimper and mother came over immediately and laid her
> on the bed. Mother looked at her and said, putting her hand onto Rosa's
> tummy, 'Aren't you growing into a fat little baby!' Mother prepared her
> left breast. She supported Rosa's head with her left arm and held her
> breast with her right hand. Rosa lay across mother's lap fairly close to
> her body; she placed her right hand under the breast and used her left
> hand to hold one of the fingers of mother's right hand. Rosa sucked
> steadily for four or five minutes. Mother then put Rosa up onto her
> shoulder and patted her gently, saying 'She is still a good baby.' After a
> few moments she placed Rosa into a sitting position facing her and
> shortly Rosa produced some wind. Mother asked me if I would like to
> hold the baby and handed her to me. (I am still taken a little by surprise
> when she does this.) I took Rosa and held her over my shoulder. I noticed
> immediately that she felt different from when I held her two weeks
> previously: there was feeling in her body although she did not snuggle in.
> Rosa's eyes were open and she appeared to be weighing me up as she
> looked into my face. I talked to her and she remained alert and poised.
> After a few minutes, while continuing to hold my eyes, Rosa put both of
> her hands on my chest and with remarkable strength pushed herself
> away from my body. I said to her, 'I think that you would prefer to sit on
> my lap.' Rosa sat apparently contented sitting on my lap facing me, her
> eyes and mouth were open. Then she yawned and began to whimper a
> little.

What followed was a sequence of the friend holding Rosa, Rosa being
returned to the crib and Emma shaking the crib violently.

Rosa lay quietly for five minutes or more; her eyes were open and her right hand was holding her nose and her left hand. Mother asked if Rosa was asleep. She said, 'She cannot have another feed because her next feed is due at 5 o'clock.' After a few minutes when mother could see that Rosa was still awake she put her finger in Rosa's mouth. Rosa sucked and mother picked her up saying, 'She wants another feed'. Rosa went straight to the breast when it was offered. Mother said, 'Sometimes she likes to suck without taking any milk.' The two mothers then talked about the crucial time about two weeks after the baby's birth when you wonder if you will have enough milk to continue breastfeeding. Mother said, 'At the moment if I do not feed Rosa every three hours, the milk starts to dribble out. If Rosa cries at night my breasts immediately start to tingle.'

Mother held Rosa to bring up her wind, saying, 'I hate bringing up her wind, it takes so long.'

Rosa expressed herself powerfully and effectively from the beginning: through her vocalisations she made her presence felt and communicated her need to be fed. Through her show of physical strength she indicated to me her discomfort about being held in a particular way. She used her eyes to scan her environment, to weigh up and to differentiate. The observer felt rather surprised by these observations and in particular her apparent capacity to use different sounds and to differentiate between mother, Emma and observer. Rosa seemed fundamentally contented, but more painful emotions were being experienced by others. The observer felt quite hurt when Rosa pushed herself away; mother was sad that she was no longer inside; Emma was struggling to find a new place for herself in the changed family constellation. In these first observations, mother and baby together seem to be trying to cope with the trauma of the birth and to negotiate the space now between them following the physical separation of birth.

By the third week there were marked developments. Rosa nestled closer to mother's body and held the breast and one of mother's fingers. Later, Rosa perhaps recreated the experience of contact with breast and nipple by holding her nose and left hand with her right hand. In contrast to the evident development of closeness and intimacy between mother and Rosa was the observer's experience of Rosa forcefully pushing herself away from her shoulder. The slightly passive infant of the first week has become a force to be reckoned with; Rosa is perhaps protecting her sense of wellbeing by projecting painful elements of her experience, particularly a sense of rejection.

The second month

In this period three themes stand out: mother's preoccupation with weight and with establishing a pattern for Rosa's feeds and Emma's intense preoccupation with the baby.

Observation at 5 weeks

Emma was sitting on the bed. She was putting a little drawing of a baby into a matchbox lined with cotton wool. She allowed me to see what she was doing, but when mother returned with the coffee she gave up her play and climbed down from the bed.

Mother told me that she had been trying to diet this week. She thought 10 stone 4 lbs was too much for someone who was only 4 feet 10 inches. She had noticed that her husband was able to be more active with Emma. She got puffed easily. I asked her if she had always had a problem with her weight. She replied that it had started when she was ten years old; she thought that nobody loved her and became a secret eater. Rosa started to stir and made little grumbling sounds. Mother said, 'She is waking up, she is still a good baby.' I asked about Rosa's pattern of sleep and mother said that they seemed to be developing a mixed pattern of feeding on demand and on schedule. One night Rosa would sleep right through and on into the morning, but then the next night would wake up every three hours. Mother said that sometimes Rosa's face went blue after a feed. She thought that this might be caused by the increasing richness of her milk. Rosa did not waken during this visit and did not utter another sound.

Observation at 6 weeks

I was introduced to mother's sister. Rosa was lying on mother's lap, her eyes were closed and I thought she looked considerably older. She was wearing a grey jersey and navy blue tights and looked more like a boy. Rosa continued to sleep. Mother reported that Emma had bitten Rosa's cheek. She also said that her husband wondered if she had enough milk for Rosa.

Mother lifted Rosa up and prepared to feed her. Rosa was close to the breast and as she sucked steadily she gently touched it. Rosa's face was red after the feed and mother thought that she must have a full nappy. Rosa brought up wind easily.

While mother changed her nappy, Rosa moved her arms and legs as if exercising and watched her mother. Mother commented on the fatty lumps on Rosa's legs. After she had put the clean nappy on, she said, 'Now you will dirty it but I won't change it.'

Mother handed Rosa to me. Rosa felt solid and 'alive'. She watched Emma, her expression was serious, almost frowning. I talked to her and she made an O with her mouth. I thought that she was imitating my mouth movements. There was a trace of a smile in her mouth and eyes.

I put Rosa on my shoulder and she whimpered. She was content for a while when I returned her to my lap but soon became sleepy and restless. Mother took her to the breast and she sucked steadily for a further five minutes.

Mother told me she was down to 9 stone 8 lbs. She is pleased that Rosa is becoming more responsive; she does not really like little babies. The midwife said that Rosa was a good size.

Mother's concern about her own weight and her thoughts about the rich milk, which nourishes Rosa but might be too much for her (turns her face blue), and about Rosa's fat legs suggest an intertwining of perceptions of herself and the baby. This partial confusion of identity excludes a relationship with father, whose reported worry about an inadequate supply of breast-milk seems to betoken some hostility to what is going on between mother and baby, and also Emma, whose biting of Rosa's cheek seems a furious protest at the special intimacy of nursing mother and baby. But when Rosa seems in mother's eye to embody the disliked aspects of herself (the fatty lumps) Rosa is at risk of rejection, as mother's threat not to change the clean nappy if she dirties it demonstrates. When mother speaks of her as 'still a good baby' the apprehension of the not-good baby is powerfully felt.

Observation at 7 weeks

Rosa was asleep for the first half hour of my observation. Her hand was over her nose and mouth but then she moved it away and only a finger was touching her face. Later Rosa put her hand to her face again and it looked as if her thumb was just in her mouth. This is the first time I have seen Rosa's thumb anywhere near her mouth. Several times Rosa's eyes flickered open. I was struck by Rosa's stillness and her air of contentment. Once towards the end of the sleeping period Rosa pushed herself up on her hands, turned to the other side and then immediately turned back again.

Mother said that she had a bad night; Rosa had been awake and she fed her at 4 a.m. and then kept her in bed with her. At 6 a.m. mother asked Rosa if she was awake and Rosa responded with talking sounds. In the dim light of the street lamp mother could see that Rosa was smiling.

Rosa was due for a feed at 2 p.m. When the time came mother went over to the crib and spoke to Rosa and after a few minutes pulled the covers off her. Mother apologised to Rosa for wakening her and slowly, reluctantly, Rosa began to stir. Mother gave Rosa a little time to waken and then picked her up and held her facing away from herself. Rosa opened her eyes, they were glazed. Mother stood for a while and then prepared to feed Rosa. Rosa snuggled in close to the breast and continued to feed for five minutes.

Emma and I moved close to mother and the baby. Emma picked up a 4-inch whistle, laughed and then blew it. Emma was rough and aggressive as she put the whistle into mother's mouth and then into mine and laughed again. She soon gave this game up and spat at me; she was quietly reprimanded by her mother. This seemed to stimulate a second attack and Emma slapped me across the face, but then sat close beside me on the floor, leaning on one of my legs. Then she got up to find a soft yellow duck: she lay on the floor, held the duck in both hands and chewed the duck's beak. Then she went to the kitchen, found a baby's bottle and after teasingly almost spilling it she began to suck the teat. Rosa continued to feed but was becoming sleepy. Mother decided to change Rosa's nappy before putting her to the second breast. As Rosa lay on the bed Emma climbed onto the bed and put her face beside Rosa: Rosa visibly tensed. Mother noticed and made Emma get off the bed. Emma then poked her finger into Rosa's bottom. Emma wanted to hold the baby before me but as soon as she got close to Rosa she asked for her to be taken away. I held Rosa on my lap facing me. She looked intently into my eyes, half smiling as I talked to her. Her eyes closed and in her sleep a smile flickered across her mouth and she opened her eyes. She repeated this several times. When Emma came into her vision she frowned and licked her lips.

Rosa appeared in these observations to be more gathered together, both by mother and by herself. Mother felt her to be more responsive and reported on the 'bed talk' and smiles in the early morning. They were observably closer physically and the observer could feel Rosa's muscle-tone firmer. Rosa had found first her nose and then her thumb as substitutes for the nipple to gratify herself when she was separated from the nipple and breast.

It is difficult to tell how much Emma's transparent desire to have a baby (the baby in the matchbox) and to be a baby (sucking the baby's bottle) and her ambivalence towards mother's and Rosa's togetherness affected the mother-baby relationship. Rosa showed tension when Emma approached and the observations show how Emma tried to disturb and spoil Rosa's feeding relationship with mother. Rosa licked her lips and frowned in response to one of Emma's approaches. Was she comforting herself and trying to allay her anxiety? Mother's account of Rosa's hours in her bed gives a glimpse of the impact Rosa might be having on the relationship between the parents, as father is not mentioned at all. The night-time feeds are, of course, free from the complications of Emma's presence and mother might enjoy this as much as Rosa does (the smile).

Weaning and playing

The following observations over an extended period show the progress of weaning and the development of more elaborate forms of play, some of it quite evidently connected with the experience of weaning. This material may also throw light on psychological aspects of Rosa's poor weight gain. At one year of age she weighed only 14 lbs instead of the anticipated 22 lbs.

Observation at 20 weeks

Rosa lay on her tummy, her head held high. She scrutinised me closely for a long time. Her expression was serious and she held my eyes with intensity. For the next ten minutes Rosa seemed keenly aware of her body. The impression given was that she was feeling it from the inside out; on the threshold of being able to move it and control it in new ways. Although highly self-conscious she was also very conscious of me and commanded my attention. She made 'conversational' sounds. I responded by saying that she seemed quite pleased to show me what she could do. Rosa smiled and responded with more carefully enunciated sounds. There was a sense of her controlling her tongue and not just babbling. Rosa became silent and concentrated on herself but continued to absorb my attention. For twenty minutes she alternated spates of conversation with periods of silence. She was a little sick several times.

Later I took Rosa onto my lap and she played with her hands: she picked at her dress with her fingers, using both hands which were far apart. She then brought her hands together by interlinking her fingers and put both hands in her mouth. She repeated this sequence several times but sometimes she only put her thumb in her mouth. Rosa was also feeling her feet and enjoying pressing up into a standing position.

After fifteen minutes or so I noticed that her gaze was going to my jumper and she appeared to be focusing more and more intently on my left breast. Soon she began to cry. I knew that she had had ground rice for lunch but I did not know if she had had her breast feed. Mother then said that she had had one breast; now that she is on solids she does not always have the second. Mother put Rosa straight to her left breast and Rosa sucked steadily for ten minutes and then went to sleep in mother's arms. Mother said that Rosa had nipped her several times and her teeth were quite sharp. Mother does not scream because that seems to make her bite more.

When mother placed Rosa into her cot she began to cry. This is something new; she seemed to want to be picked up. Mother put her finger in Rosa's mouth and then showed me the bite mark. Rosa continued to cry but not desperately.

Observation at 21 weeks

I sat on the floor beside Rosa's cot. Rosa lay on her side and observed me steadfastly, without a smile. I had the feeling that she was trying to sort out who I was.

Mother told me about the death of a friend's fourteen-month-old baby last week; he had choked to death on an apple.

Rosa was under covers and pulled the satin edges into her mouth and then cried. Mother picked her up. At Emma's request, mother put Rosa into Emma's toy car. Rosa was pale and tense and her eyes 'stood out on stalks'. She seemed both frightened and watchful. As Emma was in desperate need of attention mother handed Rosa to me. Rosa sat with her feet pushed into my tummy. She looked at me and then at mother. Rosa held her hands together and then put both thumbs into her mouth. Then she put her left thumb into her right hand between her thumb and index finger. She turned frequently to see her mother.

Mother told me that Rosa now had three solid meals each day. Rosa cried and I thought she wanted to go to mother. Mother took her but did not proffer her the breast. Rosa opened her mouth and mother told her that there was no more food.

Mother put Rosa on the floor and she lay on her tummy looking at a teddy, whilst mother read to Emma.

Mother was distressed about the death of her friend's baby and talked about it quite a lot during this visit.

Observation at 23 weeks

Rosa seemed more at home in the baby bouncer. She has discovered that she can make a spitting sound which she alternates with more carefully enunciated sounds; I could hear a trace of the sound of B. Rosa dribbled as she spat and mother thought that it might be a sign of more teeth coming through. Rosa stared at her rubber teething ring, but most of the time she was swinging herself round in the bouncer and engaging us with her sounds.

When mother gave Rosa water from a bottle (to loosen her stools as she has been having some difficulty since she went on to solids), Emma wanted to hold the bottle. Rosa however held the bottle herself with both hands and mother helped to keep the angle up. Emma took the bottle away every few minutes and put it in the fridge.

I held Rosa on my lap and she bounced herself into a standing position. She was very animated, but less intense and made her own moves towards fleeting physical closeness. She tweaked my left breast several times and for the first time touched my face.

Both children became dejected when mother was showing me the plans for their new house.

Observation at 30 weeks

This was the second visit after a three-week holiday break. Mother reported that Rosa had been following her all over the flat this week, crawling with speed: she does not like to be far away. Mother also noted that Rosa is more nervous than Emma. For example, she cannot tolerate the sound of the hoover and mother cannot therefore clean straight through as she likes.

Rosa was brought in from her sleep. Emma refused to relinquish her place in the high chair, so mother fed Rosa on her lap. Mother was not sure whether Rosa would like the vegetable lunch. However, Rosa approached the food eagerly and sucked the food off the spoon with obvious enthusiasm. Emma continued to refuse to give way in the high chair, and irritated mother by the mess she was making.

When mother had finished feeding Rosa, Emma climbed down from the high chair and I held my breath as Emma managed this manoeuvre, carefully yet confidently. Mother then popped Rosa into the chair and Emma immediately climbed up and tried to squeeze in beside her. Rosa looked tiny but quite grown up as she sat in the high chair; she was quiet and studious and regarded my face with great intensity. Then mother came and touched Rosa's cheek, laughing as she did so. Rosa began to chuckle freely.

Later, in the living room, Rosa raised herself to a sitting position and sucked several toys which were lying on the floor. Mother suggested that Rosa should demonstrate her ability to stand up, and put her hands on the seat of the trike. Rosa stood at a 60 degree angle to the bike, her back arched and her bottom sticking out. Emma came and took the trike. Mother tried to persuade Rosa to push Emma in the baby walker, but Rosa preferred to play with toys which had been thrown out.

Mother left the room and Rosa quickly followed her. She started in a crawling position and then moved by throwing her hands forward and pulling her body along behind.

Observation at 31 weeks

By the following week Rosa was crawling properly. Mother told me that she and her husband had fasted 'for Emma' for two days last week because they were not happy about some of her behaviour. They were doing this to help her. Mother said all this as if it were a very ordinary response to concern about a child's character.

Observation at 32 weeks

Rosa looked more at home in the high chair, sitting in a straighter position and more confident. (Emma was not in the room.) Rosa sucked a spoon which mother had dipped in honey and banged it on the tray. She chatted away and was more vocal than ever before. Rosa threw the spoon onto the floor and mother retrieved it. Rosa played with it for a few minutes and then threw it on the floor again. Mother ignored her and Rosa leaned over the side of the chair and stared at the spoon, but mother continued to ignore her cue. Rosa began to suck her hand and momentarily put her thumb in her mouth. She gradually slipped down in the high chair and I thought that she would slip right out onto the floor. Mother then noticed and straightened her up and gave her the lid of a toy teapot which Rosa immediately popped into her mouth.

Mother said that she had noticed some development in Rosa's speech this week. She was beginning to say Dada, and she has her own version of hello. Mother has also noticed that Rosa has a special interest in music; she rocks to the classical music on the radio.

Observation at 35 weeks

Rosa was just waking up when I arrived. She got herself into a crawling position and then stood up, smiling. Emma stroked Rosa's head and climbed into the cot. Mother said Rosa needed a cuddle and picked her up. Emma stayed in the cot, jumping up and down. Mother placed Rosa in the middle of the living room floor and Rosa crawled over to me and gently touched my cheek with her hand. She then put her thumb on my lip and plucked it for a moment. She then played on the floor nearby. From time to time Rosa stood up and looked intently at my mouth; once she held my nose.

Rosa was playing with the ting-a-ling, a musical drum on a long handle. She repeatedly put the large knob from the handle into her mouth and at one point she appeared to be organising herself to put it into mine.

Observation at 41 weeks

Rosa sat on the floor feeding herself from a bottle, almost totally absorbed; she held the bottle in both hands and sucked steadily.

Mother told me that she had taken Rosa to her GP this week because she was worried about Rosa's persistent cough and her thinness. She had been worried for several months but had not been able to do anything about it. She also reported that Rosa had fallen out of her high chair and had given herself a large bump. Mother had thought that she was 'finished' as she had been so quiet for several hours. This was said in quite a matter-of-fact fashion.

Mother went to the bathroom in response to Emma's call for help in wiping her bottom. Rosa put down her bottle and followed at great speed. When the three returned Rosa took her bottle but it was quickly commandeered by Emma. She took it with her to the settee where she lay with the bottle for half an hour covered up with cushions, as if she were in bed. Rosa crawled to the settee but did not attempt to retrieve her bottle. She took the drawing which Emma had given me earlier and squeezed and sucked that. Mother tried to interest Rosa in the baby walker without success. Rosa stood by mother's lap and tried to pull herself up. She was crying. Mother eventually picked Rosa up and stood her face to face. As Rosa pulled mother's hair she was smiling. Mother put Rosa down and the scene was re-enacted. This time mother told Emma that Rosa wanted her bottle back. This elicited no response from Emma. Once again mother put Rosa on the floor and this time she put a shirt over Rosa's head; at first Rosa was startled but it quickly turned into a game, with Rosa pulling the shirt off and mother saying 'Boo!' This turned into a tickling game.

The emotions aroused by the weaning process

The weaning of Rosa began when she was five months old and was completed by ten and a half months. At first mother put her onto solids and then only gave Rosa one breast at lunchtime before dropping the lunchtime breast feed altogether. This change coincided with Rosa nipping the breast at times and more so if mother screamed out at her. It also coincided with Rosa becoming distressed when she was put into her cot and crying to be picked up. By the time Rosa was seven months old she was crawling proficiently and followed her mother everywhere. Mother observed that she was frightened of the hoover. This of course may be related to the fact that Rosa was on the floor a great deal by this time! Possibly her 'nervousness' was linked to her own sadistic impulses: did she fear that the hoover would gobble her up into its bag, just as she nipped the breast and in phantasy devoured it? Coincident with these observations was the first report of the parents fasting 'for Emma'. The fasting seemed to be their way of purging the sins which they felt had been perpetrated and of making their children into 'good' babies. Strikingly, mother later told the observer that the final weaning (from the morning and evening breast feeds) were accompanied by mother's 30-day fast for Ramadan. Mother said this was a time when she had struggled 'not to think bad thoughts'. At the same time there had been worry at a hospital check-up on Rosa about possible coeliac disease. This was later discounted as the cause of her low weight. Mother seems to have perceived eating as a potentially damaging activity (recall mother's secret childhood eating-for-comfort and the tragedy of the baby who choked on an apple) and thus to be particularly open to the anxieties of her children about food – Rosa's anger about the going-away breast, and Emma's overt jealousy and intrusion into Rosa's feeds were both hard for mother to deal with.

It is worth noting that the observer also felt distressed and guilty that she had not noticed that Rosa was not putting on weight. The painful aspects of the weaning could not be noted or thought about for a considerable period. Attacks on the feeding breast and baby couple which were uncontained (particularly Emma's interference) put Rosa at physical risk both literally and because ambivalent feelings were expressed somatically as they had not been contained in mother's mind.

Developments in thinking and communication

Between five and ten months one can trace some of the developments in Rosa's thinking through the gradual elaboration of her communications. At seven days old Rosa gave the impression of making 'conversation'. Through the next six months 'pre-speech' activity culminated in her ability to make a 'bu', 'controlling her tongue', 'more carefully enunciated sounds' (five months), 'a spitting sound with more carefully enunciated sounds' (nearly six months). By seven and a half months she can say 'Dada' and has a form of 'hello', 'she chatted away and was more vocal than ever before'.

The elaborations of play are also very gradual but show Rosa's developing capacity to bring things together and to differentiate internal and external reality. For example, by the fifth month a symbolic representation is clearly evocative of breast and nipple as she plays with hands, fingers and thumbs. One can conjecture that in exploring her own chest she had discovered no breasts and then by interlinking the fingers on both of her hands she was able to create an imaginary breast and nipple which provided some temporary allaying of anxiety about the absence of the real breast and nipple which she had been biting: 'Her gaze was going to my jumper and she appeared to be focusing more and more intently on my left breast. Soon she began to cry.' She created different versions of this preoccupying absent object; the satisfaction of nipple in mouth is represented by a thumb placed between her other thumb and index finger; then the honeyed spoon which she throws away and mother gives back to her. By the time Rosa is putting the knob of the ting-a-ling in her mouth and thinking about putting it in mine her preoccupations seem to be changing to a form of link which can make music, like the knob on the radio which made the exciting music. Possibly the Dada whom she now could name is also perceived as linked to mother's aliveness. Rosa is becoming interested in the parents' relationship with each other.

Rosa's temperament included a capacity for intense feelings and considerable reflectiveness; this observation recorded clearly some of the ways in which these traits influenced Rosa's experience of and adaptation to life in her family. Her mother's personality and in particular some of her personal anxieties shaped her care of the baby in important respects; most striking are the observations of mother's temporary incapaciity to notice what is cause for worry. Emma's jealousy and neediness seem likely both to have awakened Rosa's wariness and to have made demands on her to cope from the beginning with sharing her mother with her sister. This factor probably played a part in the thoughtfulness and seriousness of Rosa's play. There was very little opportunity to observe father's role and position in the family constellation. However, the observer may herself have functioned psychologically as a paternal figure at times, and the feelings evoked in her may throw light on some characteristic patterns of emotionality in this family.

8

Harry

I contacted mother through an ante-natal class organised by the National Childbirth Trust. She was very willing to be observed with her baby, Harry. He was her second child; her first child, George, was just two when Harry was born. Both father and mother were graduates. Mother, who was English speaking, had left her family in her country of origin to come to England to complete her studies.

Observation at 26 days

The house was a large detached one, in a secluded position in a leafy lane. It was quite hard to open the gate and my walk to the front door was made difficult by the advances of a large, lively labrador.

An au pair opened the door and told me mother was upstairs, then showed me into a living room to wait while she called her.

Mother came downstairs. She looked tiny, fragile and childlike, despite her large breasts and abdomen. Her long straight hair hung loose and her eyes seemed enormous in her pale face. As she said hello, she smiled warmly and told me she'd been snatching forty winks while the others were napping. She asked me to join her in a cup of coffee and I followed her into the kitchen. There were no signs of children around. She said she'd peeped in on the baby who was stirring so would shortly be ready for his feed. She told me she'd fed him at 6 a.m. when he'd woken, then again at 11 a.m. when she'd had to wake him.

She said he was quite good and often went for long stretches through the night, which she liked because it was exhausting to feed at 2 a.m. and 6 a.m. George had been difficult and hadn't gone through a night until he was five months old. He had cried a lot before and after feeding; she had spent two hours out of every four feeding him. She told me that this baby is called Harry and that he's a very hungry baby. He cries a little when he's put down after feeds but this doesn't last long. The au pair brought in George. He was very sleepy. Mother told me he was a real 'firebrand' normally. All this time the dog was bounding around.

Mother asked me about the study I was doing and what my job was. She remarked how long one's studies could last. She said she feeds the baby upstairs in the daytime and would I like to go up. She told me about her degrees and how subsequently she had worked as a P.A. 'It was like being a nanny,' she said.

The baby was in his parents' bedroom, sleeping in a basketwork crib under a window and by a radiator. A furry animal was attached to the crib above his head. The bedroom was chaotic with baby bits and pieces. Harry was lying on his tummy. His head was towards the wall, his arms were raised so there was a clenched fist either side of his head. He was asleep. His head and face were very pink. He had a lot of dark hair. Mother pulled back the blanket. I noticed Harry's legs were drawn up close to his body. She put both hands on Harry's back making a slight movement to wake him. He stirred slightly, moving his hands, but didn't open his eyes. Mother paused to pin her hair up to get it out of the way for the feed. She also folded a nappy and laid it ready on the bed. She said she would wake Harry as he didn't seem to be going to wake alone and said he hadn't really woken properly for the 11 o'clock feed. She picked him up. His head dropped back, otherwise he stayed in the same position. She told me he had no control over his head. She laid him on a plastic changing mat on the bed and said she'd change the bottom sheet on the crib while he was waking. Harry stretched out his limbs and cried. His head was turned to one side. His eyes were not properly open. Mother changed his nappy quickly and competently. He cried loudly as the nappy came off and she said to him, 'Yes, it's cold, isn't it?'

Mother explained that when the baby was eleven days late she'd been taken into hospital for an induction. Once in hospital she'd gone into labour naturally. After fourteen hours they'd told her that if the baby was to be born alive she would have to have a Caesarian because the baby was stuck. The baby's nose had been squashed and his head had been caught back which is why he now had difficulty in controlling it. She told me both her sons should have been born in the same month but this one had been late. She had expected a girl. The doctor hadn't wanted her to get too big and heavy because she's so small. She praised the treatment she had had in hospital, saying it had seemed chaotic at first but had turned out to be much better than the hospital where George had been born, which was OK medically but not in other ways – she had been so doped up that she can't remember the birth at all. She hadn't wanted to repeat that experience so she'd contacted the National Childbirth Trust and had attended their classes. They had suggested this hospital.

She picked the baby up and put him on her shoulder. He was curled up with his arms and legs close to his body. She settled herself on the bed to feed him, leaning back against the wall with her legs stretched out in front of her, a cup of coffee and a box of tissues close to her left hand. She suggested I sat on the bed or on the chair at the foot of the bed. I chose the chair although this didn't give me a good view of the feed. (To have had a good view I would have had to sit right next to them on the bed.) She pulled up her jumper and offered Harry her right breast. He stretched out his limbs and yawned and then resumed his curled up position. Mother made encouraging noises, 'Come on, come on.' He turned his head and found the nipple. He sucked vigorously and noisily. Mother winced and said he really sucked hard and that she had been very sore and had had to use cream although she had fed George without problems. She had thought Harry might learn he didn't have to suck so hard after a while, but he hadn't. I asked if he sucked as hard right to the end of the feed. She said no, but that he never went to sleep at the breast as George had done – even if he nodded off he would wake up again before she put him down.

Harry continued to suck, his legs, which had been tightly drawn up, were slowly extended. His inner arm was raised, first clenched, not touching the breast. During the feed he unclenched his fist, seemed to relax and sucked more calmly. After about five minutes he left the nipple, made slight hiccough-like noises (not actual hiccoughs) and then nuzzled the breast. Mother commented that he'd begun to play like this, letting go of the nipple and then finding it or sometimes having to be given it. She gave him the nipple again. He sucked noisily at first and then more calmly. All this time mother was sipping coffee and chatting to me. She glanced down at Harry occasionally. She seemed relaxed and happy to let him take his time. He again let go of the nipple and spluttered a little. Mother asked him if he had a bubble and sat him up. He burped loudly and brought back some milk. She laughed and said neither of her sons is particularly refined. She put him on her shoulder and patted his back. He brought up more wind. He pulled his head back to look at her and then nestled back against her. He was in his curled up position again. She put him back to her right breast where he continued to suck quietly for a while. I couldn't see his hands. His feet were mostly still, he just kicked occasionally.

Mother said she tried to keep a vague eye on the time and also that she supplemented some feeds with a bottle although he took very little from it. She had no idea how much milk he'd been getting since she came out of hospital. Harry continued to suck quietly. There was so little movement I wondered if he had dozed off. Mother told Harry that she thought he'd had enough time on that breast. She sat him up to wind him. His head lolled around. He quickly brought up wind. She put him to her shoulder again. He huddled up sideways to her in a little ball. He stayed quite still. Mother then put him to her left breast. After some hesitation he began to suck vigorously once more. This time she didn't hold him closely across her body. His legs stretched out diagonally away from her. Later she did turn him round and move him closer.

Mother told me that her mother had not been able to come this time as she had done for George's birth. She had suggested a nurse but mother had been reluctant as she wanted to look after the baby herself and only wanted 'an extra pair of hands'. So they'd got an au pair. She said George was much better with Agnes than with her. Difficulties came at morning feeds when Agnes wasn't there and George always wanted something while she was feeding. I asked if she had grown up in England and she told me about her country of origin and that she had come to England to study. She told me of two classes she was attending; the au pair looked after the children while she was at one and while at the other she left them in a creche which she felt was excellent. She said she enjoys getting out, but hadn't been out with Harry yet because her sore tummy makes it hard to push the pram. Harry was feeding steadily. He seemed calm and relaxed. He hardly moved.

She said she had thought of teaching young children but her husband had deterred her by saying she could hardly raise her voice above a whisper. She went on to say they'd bought a house with a big garden for her but that she'd hardly done anything to it, being either hampered by a toddler or too pregnant. She added, laughing, that she thought Mothercare would have great success with a toddler's ball and chain.

She returned to the subject of bottlefeeding: she was thinking of giving

Harry a bottle regularly in the evening as she did not want to get stuck the way she had with George, who basically wouldn't have anything to do with a bottle, which had made weaning difficult. She had breastfed him until he was nine months old. She had found this a tie. She had left him with neighbours when he was six weeks old and he had just screamed. She wants to be able to leave Harry and needs to know how much milk to leave.

Harry had left the nipple again. Mother picked him up and put him over her left shoulder. This time he kept stretching his legs, pushing them into her abdomen. She remarked how uncomfortable this was and moved him higher. He gave a little squeal and she said, 'No, not in my ear.' The dog bounded in. She shouted at him to get out. Harry whimpered at her raised voice. (Throughout the feed George's shouts could be heard but Harry seemed not to notice.) Mother put him back to the breast where he sucked peacefully.

Mother returned once more to the subject of bottlefeeding. She told me of the idealism of some National Childbirth Trust members who felt bottles were right out. She felt this was unrealistic and she had learnt with George you had to do what you could manage. She went on to say she'd felt betrayed when George had first taken from a bottle, 'I thought, he'll be leaving home and getting married next.' She laughed at this. She told me she hadn't been able to feed Harry for the first two days because of drips and things. A nurse had brought him to her bedside and bottlefed him. On the third day they had seemed determined she should try. She said she didn't mind. She had managed to breastfeed him, propped up on a pillow with him lying beside her. She said she had felt depressed this time as she had after George's birth when she had felt very tired and had to take librium. She told me other Caesarian babies had been put in incubators but Harry had cried right away so it hadn't been necessary.

The sound of a band could be heard in the distance. Mother said to Harry, 'Listen to the music.' Harry stopped sucking and made gurgling noises. She picked him up to wind him. She said, 'I think you've had enough,' and sat him facing her. She picked him up and kissed his forehead and then sat him back down. Looking at him she said, 'Oh, you don't agree,' and put him back to the breast again. He sucked a little and then paused. She took him from the breast and put her hand on his stomach and said, 'This must be full.' She put him back to the breast which he took again. She said, 'Little piggy.' He sucked a while and then began to cry. She picked him up and sat him on her lap saying, 'There you are, now you've got a tummy ache, haven't you?' (The whole feed had taken about an hour.) He whimpered. She got up and walked about the room with him over her shoulder patting his back. He was immediately quiet. She told me, 'I reckon it can't be bad if he stops when we walk around. You don't worry so much with the second one.' She walked around a little longer and then said she thought she'd put him down. She stood still holding him. All the time she'd been standing he had hardly moved, he was nestled close into her, one arm raised, the hand clutching her polo collar. When she stood still he looked around a bit; his eyes wide open and he gazed at me briefly.

Mother laid him on his tummy in the crib. She said he wouldn't cry immediately. He liked people and would be quiet as long as he could hear her moving around. Harry lifted his head several times and then lay down with his eyes open. Mother said George at this age already had strong neck muscles from yelling with rage. I said I would go now. We went downstairs and said our goodbyes. Mother asked if I had been satisfied with what I had seen. I assured her I was and thanked her. The baby was still not crying when I left.

This observation illustrates two contrasting facets of Harry during his early life – his sleepy lack of interest, even to the point of hardly waking to be fed, and his eagerness. His strong sucking seems to demonstrate his vigour which his mother had felt was apparent in his not requiring an incubator even after a long and difficult delivery.

It also shows how mother helped Harry to feed by talking, gently stroking and prodding him if his concentration wandered or if he was unable to focus on the breast. Mother allowed him to have the breast and return to it until he had had enough.

The way in which the observer is received into the household and allowed to observe the feed also seems to indicate mother's own sense of competence in establishing a relationship to her baby.

Yet there also seems to be signs that she is under some strain. Her own family are not available for support. Mother makes passing references to feeling depressed with both children and to her husband's view of her as being unable to speak above a whisper as if she were too fragile to be a teacher. Harry's birth must have been a disappointment, particularly as she had taken steps to try to ensure that she had a better experience this time (than she had had at George's birth) – one which she would consciously experience and would be able to remember. She defined this as a wish for a more natural birth (Trowell 1982).

Although she seems to be recovering from the birth, and breastfeeding is, to all appearances, established, there are some indications of mother's uncertainties.

Mother and Harry are only at the beginning of a breastfeeding relationship and yet weaning is already in her mind. Perhaps the hospital recognised some reluctance to begin feeding and therefore put some pressure on her to make a start? Mother did not seem aware of this in relation to Harry although she spoke about being unable to leave George because of breastfeeding and resenting this tie. As she describes it, with George breastfeeding made her feel stuck while bottlefeeding meant total separation. She talks in a very rational way about the need to sort out what you can manage as between breast and bottle but perhaps she is finding it difficult to establish a balance within the intimacy of breastfeeding.

Although mother's conversation during the observation seems to indicate, often rather obliquely, some of the difficulties of her situation, the overwhelming impression which the observer received was of a confident mother in a careful, gentle relationship to her baby.

Mother seems able to cope with the interruptions during the feed and to be able to allow for the uncertainty as to what was the matter and what would relieve Harry's distress. The fact that she can then offer him the breast again seems to indicate her confidence in what her breast offers and in her ability to re-establish contact with him and provide comfort. At the same time the observer noted a particular quality to Harry's crying. Its sound was thin and high-pitched and he seemed unable to cry wholeheartedly. This very distinctive kind of crying was quite different from the lusty rage he sometimes displayed when held by the observer, when he would throw his head back, arch his neck and yell.

Observation at 7 weeks

I rang mother at 11 a.m. to arrange the visit as promised. She said Harry had been fed at 8 a.m. and was now crying but she didn't want to feed him. He had been going between 4 and 6 hours so that he'd be ready between 12 and 2 p.m. The observation was arranged for 12.

Harry was crying loudly when I arrived. Mother said she had waited because there would be no one to let me in. She went into the kitchen and emerged with a cup of coffee in each hand. I apologised for what appeared to be a feed delayed on my account. She said she wasn't worried and had lots to do before feeding Harry.

We went upstairs. Harry stopped crying as soon as we went into the room. Mother went to the crib, talking to him all the time. 'It's not fair is it?', 'What a naughty mummy', 'It won't be long.' She put him on the changing mat at the foot of the bed and swiftly changed his nappy. She said how much he'd grown. He'd had his six-week check-up that week and weighed almost 13 lbs. She said she'd been for coffee with some NCT mothers, one of whom was worried because the Clinic had told her that her three-month-old baby was too heavy at 13 lbs. Mother had said that Harry was almost that at six weeks. She said he really only had breast milk and the occasional bottle and not any cereal; he was long and big rather than fat. He had been half a pound more than George at birth but was now 1½ lbs more than George had been at that age. She attributed this to his being a more placid baby.

Harry had been gazing dreamily in my direction. He had stopped crying but kept opening and closing his mouth. Mother began to tell me about their visit to the Clinic and how unsympathetic the doctor had been. The doctor had asked if Harry always lay with his head to the same side. Mother said she thought so, but that he was always on his tummy in the cot and didn't often lie on his back. The doctor had told her to turn his head round or it would be misshapen.

Mother said she had been worried about his head after she'd got over feeling angry. She told me she had looked at it carefully and had seen no sign of damage. She added that she had to see her GP in the week and would ask her to look at Harry's head. The Clinic doctor had been better with George who had had his two-year check-up. She went on to say she had gone to her GP for pre-natal check-ups and thought this was better as it meant you saw one person who already knew you and then they would also know the children from the word go.

While talking mother had picked up Harry and had gone to where she normally feeds him. As he prepared to feed him he made excited little noises, waved his arms and gazed up into her face. She offered him her left breast. He took it immediately and sucked noisily and vigorously. He continued to suck at a steady pace, his arms and legs quite still, for a while. Then the rhythm was lost, his sucking became intermittent and his limbs moved more and more. He finally drew back from the breast and gave a cry. Mother sat him up and he immediately brought up wind. He remained sitting up for a short time and seemed quite lost in himself. His head nodded forward a bit. Mother lifted him to her shoulder to pat his back. He wailed in protest. She put him back to the same breast. He sucked peacefully and regularly, making very little other movement until she told him she felt he had had enough and took him from the breast. He did not resist.

She sat him up to wind him. He brought up wind and quite a lot of milk. She told me how George cries when Harry is sick and he can't bear it. She also mentioned an item on 'Play School' when a dog had gone to fetch a stick in a pond. She had heard George's crying from the kitchen. She went to see what was wrong and he had wailed, 'Dog in water.' She said he couldn't bear to see anyone diving or jumping into water. While she was talking Harry put his head back to watch her face. He stayed quite a while cradled in her arms staring up at her. He was quite still. She smiled at him and encouraged him to smile at her. She said to me he couldn't quite make up his mind to.

By now George, whom we had heard talking to himself in his cot at the beginning of the feed, was whining intermittently. While Harry was still gazing into her face mother turned him round and put him to her right breast. He took the breast immediately and sucked steadily for quite a while. He paused and mother said, 'I think you've got a bubble,' and sat him up to wind him. He brought some up immediately. Mother told me that the previous week's wind problems had disappeared at the beginning of this week and that Harry had been having an evening feed at 7.30 p.m. and then going until 1 or 1.30 a.m. and then until 7 or 8 a.m. She was pleased and said she hoped soon to be able to switch it round to avoid the middle of the night feed.

While sitting on her lap Harry was looking around. His eyes wandered from the large window above his crib to a small window beside the bed. He didn't fix on either for long. Finally his gaze seemed to settle on the shade of the bedside lamp. Mother confirmed that he was looking at it. It was trumpet-shaped and the light – which was on – caught the top, making it a different shade of beige from the rest. Mother said to Harry, 'Is that the most wonderful lamp you've ever seen?' He was not distracted by her voice. Mother told me she sometimes puts him down on the floor in front of the fire and props a magazine by him and he gazes at a picture of a woman's face. She said she thought he must think it's her or at least a mummy-like person. He gazed at it and gurgled. George got jealous and insisted the magazine was his. Mother interrupted Harry's gazing to return him to her breast. I could hardly hear him sucking and he seemed quite drowsy.

At this point father came in with the dog. He spoke to me. The dog approached me and was then told to leave me alone. It repeatedly returned. I was totally distracted from Harry. George was whining in the next room. Mother wanted father to see to him. She commented to me, 'Get the big guns out.' When father left she called out to him to attend to George but he was out of earshot. She took Harry from the breast and sat him up. Soon she said, 'I'll have to go and speak to George.' She put Harry on his tummy on the plastic mat and left the room. I could hear her speaking sharply to George and threatening him and then her voice lowered.

Harry gurgled quite happily and pushed his head and shoulders back. He looked around. He looked at me and then over my left shoulder at a pattern the sunlight was making on the wall. Later he left that to gaze wide-eyed at the window. Mother returned and told me George had been miserable because he had thrown some rugs out of the cot and couldn't reach them. When she sat on the bed Harry's gaze left the window and he turned his head to look at her, putting his head on the mat in order to do so. He then lifted his head again and returned to gazing at the window. He brought up a lot of milk. She said, 'I was going to ask you if you wanted some more but it looks as if you are full to overflowing.' Harry still had his head and shoulders raised and was making squeaky noises as though he was about to cry. Mother picked him up and sat back on the bed with him, cradling him in her arms in a sitting position. He nestled into her. He soon looked sleepy. When mother turned slightly the lamp caught his interest and he gazed at it but not with the same concentration as before. Mother said, 'Oh, you're back to your lamp now.' She told him she was going to put him down so he could get some sleep. She made jokey snoring sounds and rocked him. She took him to his crib. As she lowered him into it, he opened his eyes wide and glanced at her. He yawned. When in the crib he lifted his head and shoulders right up and looked over the top at me. Mother said, 'You're showing us what you can do, are you?' He looked around and then lay down, his eyes still wide open. He began to whimper. Mother said, 'It's no use trying that on me. You know I won't take any notice.' She left the room. Harry now cried loudly, his legs kicking, his hands plucking at the sheet. His head was quite pink. Mother returned for a moment and we both then left.

The observation marks the beginning of an overt change in mother's relationship to Harry but it also illustrates a marked contrast in mother's attitude to Harry between the times when she is with him and the time when she is not. When they are apart, she seems to be in every sense cut off from him, indifferent to his distress and preoccupied with her own activities. Once they are reunited she seems to be again in touch with him, aware of what he needs. This seems to echo her comments on breast and bottlefeeding George in that in both cases her experience seems to have become very polarised.

This was not an isolated incident. It became the pattern of things. The observer was sometimes told on arrival that Harry had been crying for an hour or so. It is difficult to know how to understand this change. It did not seem that she made a conscious decision to leave Harry to cry; more that it happened almost without her really noticing what she was doing. It is also unclear what part the observations played in this situation. While it did not seem that the feeds were really being delayed for the observer's benefit, it is striking that these sharp contrasts were so dramatically and repeatedly displayed.

Despite his long wait Harry accepts the breast easily when it is offered. There then comes a moment when he loses the rhythm of sucking, draws back from the breast and emits a cry. Perhaps this is the pain caused by wind but it also might be a moment in which the discomforts and distress of his long wait repossessed him. He spends a lot of time gazing at mother's face as if he is re-establishing contact with her and perhaps trying to get a grasp on her state. At other times he stares fixedly at the light in preference to mother or her voice. Mother, too, has noted his attachment to the light.

This observation also gives some idea of the difficulty she was apparently having in handling George. In the first months of observation he was conspicuous by his absence. There was little sign of him or of toddler life. There seemed to be some evidence that mother felt their relationship was mutually destructive. Her hope of having a harmonious relationship with her second child may have led her to exclude George and his 'firebrand' temperament which she was afraid could upset things.

Following an observation when Harry was nine weeks old the observer noted the following general thoughts: Mother's contact with Harry was more superficial. Outwardly she was loving and affectionate but she seemed less in touch with him, not noticing, for instance, that he was in an uncomfortable position while feeding. She was more withdrawn into herself. There was an intensification of her demands on me for conversation. I sensed her loneliness and isolation despite her frequent references to social contacts. There were many references to her family and to the experience of living in a foreign country. It was also becoming clear that her husband's work meant that he was away a great deal.

This marked the point at which the observer noticed a change in mother's attitude towards Harry when she was actually *with* him and follows the pattern already noted when she was apart from him. During the observation she mentioned that she had left Harry with a neighbour while she went to a wedding. He had fed from a bottle and had been very good. The latter was said with great affection.

It may be that while she was ostensibly pleased with Harry for adapting so readily to the bottle, she had actually experienced this as a rejection which had provoked her withdrawal and sharpened her feelings of loneliness and isolation. Her contradictory feelings would have been painfully confusing for her.

When Harry was eleven weeks old the observer first saw him bite his mother's nipple, causing her to withdraw it. This occurred during a feed when mother was unable to concentrate on him and he was consequently restless. Three weeks later the observer saw him bite her again and then while sucking look up searchingly into her face. This time mother threatened to wean him. This was during a feed which seemed quite pleasant despite interruptions from George. However, during the same feed mother reported an incident in which she had thrown merchandise at a saleslady who had ignored her. This seemed a clear indication that her control was breaking down.

Observation at almost 14 weeks

Harry was feeding steadily without moving and then lifting his outer arm and exploring with his hand. This time he brought his hand right down to the nipple and let it rest there cupped round with the fingers prodding occasionally. His legs were quite still. Towards the end of the feed mother squealed, 'Ouch!' and withdrew her nipple. George turned and gazed at the couple. She said, 'That's naughty,' but smiled at Harry and tickled his cheek so he smiled back. They smiled at each other in this way for a while and then he began to feed again.

It is impossible to know whether Harry's repeated biting was a response to mother's withdrawn mood or vice versa. Harry's early bid for independence or adaptation to mother's withdrawal, suggested by mother's account of how he readily accepted a bottle, may have caused mother's depression or resulted from it. The issue is whether these painful experiences could somehow be acknowledged between them and thought about by mother or whether they would by continuing to smile at each other, collude in pretending it was not happening. This would also tend to leave both mother and baby confused.

Observation at almost 21 weeks

Harry fed for about five minutes and then pressed his head back to look out of the window which was behind him. Mother said, 'Oh no, not another dirty nappy.' (Harry often loses concentration during a feed if he defaecates but there was, in fact, none of the usual accompanying restlessness.)

Mother prodded him gently in the side but he remained fixed on the window. She tried to lift his head but he resisted. She lifted him up to her breast but he noticeably pushed back. When his face was near the breast he began to make sucking movements with his mouth. He took the nipple and in fact seemed interested in continuing to feed. He continued to suck for some time but gradually lost interest in the breast. His head fell back and he returned to gazing at the window. Mother lifted his head gently several times, jerking it slightly, but he continued to gaze. She then sat him up very abruptly. He became very pale, his lips went blue for a moment. He looked very shaken.

The struggle between mother and baby continued throughout the observation. I was struck by his tenacity. At the end of his feed I observed:

After feeding peacefully for about ten minutes he threw his head back to gaze out of the window behind him. Mother forced him back to the breast. He sucked for a few moments and then returned to his gazing. Mother again lifted him abruptly saying she felt he couldn't be very hungry and she wasn't going to force it on him. He sat on her knee and brought up wind. He seemed dreamy and far away. He was certainly not as startled as when his gazing was interrupted before.

Mother was able to remain sensitively in touch with Harry during the early feeding period when his need for her seemed clear and unequivocal. In this situation Harry's need and pleasure in feeding seemed to support her identity as a good mother (in contrast to the time between feeds). In this way mother is in a sense dependent on Harry for her sense of well-being. As Harry develops, unavoidable changes begin to manifest themselves and the issue becomes who is to bear the brunt of the pain which these changes cause – the pain of steps towards weaning. The first relationship between mother and Harry is characterised by too great a degree of self-idealisation as against a real awareness of her baby's needs, so that she is in fact unprepared for the pain of weaning although she has spoken about it since the first observation.

Harry's turning away from the breast did seem to be a response to the change in his feeding and the beginning of weaning. The following observation shows his first responses to solid food.

Observation at 18 weeks

Mother crouched in front of Harry and fed him from a mug about 6-7 spoonfuls of the food. He took it quite willingly but not enthusiastically, making noisy sucking sounds on the spoon. He showed no signs of pleasure and kept his hand clasped in front of him ... For the last two spoonfuls he sucked harder on the spoon retaining it for a short time in his mouth. Mother spoke to him as she fed him and he occasionally looked up into her face but his face was expressionless. When the mug was empty she wiped his face with a damp cloth and then left him a couple of minutes before we went into the sitting room. During this time he sat quite still in his chair.

Later in the same observation, following the breastfeed and bringing up wind:

> Mother lay Harry down on his front on the towel making an arc of toys around his head, within his reach. He held his head up briefly, moved his legs a bit, bringing them up and out. When mother spoke to him he raised himself up to look. He didn't seem to be enjoying himself at all. There was no laughing or gurgling. Mother squeaked and rattled some toys. He turned in the direction of the noise. He brought up wind and was slightly sick twice. Having done this he was livelier and reached out for the toys. Mother told me he'd recently managed to catch hold of a toy and suck it. It was time for me to go so I left reluctantly, wondering anxiously if Harry would perk up a bit.

In this observation Harry seems to have lost some of his spontaneity and to have become slightly depressed. This was most likely part of his response to the new food which he eats without pleasure. His face is blank and he is still after being fed. Following the breastfeed it seems he has to rid himself of an unpleasant or uncomfortable feeling, which may have been associated with the new food, by bringing up wind and vomiting, before he feels free to play. He was still subdued when the observer left.

However, the change in feeding also spurred development and stimulated curiosity. He was looking for other satisfactions both outside – looking at his brother's play and looking behind him – and inside himself – his gazing at or through the window. The latter was a long-established practice following a feed, moments in which he seemed to be digesting the experience, recreating it and holding on to it mentally. In the observation at twenty weeks he is snatched right out of this process by his mother. His reverie is interrupted and he is dragged back to face a furious mother who feels she has been spurned. In the end, when his gazing is finally interrupted, his reaching out and exploration seem to stop. As they have proved unacceptable he gives up. Mother's difficulty in absorbing the painful feelings aroused by weaning seems to leave her feeling too persecuted by these developments to see them as such and so she is deprived of the solace and pleasure which her baby's progress could bring.

From this point onwards Harry's interest in the breast gradually diminished. He seemed under the sway of two attitudes – the desire to wean himself and a desire to control the breast omnipotently and have it at his beck and call. The former was predominant, supported by his interest and pleasure in discovering new objects and his growing control over his own body. This could be seen as a naturally occurring development but given a particular quality because his growing independence was not a process which mother could really bring into a loving contact with her since she found it too painful.

Observation at 28 weeks

Mother came down carrying Harry. She stopped in the doorway and turned him towards me so I could look at him. He stared at me wide-eyed and held his gaze unblinkingly. Mother took him over to put him in his chair. He turned his head to continue gazing at me. She lowered him into his chair and I went nearer. He sat forward in his chair and continued to gaze at me intently ... mother crouched in front of him with some food. He turned towards her and his expression altered completely. He smiled and his face, which had been blank and set, softened and came to life. Mother wanted him to lie back in the chair to feed and moved him. He frowned and looked crossly down. He continued frowning until the first spoonful arrived. He ate willingly ... Sometimes he became very excited and bounced up and down waving his arms and cooing. Mother warned him we'd have 'big smacks' like yesterday: 'You get so excited about food.' He did this several times, each time she paused and spoke warningly, 'Now then,' and fed him only when he stopped.

Harry begins in this observation to stare anxiously at the observer when she appears. At the same time he displays extraordinary enthusiasm and pleasure on seeing his mother, and goes on to smile at her and give her soft looks. Harry may, in this way, be able to separate wildly opposing feelings. Mother found it hard to cope with his developing independence and his taking pleasure in things other than her breast and herself. He seems to respond to her difficulty in tolerating their greater separation as individuals by seeming to reassure her of her goodness and desirability. By doing this he both spares his mother and avoids her possible retaliation, such as when he is angry with her for moving him before feeding him he frowns, but looks down rather than at her. It could be that he viewed mother as both too fragile and too dangerous to receive his anger.

In this feeding situation they are more separate than when breastfeeding. For Harry the loss of the breast seems to promote development. He has found his backbone; his sense of his own strength is shown by the way he sits and then resists being moved into a more passive position. For mother the fact that he is more independent seems to mean that they are now totally separate and that she is no longer needed. She cannot tolerate his excitement about food and becomes actively hostile and punitive. At this point she offers him little encouragement to develop further.

Conclusion

Although mother talked quite openly about her feelings at times there were also moments in which she gathered up a sense of competence and seemed to convey to herself and others that she was on top of things. This process emerges in the first observation when she talks about the idealistic outlook of other NCT members while saying she knows 'you have to do what you can manage'. She also remarks that it's easier to know how to respond with second babies. Her sense of being competent seems to depend on the belief that others are not; other NCT members or herself as mother of a first baby. It also seems to be bolstered by the presence of an observer – someone to whom she can portray a picture of a good mother, which could also serve to hold together this picture for her and therefore enable her to cope. The observer was, however, also to witness many difficult moments between mother and her children, and to feel the strain of the sudden shifts of feeling.

The extent to which vulnerability and incompetence are located elsewhere seems to be illustrated by the fact that the observer felt that, after the initial impact of mother's fragility, she failed to notice for some time the many indications of the difficulties she and the baby were having. Looking back, Harry's inability to cry wholeheartedly in the early weeks might have been thought to be due to his experience of mother's inability to cope with the full experience of his anger and pain. Even though the observer was aware that mother had been leaving Harry to cry for long periods she did not really absorb at the time the implication of this but continued to think of her as an attentive mother. The observer's avoidance of the pain of recognising these things may have been exaggerated or instigated by mother's own avoidance. The violence with which these feelings reasserted themselves within mother at a later point, and the way in which the observer is taken by surprise in the observation when Harry was five months old, would seem to confirm the degree to which the mother's and observer's capacity to notice had both been reduced.

The prominence which feeding Harry played in so many observations is also a notable fact. The timing of visits probably played a part, but possibly mother, who certainly controlled the timing of feeds, was wishing to communicate how crucial the negotiation of feeding her baby was for her. She perhaps hoped intensely for a better fit of mother's and baby's needs with her second child and intensely dreaded a repetition of what felt wrong with George. While some degree of difficulty in weaning is experienced by almost all mother-baby couples, the situation for mother and Harry was extreme. Harry's inner pressure towards development and separateness conflicted painfully with his mother's need for a harmonious relationship with a dependent baby.

This observation illustrates some of the problematic counter-transference reactions referred to in Chapter 1, and provides an example of the way in which the observer may be unconsciously drawn into the psychological problems going on within the family. This mother's need for a third person to help regulate the relationship with her children was not met by a very busy and much absent husband, nor by other extended family members, and it is interesting to note that the observer rarely seemed to be able to function as a helpful outside figure during the first year of observation.

During Harry's second year the situation in the family deteriorated. Mother was finally completely overwhelmed and, after a period of medication, sought psychotherapy shortly after the observer stopped visiting. She continued to contact the observer to ask for help when either she or the children were in difficulty over a period of years.

9

Steven

Steven's father and mother were a couple in their early thirties, whose first child, Karen, was born to them after about four years of marriage. The little girl was very nearly three years old when their second baby, Steven, was born. Father worked in the building trade, and mother had not worked since Karen's birth. She had been a shop worker and a clerk, and had liked her work. Both sets of grandparents were born in a remote rural district. Mother had spent most of her childhood in the city. Father had come from the country when he was older, and his accent was marked.

The family lived in a privately rented attic flat, at the top of an old Victorian house, the entrance and stairs of which were somewhat shabby. The flat was immaculately clean and tidy; very long from front to back, with a lot of rather dark corridor between. The baby slept in his parents' room for some weeks, and later shared with his sister. The flat had no central heating, and could be damp and cold in winter and very hot and sunny in summer.

Mother went into hospital at 12.30 p.m. and the baby was born at 3 p.m. I know little about the birth other than that she described it as easy and normal, and that she left hospital after four days. She had been regretful about this, because a student nurse had asked if she could be a 'case study', but she had left too soon for that to be possible. This linked, for me, with the warm welcome she gave me, when I visited with her Health Visitor to ask if I might observe her baby. She was delighted. She also told me, on that occasion, that her husband had been in a real tizzy about the baby's birth, with a sympathetic nervous tummy. He hadn't gone to work on that day, and he couldn't settle to his paper or to the TV.

The baby was weaned the week after I first began to visit the family, when he was four weeks old. I later learnt that, at this time, a close friend of mother's had died. With the Health Visitor, mother had discussed wanting to wean the baby who had been unsettled the previous night. She directed comments to the sleeping baby, 'You're all right now, aren't you? You weren't in the night, but you don't care now, do you?' She had been giving occasional bottles, anyway, convinced she

163

was unable to give him enough, and adding that, in any case, she would have to wean him because his feeds would interfere with his sister's routines – needing to be taken to and from play group. Breastfeeding had been difficult anyway, because Karen demanded attention, needed her knickers pulling up, or to go to the loo as soon as mother began to feed the baby. Being plonked in front of 'Playschool' on TV hadn't held her sufficiently either, which seemed to mean she wouldn't be kept quiet.

When I saw her the following week, for my first proper observation, she told me of her best friend's death, and of going to her funeral in a few days' time. In the same sentence she said that her husband had not been to the Registry Office to register the baby, telling the baby, 'You'll be Steven then, won't you?' She sounded sad, in a rather distant way, and also absorbed in the baby in her arms, to whom, from time to time, she addressed remarks about his not caring.

Observation at 4 weeks

Steven (in the carry cot) began to move. He rubbed his head against the mattress as if it itched and began to frown. The dummy had fallen from his mouth. His face became a deep pink and he made light, grumbling noises. He almost seemed to lift himself up and round, fell back on his left side and started to cry. The cry was an insistent noise in the back of his throat, he gasped for air. His mother allowed him to cry for a few minutes and told me he was probably hungry again; he had last been fed two hours ago. She told me, as she lifted him up, that he wanted his cuddles, just like his sister. She wrapped him more firmly in his blanket, holding him against her shoulder, and then away, to look at him. He stared up, at the light, for a few moments; his colour became paler and the crying stopped. His open mouth seemed to be gulping for air. She held him in the crook of her arm, felt his hands and said they were cold ... Steven, now back in his carry cot, sucked regularly on his dummy, then stopped suddenly and lay still. Mother was saying that he probably had been cold, that today is Karen's birthday, that her friend's funeral will be next Thursday, and that Steven will be registered on that day. She added that it is amazing, babies sleep anywhere, 'in their mess', as her baby book says. 'After all they've been swimming around in water and stuff for nine months!' She didn't want kids before she had them, and didn't like them. 'It's different when you have them, you grow to understand and learn.'...

Later, in the sitting room, the baby was asleep in the carry cot, yet he seemed to be constantly on the move; his eyes moving around under their lids, right hand moving to his cheek with too much force, as if he couldn't do anything to regulate it: his eyes seemed to roll more when his mother returned from the kitchen. She looked at him and his dummy affectionately, saying dummy was a bad word, she preferred the old-fashioned term, comforter, because it described what they did. She told me babies suck anything, hands, people, dummies. Karen says 'He's eating me' when she goes near him. Before she was married, mother's cousin's baby, who was weaned abruptly, got something wrong with it, because of that. The baby used to go for her nipples and she was embarrassed and wouldn't hold the baby when her husband was present.

So, here, in my first observation, were references to things going wrong with babies who are abruptly weaned, at the very moment when her own baby had been abruptly weaned, in less than a week. She was preoccupied with his wish to eat everything, with how cold he was, and with a need for an oldfashioned comforter. Her way of talking, which I came to understand was typical of her, was rather flat, matter-of-fact, as if apparently understanding with ease what her baby might need and how to provide for him. Yet there were hints of something else. What was hinted at, and seemed to have some connection with anxiety about the effects of abrupt weaning, was, perhaps, that she had not liked or had been embarrassed by breastfeeding. The sadness, again the merest hint, may have been felt in connection with the loss of breastfeeding, or at the loss of her best friend. Certainly, too, in view of her comments earlier in this observation, that I wouldn't want to watch a sleeping baby, and that they are much more interesting when they are a few months older, I think she was saying something about the difficulty of focussing on very young, vulnerable babies, and perhaps hoping that I might, as observer, be interested in her as well as Steven. (She had wanted to be a 'case study'.) At the end of that observation, Karen had returned from visiting the flat downstairs. Although it was her birthday, she and her mother seemed to be waiting to celebrate it. She kept asking, her mother reported, 'When is my birthday time?' It seemed to be being saved up, as something to look forward to with excitement, as something she and her mother would do on their own, later.

I want to look at further observations, which link, in some ways, with this first one, in order to consider the way this mother and her baby found ways of creating a fit, of moulding to each other.

The baby had already been described as 'good', in his 'not caring', in his willingness to be comforted with the dummy. He already often slept right through the night. He developed quickly into a baby who made little protest. He rarely cried, and learnt to tolerate his mother's frequent comings and goings. He seemed to be patient about the demands on mother's time which his sister made, and to get what he could in between.

Some of the following extracts include material which illustrates how he developed his own ways of containing himself. He also became very attached to his bottle, in a very particular way, which seemed somehow to be different from his attachment to his mother, as a person, during his feeds.

She, in turn, was preoccupied with how special or particular was his interest in her, how rarely she got the first smile, how easily others got it from him. She remarked frequently how he was 'all for his bottle' but not, apparently, for her. She recognised that there was 'something' which bothered her about it, but did not pursue this idea any further. She cared for him with skill and gentleness, worried about his physical health, and often complained of her own tiredness.

While mother seemed to focus her anxiety about the baby on his physical state, feeling how cold he might be, wondering if he was hungry or tired (see above), the baby rarely showed strong reactions, except when he wanted his bottle. He cried very little, protested rarely, could easily withdraw into himself and become absorbed in his own activities, whether mother was present or not. While he was ready to smile at everyone, for much of the time, he rarely showed intense emotion of any kind.

Later, after about five weeks, there came a development. The nappy changing with his mother became very special, and was remarked on often. The character of these moments was in marked contrast to the lack of warmth and intimacy when the baby was being fed.

Here is the baby being fed the following week:

Observation at 6 weeks

The baby, in his mother's arms, is very quiet and still. I sit near them, on the sofa, and have some difficulty in seeing the baby feeding, as Karen is noisy, jumping up and down, talking. The baby in contrast looks very sleepy, eyes blinking, almost closing, arms across his tummy. Mother can't get him to burp when she takes the bottle away, and Karen is constantly wanting me to catch and throw a rubber ring with her, and dancing around. When given the bottle again, the still, sleepy baby sucks regularly and quietly from the bottle, gazing outwards, away from mother ...

In the baby bouncer, when mother leaves with Karen to make coffee, he is facing the door, quiet, only his hands flexing slightly. After about ten minutes his hand movements become more marked and he looks as if he is trying to escape. Karen returns to ride the sofa, to tell me, 'I can pull up my knickers at the convent', to turn somersaults, showing her knickers, and to ride a little stool. The TV is on, as usual. The baby continues to flex his hands, and to make little moaning noises. Mother returns, Karen approaches the bouncer from behind and pushes the baby's head. Her mother warns her not to, she continues, and the baby smiles. Mother and Karen smile too. Mother tells me she had a bad time at the funeral on Thursday, as an aside, while showing me a chapter in a baby book about six-week-old babies. Karen's boisterous play results in a warning and, on her mother's lap, she is smacked. She leaps up to change the TV channel instantly. The baby lies waving his arms, kicking slightly, playing his tongue inside his mouth, pushing at his lips. Karen wants me to watch her all the time, and eventually I give her some of my felt pens to play with.

I recall that I felt immensely over-stretched after the observation, wondering if I would ever get the chance to observe the baby for a continuous sequence. Karen's constant activity and demands evinced anger and resentment in me as well as her mother. By contrast the baby did seem uninteresting, undemanding, and somehow capable of looking after himself. Again the next week, I watched the end of a feed:

Observation at 7 weeks

The baby is being fed when I arrive. Mother has asked me how I am, and had answered for me, 'Cold.' She clearly has a cold herself. The baby, on his mother's arm, is sucking regularly and fast, a little breathlessly with his eyes closing. I cannot continue to observe him, for (as last week) Karen is running up and down and telling me to look through the tower she has made at play school. She pushes it on to my eyes like a telescope, but the other end is blocked. I can see nothing! Mother says Karen is crotchety today. When I next get to see the baby he is looking out, in my direction, but past me, at the wall, or the reflections of light on the ceiling, blinking slowly, quiet. Karen wants her mother to play with her, the baby burps, mother says he is a good boy, he's been all smiles today, and he's wet. She asks Karen to come with her to make coffee and asks me if I would like to hold him. She organises an apron for me because he will be milky, and I feel unable to refuse. He is restless but keeps his arms and legs still, looking up beyond my shoulder. His tongue works inside his mouth, pushing the skin out near his lips, then poking through, around the inside of the lips and back in again. I am aware of an increased restlessness as he gazes at me, but not registering somehow. His breathing is shallow and fast, he shudders suddenly, and I think he might be at my right breast. Then, he seems to gaze rather than look; his arm definitely brushes my right breast, brushes his own left cheek and my breast again. He repeats the movement several times, touches my arm with sudden, surprising force, and suddenly tugs his ear hard. Now he becomes increasingly restless, struggling, kicking, his brow furrows and he makes little noises in the back of his throat.

His mother comes back and takes him from me, asks if he's been good and whether he will smile for her. He seems, lying on her lap, to be more focussed, his arm movements continue, he looks at her intently and makes little noises. She asks for a smile, saying rather wistfully that he's been all smiles today, he doesn't usually smile for her, her own mother gets one easily from him. As she continues to talk, looking at him, he beams at her, she holds him up as he blinks sleepily, and kisses his mouth. Now, holding him, she asks Karen to get a smile. Karen growls, the baby gazes intently at his mother and pulls his own cardigan. She starts to talk to me about visiting the clinic for a check-up. The baby peed on the doctor, she says, laughing cheerfully. The doctor waved two red balls in front of his face to test his eyes. 'I could have told her. She doesn't know him, he can pee a pint, or it seems like!' Karen smiles too as mother asks if she remembers. She holds the baby very close, kisses his mouth again, and shifts him to her side. His head lolls, she says, 'I know ...,' and stops. Then, just as suddenly, she says the baby is tired and asks him when he last slept. There is a pause, when I feel she suddenly doesn't seem to know or to be able to think about anything. She recovers in an instant – says she'll change him and takes him into the bedroom.

At this time, the baby had still not been officially registered. There was a sense of disorganisation and of a mother who felt there were a great many calls on her time and energy. She clearly had a great deal to do, and would then add to it – for example, it was always important that I be given a cup of coffee. I couldn't say no; she seemed determined to take care of everyone, in a practical kind of way. While she seemed to be taking care of things, in her way, she only ever seemed to touch on her own feelings fleetingly.

The baby, in his turn, seemed to have ways of coping through absorption in himself. In his baby bouncer, or mother's arms after a feed, there was little eye contact. His tongue in his mouth seemed to fulfil the function the teat had done only minutes before. His very small noises, not cries or screams, seemed to show a lack of distress, a way of keeping himself at a distance. While he was left with me, in his mother's absence, his restlessness did increase, as if his way of holding himself together by using his own tongue to fill his mouth, not to notice an empty space, a missing mother, was not working quite so well. He also may have been telling me something about noticing a breast, about wanting to touch and be in contact with a feeding mother, from which he quickly retreated to touching his own cheek, tugging his own ear, as if turning the need and its frustration on to himself. There seemed to be a sense of his not communicating any feeling very strongly, and of his not then suffering any disappointment if his needs were not met.

I have mentioned that mother only remained fleetingly in contact with painful or depressed feelings. Her own inability to stay in touch with them herself may have led to her need to maintain some distance from the baby, especially in the tricky bottlefeeding relationship. The incident she reported with the doctor raises a question about the kind of response, the kind of communication there might have been between mother and baby, had she been less distant, or he less 'good'. Mother's and Karen's delight at reporting his peeing on the doctor may suggest some pleasure at his showing anger on their behalf. His mother was certainly reporting a baby who was reacting strongly. One might wonder about some anger in him, using his pee as a weapon, a protest against having something done to him (red balls flashed in front of his face). In the same way that, in my arms, he seemed to be interested in exploring something (possibly to do with a breast and feeding), he might have been telling the doctor something about his anger at things going out of sight, communicating this through his urine to someone whose purpose, in a developmental test, was to get a response from him. It may have been that a memory, perhaps a painful one, had stirred in his mind.

His mother's fleeting 'I know ...' faded, as if something stirred in her mind too, emerged in telling the observer, and subsided again. She was unable to pursue it, to find what might have been there, to be known, in her own mind, and to be thought about in relation to the baby. Her own 'knowing' (in the sense of being in touch and able to think about a powerful, emotional experience) ceased, and she became again the mother relating to her baby in terms of his tiredness, and need for a nappy change.

After a few weeks, a coherent pattern began to emerge from what had seemed, to the observer, like random events. The baby's way of feeding, for example, was a constant. He was always still, protesting only when the bottle was taken away because his energetic sucking flattened the teat. He rarely looked at his mother during a feed, he was often apparently sleepy, eyelids drooping. His attachment to the bottle was strong, and his hand came increasingly to hold his mother's, holding the bottle. Karen's demands continued, and there were comments about how she used up baby things, like the shampoo and the Farley's Rusks. Whenever possible, especially in the living room, she filled up the observation times with games which involved her mother – especially 'shopping' for clothes and for cigarettes. (Mother had begun to buy herself clothes from a charity shop each week, and to show them to me. She was also a heavy smoker at this time.) Karen also carried around my handbag, examining its contents whenever she could, and asking to use most of the many pens and pencils she found in it.

There were illnesses almost constantly between October and Christmas. The baby seemed to have a chesty cold almost every week. Mother often had colds, and, on two occasions, gastric flu. She was preoccupied with guilt (her word) over the baby's nappy rash, which seemed to be constant, and with which she felt neither clinic nor her own doctor helped her. She was always seeking reasons for it, worrying about the nappies she used, the flannels she washed him with, or whether water and washing irritated his skin. The baby seemed untroubled, even when, as she reported to me, she found his chest covered in blood one morning. The rash often spread down his legs and up to his chest. Anxieties and symptoms of anxiety (if that is what they were) seemed to be firmly located in the realm of the physical.

While feeding him Farley's Rusks crushed into his bottle milk, she commented, more than once, that the clinic said the baby was too heavy for his age. She dismissed this, saying that he was hungry and she fed him. Yet there were also some times, when he had just been fed, and he persisted in putting fingers, clothes, toys, into his mouth, when she would say to him, 'You can't be hungry, you've just eaten.' She would refer to Karen's comments that the baby 'ate' her when she came near to him, and very often, to the dummy/comforter he needed, and which she sometimes held in his mouth until he quietened after a nappy change. She seemed to need to fill him up with something, to 'comfort' or to quieten him, as much as he sometimes did it for himself with his own tongue. A physical filling seemed to enter her mind, as if it wasn't possible, very much, to think about other needs he might have – needs which were not easily communicated and which she seemed unable to explore or to develop with him, or on his behalf.

Indeed, mother would also deny her own neediness. For example, although I knew that, after a few weeks, she clearly came to look forward to my regular weekly visits, she never seemed to mind if I was late, or had to change the day I came. But I came to realise that after I had disrupted the routine, there would often be comments about other members of her family who had let her down, or used up *her* things, or she would tell me that, had I come at the pre-arranged time, *she* would have had to put *me* off anyway! Her own anger and the objects of her disappointment were located elsewhere.

Observation at about 11 weeks

It was just before Christmas. I came to suggest that I visit when my own bad cold was better. Mother told me to come in, they all had a cold themselves.

The baby is asleep in his carry cot, lying on his side, pink faced, mouth slightly open, still. His mother tells me his cold makes him all choked up and chesty, she'll take him to the doctor in the morning. The doctor has already given him penicillin which makes him bring back his milk, so she's stopped the medication. She goes out to make coffee, and Karen comes in and out playing fastening and unfastening my handbag. The baby stirs, his face begins to crumple, he holds his hands together in front of him, his face relaxes and his tongue pokes in and out between his closed lips. He struggles for breath and his face crumples again, his complexion reddens and he gives all the appearances of crying – but is completely silent. He settles a little, face now paler, and he kicks more; he appears to be struggling with arm movements. His mother comes in, removes his bonnet, holds him on her arm, saying, 'Poor boy,' as she goes to get his bib and bottle and sits with him in the usual chair near the fire. He struggles, moving his arms, turns his face and makes complaining noises as she uses cotton buds to wipe some matter from his eyes. She says, 'You want your bottle, don't you, then you'll be quiet.' He sucks rapidly, pausing only for gulps of air, his feet kicking rhythmically, arms held quietly across his tummy. At one moment mother takes the bottle from him, he protests noisily, she says he's sucked the teat flat, and puts it right. He sucks eagerly again as she says he's always like that over his bottle. Meanwhile as he feeds she talks to me and to Karen. She asks chattily about my Christmas arrangements, and then returns to the subject of going to the doctor tomorrow. Steven's cold has just come out today, he's always been chesty. Karen didn't have penicillin until she was two. She crosses her fingers as she speaks, says she's had gastric flu again, the second time in two weeks, and adds that she needs a tonic since this baby. The door bell goes and she hands the baby to me. He holds the fingers of my right hand and looks at me and Karen. His mother returns and finishes the feed, his hand touching his mother's which is round his waist. His breathing is noisy, he burps twice and mother holds him in her right arm, from where he looks at her and around the room. His hand goes to his mouth, he sucks his fingers, there are bubbles of milk at his lips and he kicks and waves his arms, becoming fascinated by his own left arm and hand. His tongue works between his lips, eyes shining, then he notices his mother's hand and touches it with both hands, pulling the skin, then touching his own thumb and first two fingers together.

Later in the same observation:

The baby is lying on the changing mat, on the bed, looking up at his mother, eyes shining, arms and legs waving. Karen shows me pictures of Father Christmas and a house. The baby turns his head to look at us as his mother leaves to get warm, clean clothes. When she returns and tickles his tummy he looks at her and laughs, then smiles as she talks to him, the tongue still working in and out of his mouth. He thrusts a fist into his mouth, and mother asks what he's doing, he's just eaten! He persists, and sucks a bit of his cardigan too, constantly looking at his mother, and smiling. His mother says how much he now loves being changed, he'll kick furiously once she gets his nappy off. She undoes the nappy and indeed he kicks, smiles happily and looks at her. She takes away the dirty nappy and when she comes back looks at him and says he'll probably spray her now. He doesn't. She says she'll clean his face which he used to hate, but is much better now. He struggles a little but still looks lively and cheerful. She talks to him and strokes his cheek, then cleans his bottom and genitals, not commenting this time on the ever-present angry looking nappy rash. She says he may be smiling now, but Karen always gets first smile of the day. She (mother) gets his bottle and he's all for that, but Karen gets the first smile: 'It doesn't seem fair.' He keeps looking at her and continues to smile, and while she powders him he seems to pull his vest up. She pulls it down gently saying she doesn't want to see his hairy chest. She sounds regretful talking about 'wrapping him up again' as she pins on the clean nappy. He seems quieter, as Karen brings Vick for his chest. He watches his mother's left hand with interest, and continues to do so as she changes his vest. He seems happy as she rubs Vick round and round on his chest and smiles as she puts him gently into a clean baby-grow.

The changing routine, in contrast to the earlier part of the observation, seemed to bring the relationship between mother and baby to life. There was real pleasure in their looking at each other, in her touching, so gentle and confident, and in his response. The moments of closeness revealed a baby far less ready to wait patiently and be 'good' when his mother left, and there was a sense of great regret in her 'wrapping him up again'. These moments, rather like the earlier waiting for Karen's birthday time, were postponed, as if to build up the anticipation in advance of its coming. Their endings left both mother and baby regretful and sad. They often brought full-hearted cries of protest from the baby, and mother often left the room, thrusting Steven into my arms for a few moments. I think there were times when she would overcome the sense of loss by leaving the scene, and there were times when she could not tolerate the baby's vigorous or angry protests when it was over. There was one occasion when she left him with me and went to get his bottle, after a particularly enjoyable nappy change. He bit me on the forehead and cheek with such force that tears came to my eyes.

I should like to illustrate further from two observations, when the baby was six months old, and which include his father, whom I met then for the first time. By this time, the baby was very physically active. He could do 'press-ups' at thirteen weeks, was always active during changing, and soon became able to roll, stretch and grab what he wanted, even if it seemed to be out of range. He adored his bath-times, often twisting and turning and trying to thrust himself into the water, where he loved to kick and splash. His mother and Karen shared his enjoyment in being held standing and dancing in the water.

Observation at 24 weeks

I am greeted at the door by a man who shakes my hand warmly saying, 'We meet at last!' I say hello and that I hope he doesn't mind my weekly visits. He says they're fine and that he'd thought I wasn't coming tonight – that I must have known he was home!

Mother is bathing Steven and Karen, their father looks in on them, complains of the heat and leaves. Karen is amusing Steven by moving a pink wobbly toy around the bath. The baby is splashing and kicking at the toy, looks up when I come in, giving me a big smile. His mother supports him standing in the water 'for his splash' before drying him. He rubs his left sole over his right foot as he splashes, seems absorbed in the activity, until his mother lifts him out to wrap him in a towel on her lap before lifting him up again to take him to the bedroom, where she lays him on the bed to dry him, kissing and talking to him. He lies still looking at her and smiling while she says he's such a good boy, and gets up to fetch something. The baby instantly reaches out to his right and rolls over completely. She says he does that all the time and gets very close to rolling off the bed. She rolls him back, asks me to keep an eye on him, and leaves. He reaches out and grabs something to put over his face, making chatty noises and smiling, very cheerfully. He begins to rock his body in an attempt to roll over as his mother returns to place a nappy under his bottom. He rolls over instantly, upsetting the nappy's position, which makes his mother laugh as she rolls him back, picks him up for a cuddle and asks him to keep still. On his back again he watches his mother then rolls again to grab his plastic pants. Mother puts them out of reach. He tries hard to get to them, then finally grabs a corner of his nappy and puts it into his mouth. His mother says he'll always try that if there's nothing else to grab. He holds his arms out, smiling, waving his fingers and looking at his mother. As she tries to hold his legs while trying to dry and cream his bottom and genitals, he makes a grab for his feet and tries to thrust them into his mouth. She notices two blobs of clotted milk on his chin and says, 'That's what you get for choking on your feet.' I hadn't seen the feet actually reach his mouth. He begins his low machine-gunning croaking noises, which usually lead up to crying before his bottle, but they turn to giggles as his mother holds his feet and creams his genitals and bottom. I comment that he seems to like that and she says he loves to have his willy tickled. He lies smiling as she puts his nappy on and works playfully at preventing her getting first his arms then his legs into the baby-grow. She turns him on to his tummy to do up the baby-grow and he drives his face deep into the bed, almost eating it and making little growling noises. His mother talks of how he nearly fell off the bed the other day and she nearly grabbed him by the willy! If, when he starts to crawl, he puts his fingers in electric sockets, he will be smacked – it's OK if done in the right way. She turns him and kisses him while he, more subdued, makes low croaking noises as if about to cry. She hurriedly gives him to me telling us both she will go and make coffee, although I say it really doesn't matter. She insists I have him 'for a chat' while she gets the bottle (and makes coffee anyway). Father comes in with Karen, whom he has bathed. He shadow boxes with Steven, whose arms go out to him as he wonders whether the baby will play rugby or golf for England. He turns his attention to Karen, in vest and pants, whom he throws on to the bed. She asks him to do it again. Steven watches her jumping about on the bed.

Observation at 26 weeks

Father lifts him out of the playpen and puts him on his knee, facing him. The baby giggles, looks around and away thrusting his fingers into his mouth. Father pulls them away telling him not to do that – the baby persists. Mother offers me a glass of sherry and takes up the playpen. Father has put Steven on the floor on his back, he instantly rolls on to his front, pressing himself up with his hands, looking at the TV. Then, as the others take away the playpen, he notices his bottle. His mother picks him up and hands him and the bottle to his father. He drinks fast, staring ahead, lying still, with hands around the bottle. He slows down quickly, and father is not really alert when the bottle drops. Mother tells her husband, 'You've let it drop.' He seems more interested in the TV. She goes on, 'Jiggle it around, take it away from him.' He does so and the baby tries to get it back reaching out with his hands, but then drinking only slowly, dropping back to sleep. Mother attributes his tiredness to the clocks going back yesterday. He had giggled all the way through the Christening on Saturday, and they'd all been to a prolonged party with lots to drink. They all went to bed very late. He now looks very sleepy as she asks him to burp and his father pats his back. His tongue is filling his mouth and he is sucking his fingers; again father tries to stop him, again to no avail. He livens up when turned to face his father, and mother wants me to take a family photo.

The atmosphere of constant movement in the house seemed to be something which the baby took in. His mother came and went; so did his father and his sister. He was put on his back and rolled on to his tummy, raising himself to look at the TV. When he was being changed he was never still for a moment. He remained still only when he had a bottle in his mouth. In the family, there was little talk and plenty of movement, 'jiggling about'. Mother's instruction to her husband, when he was feeding Steven, seemed to epitomise something of the family's way of keeping things going. The constant activity left little space.

The absence of space or calm seemed to be mother's way of marginalising her own anxiety about the baby, his survival and her own state. Steven made few demands on his mother. He did not stimulate, in her, a questioning or thinking attitude about his state of mind. He tended to withdraw, to turn to himself and his own fingers, toes and tongue. He never fully challenged or stimulated his mother's capacity for 'holding' him (in the sense of holding him in mind and imaginatively understanding his experience). His active enjoyment and pleasure in nappy changing and bathing served a dual purpose. For him too, the activity left little space to notice the impact of his mother's presence or absence (of mind or body) or to distinguish between the bottle's teat and the substitution of his own tongue. He also found, in his mother, a lively and energetic attention in the changing and cleaning. They found mutual pleasure and intimate contact there, which clearly fitted in with the established way of relating within the family.

Conclusion

What I describe as the established way of relating within this family merits some final comment. I am describing a baby adapting to a busy mother, whose own depression made her less mentally or emotionally available for him than might have been ideal. He adapted by demanding relatively little, and by substituting his own self-containment, when by himself, and sometimes in the passive presence of his mother. His generally good, compliant behaviour gave his mother little cause for concern. His bodily illnesses, however, impeded his breathing and erupted on his skin. His mother worried about them and about his physical survival. She creamed his skin and took him to the doctor. A little cycle of behaviour and response developed, a relatively satisfactory compromise. She was happy to care for him, as for others, physically. He allowed her to do so. She felt competent and took pleasure in bathing him or changing his nappy. He loved both activities. This comfortable compromise, or adaptation by the baby to fit in with his mother's strongest capacity for care, may be seen as a happy coincidence. Indeed, I think it was. However, I think something must be said about my own experience as observer when the baby was not in his bath or being changed. While he was rather blankly containing himself in the sitting room, I sometimes found myself uncomfortable and restless, longing for a change of activity for him, for some fresh source of interest. One may see this as my own boredom, projected into Steven, who rarely appeared unhappy there himself, or perhaps as my sense of disappointment in his limited opportunities. He did lack spontaneity, passionate interest, or vivacity, when not stimulated by tickling and jiggling. I rather think that my own feeling, in that sitting room, was something to do with what was not stimulated and developed within this baby's relationship with his mother. Something rather flat and depressed seemed to creep in in ordinary play and chat, and it was to be denied or to be jiggled away in the excitement and heightened brightness of bathing and changing times, whose importance increased over time.

10

Oliver

In ordinary circumstances after the birth of a baby there is a tender intimacy between mother and baby, as each has to get to know the other outside themselves. This new relationship has to be accommodated to by the father of the child and other children in the family. Each person in the family has to find a new role. In our society the father's role in the earliest days and weeks has often been to provide a protective environment for the new couple, as well as to look after the mother. Frequently the latter is also done by other women within the extended family. This period can be a vulnerable one for the father as it is already for the siblings. It is easy for the father to feel rejected, pushed out and redundant before he can settle into a new role. He may often react like a child who has been faced with the intimacy of his parents' relationship. There is still a strong feeling that birth and the earliest period of child-rearing is a woman's world, and this is only gradually changing.

The family I observed held traditional values like these, and thus my role as a male observer interested in the baby required a further adjustment by the whole family on top of that already imposed upon them by the birth of a new baby, and I suspect different from that required if I had been a female observer. I also feel that within the context of the birth of a first son, the father felt particularly fragile and responded in a defensively aggressive way. The fact that I was another new male entering into his world accentuated these feelings. It also provided an opportunity for him to use me as a focus for some of these difficult feelings.

Oliver was born after an easy labour with mother confined to hospital for forty-eight hours. He has a sister, Susan, 1½ years old when Oliver was born. Father works in connection with the armed forces. I was introduced as a student of child development by the health visitor when Oliver was ten days old. Mother struck me as a warm, down-to-earth, sensible woman, whereas I was immediately faced with father's scepticism, hostility and anxiety. The first thing he said when he saw me was, 'So you've come to scrutinise my protégé?' He appeared antagonistic to me and scornful of anything resembling psychology, betraying a strong wish to protect his new son, and saying he 'reserved the right to have an observer as part of his child's experience'. This, together with the comment that my ethnic background 'threw him in his categorisation process' made me offer him the chance to withdraw from the observation. Mother quickly intervened, saying, 'If he wasn't happy about you observing, you'd be out of the door already,' and that I shouldn't worry about him as 'He is always rude.' Father told me he was anti everything except the British and 'There are not too many of them left nowadays.' Eventually I came to feel that I was made welcome in the family by father, but that this was interfered with by negative feelings which emerged despite himself. This may have mirrored the situation of Oliver's arrival in the family.

I think the new situation in the family after the birth of a first son 'threw them' all in their 'categorisation process', with the whole family having to regroup and redefine their roles to accommodate the new member. Father sometimes seemed threatened and edgy while at other times he was fiercely proud of his new son. Mother had to adjust to being the mother of a son, and both parents to cope with having two children. Susan had to 'grow up' and be a 'big' sister and often found this very painful. She seemed lost, sad and whiney. I think many of father's negative feelings towards the new male in the household were disowned by him and located in his relationship to me. His pride in and love for his new son were so much at odds with these more hostile and resentful feelings that I believe he felt unconsciously it was safer to express them towards me and to distance them from his son.

Throughout the year father had to go away on different placements for a few weeks at a time. Each time his suspicion of me emerged, probably fuelled by painful unconscious fantasies of jealousy while he was away. He would intimate in a joking way his anxiety about my seeing mother and Oliver when he was not there. Several times when he walked in while I was visiting, he apologised for 'disturbing our rapport'. There was a feeling of his being left out. His hostility and suspicion towards me were expressed by making pointed 'jokes' about me.

Once Susan farted. Father immediately said, 'Say pardon me.' Mother retorted, 'Paul – you'll embarrass her.' This comment seemed to embarrass father and he said he hoped I was 'up wind' and that Susan should have been facing me when she did it. In the same observation while watching Oliver being changed he said to me, 'You really do see eveything, don't you?' Oliver was put into the bath, and while in the bath Susan pulled Oliver's penis. Mother stopped her saying, 'That's Oliver's tail – don't pull it.' Father saw this and groaned, saying of me, 'Susan, don't do that – he's in agony.' As I left to go shortly afterwards, with mother saying I should let myself out, father said 'Don't steal the silverware.'

It was as if all the painful, embarrassing, unwanted bad feelings were to be lodged in me. It seemed father identified me with the baby since we were both males, but at the same time was talking about his own masculine identification and feelings of rivalry, and feeling in danger of something being stolen from him. This may have referred to the loss of his previous position as the only male in the family. Again I and not Oliver was being held responsible.

Whenever I arrived at the house and other visitors were there, father would introduce me as 'the man from the NSPCC'. Possibly his disapproval and suspicion of me made him feel as though I were checking on him. On another occasion father came in from work and paraded Oliver on his shoulders.

Oliver smiled nervously. Father said, 'You don't feel like playing but you're pleased to see your Dad.' Mother replied, 'He couldn't care less – he didn't even notice when you left.' Father began complaining of a garlic smell and said it must be my after shave. He then turned to me and began telling me about his gun insurance – in case he accidentally shot someone. He said he would show me his 12 bore shotgun sometime, if I was interested, or else mother could show it to me 'next time you are upstairs with her'.

Mother's statement that Oliver 'couldn't care less' about father must have stimulated father's rivalry with me, as it implied he was redundant and excluded.

It seems again that I was being held responsible for making father feel this, and it was interesting that it was again expressed by references to bad smells. It may have represented father's image of Oliver as a good and wanted baby while he was felt to be unwanted and able to be dispensed with. His murderous feelings towards me, as a masculine rival for mother, were barely concealed. Mother's attitude fanned these thoughts and wishes; for example when she would tell me not to bother about him whenever he was abrasive in his attitude towards me. This did not help father's fragile brittleness, nor, presumably, foster a feeling in Oliver that his father loved him. However, at other times, perhaps feeling guilty as well as wanting to include father more into Oliver's world, mother would talk to Oliver in a positive way about his father. She seemed concerned that father and Oliver should get on well together. For example, while smiling, mother said to Oliver in a deep voice, 'I like my Daddy the best.' She said to me that Oliver looked around when he heard father's voice. It seemed from my early observations that Oliver hardly differentiated his father from anyone else but found his mother's face and presence special. It was as if this was the only really satisfactory relationship for Oliver. He was easily comforted by her and very responsive to her, chatting, smiling and chortling when he saw her; and mother would often comment on what a happy little boy he was. He would actively search out his mother's voice, orientating his head to her and looking out for all signs of her.

Father's initial apprehension and mother's traditional view of the male role made it difficult for me to observe breastfeeding. I had to wait to be invited in by father. Since from the beginning he had also made some alliance with me and seemed pleased I was there, he often demanded I should pay attention to him, delighting in showing me all the electronic clocks he had made, correct to the nearest millisecond. There were a large number of these clocks all around the house and for me they represented father's desire for exactness and his lack of tolerance of anything that could not be quantified. There seemed something vulnerable and lonely behind his wish to show me what he, as distinct from mother, could produce, and in his rivalry for my attention with the other male I had come to observe.

His more negative suspicious feelings towards me gradually waned, and gave way to a more trusting attitude, so that after I had observed for a month, spending large parts of each observation with Susan (and father if he was there), father casually suggested that I should go and watch mother breastfeeding Oliver in the next room. He seemed to recognise the importance this might have for me and felt more at ease and able to allow it. Mother too was shy to feed in my presence, so the first time I could see very little of what was happening because of the way she sat in relation to me. This was coupled with the fact that father, perhaps to protect the intimacy of the mother-baby couple, continually distracted my attention with talk about his electronic clocks. Precision timing at first was part of Oliver's feeding schedule. He was fed with the bottle and the breast at regular intervals. Even when it was apparent that he yearned for the breast and not the bottle mother did not allow this as she said he had been breastfed an hour earlier. But mother's regimented feeding schedule eased, because Oliver did not settle into stable feeding times. Mother changed to feeding him on demand, though often withholding the breast and giving him the bottle. Mother told me that Oliver did not like the bottle teat as it went to the back of his mouth, and he tried to get his fingers into his mouth when she bottlefed him. He had no such difficulties during breastfeeding although frequently in the feeds I saw, only the nipple was exposed. When he was bottlefed mother changed arms and winded him in between, exactly as if she were breastfeeding him. I managed to observe Oliver being breastfed more frequently as mother became less shy. She did, however, talk to me almost continuously while feeding.

Observation at 12 weeks

Oliver sucked vigorously at the breast then lay motionless. He jerked his
head away from the nipple as if he had forgotten that he had it in his
mouth. This jerking hurt mother and she jokingly said that if he did it
again she would give him a 'big cup and a straw'. After feeding, Oliver
grabbed one fist with the other and vigorously sucked on his knuckle.

Perhaps nipple and mouth were not felt to be separate, in that he may
not have attributed a separate existence to the breast but felt it to be a
part of himself. Sucking on his knuckle may be evidence that he felt he
possessed something like the nipple available whenever he wanted.
This relates to the devastating rage precipitated when Oliver woke up
to find mother not there. Then, despite sucking his knuckle, fingers,
and other parts of his body, he could not satisfy himself. It seemed hard
for him to tolerate a space or the idea that he was dependent on
something outside himself or the thought that he did not possess
everything that mother had.

Observation at 20 weeks

Later when Oliver was fed with solid food he tried to grab the cup and
hold the food, and he whimpered when the spoon was out of his mouth.
Mother commented to me, 'When the spoon is out of his mouth he thinks
all is gone.' While swallowing the food he banged his left hand on his lap
and rotated his right hand, opening and closing his fingers and toes.
When demanding food, his hands fell still and he used his voice,
whimpering and opening his mouth. He cried bitterly at the sight of the
empty cup. He became excited when he saw the bottle mother produced
and he fingered the teat, looking at the bottle, feeling it up and down
with both hands. He pushed the bottle away by extending his arms and
scrutinising it.

Mother's comment seemed to describe Oliver's behaviour well.
Bottlefeeding seemed less anxiety provoking to him than spoonfeeding,
as he could control the pace and feel more of the feeding source. I
wondered how magical he felt. Did his hand and feet, rotating and
clenching, create a sense of continual motion with no gaps?

There seemed to be little space in anyone's mind for the idea of a
relationship involving threes. The third element in the relationship
was invariably felt to be threatening and intruding. For example, I
noticed from around four months that Oliver began shielding himself
behind his arm when he saw me and he would then smile in an
uncertain way. This may have been linked to Susan's ambivalent play
with him and the 'cuddling' which sometimes he smiled at and enjoyed
and which at other times frightened him. He would cover his face when

he saw her and become quite distressed, whimpering and writhing. Often he would suck his hands as they covered his face.

Observation at 22 weeks

Oliver was fed with a spoon, crying between spoonfuls, apparently unable to tolerate any gap between them. He was then taken for a breastfeed. During the feed he held tightly on to mother's fingers. Father walked in and Oliver jerked away from the breast to see who it was. He turned back to feed, resuming sucking. He suddenly stopped sucking, the nipple still in his mouth, and looked at me. He went back to sucking but soon jerked around again. He grasped mother's hand and pushed her jersey away from the breast to reveal more of her breast. Oliver looked at me and then at mother, sucking in his bottom lip as he looked at mother, stopping when he looked at me. He then looked back at his mother and began sucking his own jersey. Mother went out of the room, and on seeing this, Oliver began crying, sucking vigorously on his jersey, as if to try to comfort himself. He then looked at me, reproachfully, as if I were responsible for this painful state of affairs. At this point mother came back in and responding to Oliver's feeling said to me, 'Been kicking him?' Mother picked Oliver up and he stopped crying. Mother gave Oliver to father to hold, reassuring father that Oliver wouldn't bite him. Father bounced Oliver on his lap and he began biting Oliver's tummy, which Oliver seemed to enjoy. Susan began bouncing on the chair and was suddenly reprimanded by mother, who hit Susan on her face with a cushion from the chair.

This sequence illustrates how disrupted and intruded upon Oliver felt in his relationship to the breast. Father was unable to protect the intimacy of the feeding relationship and was felt, like Susan, myself and to some extent the jersey, to be muscling in on the feed. Oliver seemed to differentiate between mother and me and to show this by his sucking movements when he looked at mother. Mother had told father Oliver wouldn't bite him, as he sometimes bit the nipple; instead, father played at being a biting mouth himself. Hostility and anger were passed around the members of the family, in an attempt to push these unacceptable emotions away, a process common to all families at times. In this situation the hostility was located in me by mother when she 'jokingly' asked if I had been kicking Oliver. Susan then received the brunt of the blame at the end when she was hit by mother.

Observation at 23 weeks

Mother talked to me while breastfeeding Oliver. As I replied Oliver looked up from the breast straight at me. Mother directed him back on to the nipple. He sucked a while then looked up at me again. He lay with the nipple in his mouth, his lips loosely around it, looking at me. Mother expressed Oliver's feelings about me as an intruder by saying, 'It's only him, come on.' Oliver carried on sucking, looking up at me again, easily distracted. Mother was getting irritated and said, 'Stop playing around, Oliver, have your tea.' Oliver lay there, not sucking. Mother lifted him up and rubbed his back to wind him, then put him back to the breast.

Oliver sucked more strongly and began pushing mother's jersey away from the breast, clutching at it. He stopped sucking again and looked suspiciously at me. Mother directed the nipple back into his mouth. Oliver continued sucking but suddenly began pushing her chest hard away from him and pulling the nipple with his mouth, as if ruthlessly trying to wrench the nipple out. Mother told him to stop because it hurt but he continued. Mother explained, somewhat embarrassed, what Oliver was doing. Mother grabbed Oliver's hand to stop him pushing her chest. He grasped her finger tightly and continued feeding. After a while mother sat Oliver up and he looked bewildered for a few seconds.

Here and elsewhere Oliver was preoccupied with the two nipples and the two eyes which looked down at him while he fed. These two pairs, eyes and nipples, lend themselves to confusion, and Oliver's aggression towards the nipple seemed directly connected to his experience of feeling intruded upon by my eyes watching him. He had stopped feeding and several times stared hard at me as if to push me away with his eyes and send me off so he could get on with his feed. There seemed little notion that my eyes could have been looking at him in an interested way rather than in a hostile or threatening one. It reminded me of father's comment about my coming to scrutinise his protégé, or introducing me 'jokingly' to the neighbours as the inspector from the NSPCC. Oliver may have confused the nipple with a hostile eye and so tried to attack it. He may also have wanted the nipple for himself, to continue his uninterrupted relationship to the breast whenever he wanted and not allow any intruders to have access. However, I think it is interesting to note how similar Oliver's primitive reaction is to father's defensive aggression towards me at the very beginning when I started to observe Oliver.

In this family masculinity seemed predominantly characterised by this kind of aggression. A relationship including three people seemed hard to conceive and there was much rivalry and jealousy in relation to the all-important two-person relation to mother.

Once, when Oliver was being breastfed father put on a King Kong mask which earlier he had told me frightened Oliver. He called Oliver as he put the mask on. Oliver turned round, and his face dropped. He looked very uncertain but quickly turned back towards mother and continued feeding. Father said, 'Oliver's got his priorities sorted out.' After this incident father played with Oliver, tickling his feet and playing with his toes, tickling him again and then biting his tummy. Oliver grimaced and turned away from father who sadly said, 'You love it when Mummy does that.'

Here it seems father became the cruel personification of precisely the biting, intruding monster Oliver feared. Confusion of feelings was rife. From Oliver's point of view, father now had the ruthless biting mouth, while he himself was like the breast under attack. It was as if father's genuine wish to do well by Oliver was continually interfered with by his unconscious rivalry and jealousy. The underlying belief was that only the mother can really satisfy the baby, and there is thus no real place for a good father.

Oliver was weaned at six months, rather precipitously: it was characteristic of the way the family planned things that the exact timing had been decided when he was born. Although the date had been fixed on in this way, Oliver seemed to have little preparation for it. He was said to be more interested in the bottle than the breast, however, and seemed to feel relieved to give up the breastfeeds which were so seldom peaceful. He also had more control over the bottle.

In the observation following weaning he seemed to symbolise his feelings about the breast, weaning and rivals. This capacity to symbolise and 'play out' his emotions was significant and helpful for him.

Observation at 26 weeks

He lay with a white plastic box slowly emptying the toys from it and then sucking the box. He found a toy ship among the toys and began sucking on it, pulling on it with his mouth and then leaning backwards, a motion strongly suggestive of his emptying the breast and wrenching the nipple. Later, when mother was holding Oliver, Susan was playing with father, putting the same white plastic box on her head. Oliver got furious, writhing in mother's arms, trying to force his way out. Father proudly said, 'Oliver wants to give Susan a good one.' Oliver raised his arm to shield himself when he saw father as well as me. He was distinctly unfriendly towards father, refusing to play with him, turning away. Both father and mother commented on Oliver's sudden shyness with strangers, how he shielded himself in his pram while being pushed on the street whenever someone walked past.

I wondered how much Oliver's own ruthlessness towards the breast gave rise to these frightened and threatened feelings in him. Hostility was so often lodged in other people in his attempt to get rid of it. But then it seemed to be coming back at him. Oliver felt on this occasion that Susan had got the prized white box-breast. His hostility was talked of with pride, and I suspect seen as evidence of his maleness even if he seemed afraid of other people, thinking he might be attacked. This contrasts with the family perception of Susan's femaleness, and the attitude to her feelings.

When I first arrived to start observing mother had told me Oliver's birth had been easier than Susan's; he was feeding well and was much easier to handle than Susan had been. They found it hard to accept that Susan had an emotional reaction to Oliver's birth, preferring to find physical reasons for her misery and upset which were evident for example when Oliver was being breastfed. They said she was tired or teething. Interestingly father seemed more able to identify and be in touch with the feeling that 'Susan had been green over the last few days, with lots of *me's,*' with mother adding that she thought it was because Susan had not been well. Father added thoughtfully, 'Perhaps.' Both parents seemed to revel in Oliver's maleness with mother appearing to be delighted she had a baby boy with a penis. Mother told me that she kept forgetting Oliver was a little boy, while carefully covering up his penis as he lay on the floor. She said that Oliver often sprayed her. Although on the surface she found this distasteful, she secretly seemed to enjoy it. Father told me I must watch out with Oliver as 'his penis stands up to attention and can spray the roof'. Father's infantile rivalry with his son's penis was expressed in his next sentence when he said, 'If you ever want to compete with a little boy to see who could wet a wall the highest, don't try! The little boy would automatically win.' He went on to give me the physiological reason for this. While father was talking to me, Oliver wet mother. Father congratulated Oliver on his aim. Mother said how much Oliver seemed to enjoy wetting her. What was also evident was that mother enjoyed it herself. Susan seemed to realise how much mother and father delighted in Oliver's maleness, and on one occasion she pulled his penis while he was in the bath. She was told to be gentle with him; that Oliver was a boy. Father mockingly said that at sixteen Oliver may remember his sister pulled his penis. Father told me he was dreading the day Susan started bringing boyfriends home (she was 18 months old) as if he wished to be the only man in his girls' lives.

Shortly afterwards, mother was breastfeeding Oliver on her bed and Susan became very anxious. She began searching in a magazine for a picture of a baby saying, 'Anna, Anna.' Mother said, 'You mean Oliver.' Susan found a picture and held mother's attention with it, as if trying to say, 'Here, look at me, this is a *girl* baby, not Oliver.' Father leaned over the bed towards mother, Susan and Oliver and tried grabbing the magazine. Susan pulled it away. Father told her sternly to put the magazine back. Mother said Susan would if she was sure father was not going to take it away. Father looked embarrassed.

It seemed that father found the feelings of exclusion painful as well as Susan, but that he wanted Susan to have all the feelings of deprivation in the context of the intimacy of mother and Oliver's relationship. Mother seemed aware that father wanted to inflict those feelings on Susan.

Susan often seemed irritable, listless and tearful. I felt she was depressed. Mother noticed her unhappy mood and explained it in terms of her being upset by teething and tiredness. While feeding Susan, mother expressed disgust at the food but nevertheless continued feeding her. Susan was not really allowed to express hostility directly; this seemed to be a male preserve. For example, once she tried acting out her feelings with dolls by putting some dolls in Oliver's high chair. Mother told her to take them out. As she did so, she flung them hard on to the floor. Mother told her, 'Be gentle.'

When Susan was grizzly and demanding attention, mother 'joked' with her saying, 'We should swop you for another child – a black one with curly hair.' I connected this with early remarks of father's about aliens. At times Susan was felt to be like a nasty alien denigrated baby, without a penis, of little value in contrast to her baby brother. Mother said to me, 'You couldn't tell for a long time whether Susan was a boy or a girl, but with Oliver you are certain.' Once, while being cross with Susan and simultaneously tickling Oliver lovingly, mother said, 'Sometimes I wonder how I remain sane.' It was clear that the implication was that Oliver does it for her, as she followed by telling me how contented, happy and undemanding Oliver was.

Father loved rough-and-tumble play with Oliver, who sometimes enjoyed it too. Father said to Oliver: 'You and I have a good communication we do – no chamois leather treatment for you – you like rough and tumble.' He went on to tell me that Oliver loved watching his clocks and oscilloscopes, a sort of 'like father, like son' feeling, although as I have already described, Oliver grew to like the rough and tumble less and less, especially father's propensity to bite his tummy. But father told me, 'He is my pride and joy, my son – he'll father my grandchildren some day.' This was interesting in contrast to father's expressed feelings about Susan's future boyfriends.

It was when Susan herself had actually bitten Oliver that father said they had been having some 'jealousy problems' lately. Father asked Susan why she had bitten Oliver and she replied, 'Because Daddy was cuddling him.' This rare acknowledgment of Susan's jealousy and rivalry, together with father's often locating his own negative feelings in me, was in contrast to the ability of the parents to accept and even admire Oliver's jealousy, greed and temper by attributing it to his maleness. Mother often said in a fond tone to Oliver, 'You're so greedy and impatient – a typical male.'

I think it was difficult to conceive of any other kind of masculinity. Maleness was seen as something 'sure', something quantifiable like the clocks, whereas femaleness was equated with something you couldn't be sure of, less certain maybe unseen. This would seem to be much the same as an infantile experience of the differing sensations of nipple and breast – the former firm in contrast to the latter's softness. I wonder how much emotional life in general was seen as a part of the female, as the presence of emotional responses were so often denied, and physical 'observable' causes substituted. Teeth were for ever coming up and being held responsible for Susan's unhappy mood.

Conclusion

I believe my interest in the baby and in emotions was seen as something quirky and feminine, and brought father into contact with a kind of man he couldn't quite categorise.

At the beginning my position in the family was precarious but I was none the less given a place by the family and often treated very kindly. Father and mother wanted to welcome their baby warmly and wanted to do the same for me, but this wish was constantly being disrupted by an upsurge of unconscious hostility and rivalry. The particular circumstances and belief systems of this family brought out something quite extreme, particularly in father. I cannot know if a male observer would have elicited the kind of response that I did if the baby had been female. I think that a useful aspect of the observation was that I could be used by father as a place where he could locate some of his rivalrous and envious feelings towards his and Oliver's exclusive relationship to mother. Surviving this may have been helpful for him, as well as perhaps protecting Oliver from the full impact of these emotions.

11

Jeffrey

Jeffrey is the second son of a couple in their early thirties. His brother Peter was four years old when Jeffrey was born. The parents had left the country area in which they grew up, and moved to some distance from their large working-class families of origin when they married.

The parents wanted to provide a comfortable and secure home for their children. This meant that they both worked full-time. They worked hard in order to buy their own house, a suburban semi-detached which was always very clean, bright, comfortable and welcoming.

Mother had returned to her demanding work within a few weeks of Peter's birth. She again took maternity leave for Jeffrey's birth. This time the leave allowed her to remain at home until Jeffrey was five months old; the return to work was difficult for her, and she spoke of having found that she liked being at home, and that she enjoyed Jeffrey's company. She told me, 'Women I know work simply for the money, not for a career.' She enjoyed her work very much but her priorities lay in providing a home and she took all the responsibility for child-care and the running of the house.

Jeffrey's father chose to organise his shift work so that he was often at home during the day in order to be with his family. He is a quiet and shy man, who clearly finds much pleasure in his wife and children. Peter is an energetic and talkative boy, constantly on the move. Generally he was quite tender to his small brother, but his jealousy was easily tolerated by his parents within strict rules of 'how one behaves'.

Mother is friendly and welcoming, but I was always aware that she maintained her privacy. She did not confide in me, nor talk of any matters of family intimacy. Although she always asked about the welfare of my family, she clearly did not expect me to talk of my life and was content to accept me as a student who came to observe and think about Jeffrey. Indeed, she used my visits on many occasions to pause from her domestic work. She would sit down to watch and be with Jeffrey herself.

Jeffrey was born at home. He was a large baby and mother was pleased that the birth had gone well. She told me that she 'had good feelings about the whole thing', but she never told me details of the labour and birth. I see this now as my first encounter with the reserve of this family. Jeffrey slowly found his place within this close yet undemonstrative family; a place secure enough to weather the difficulties of infancy and, in particular, his mother's return to work.

Mother told me, on my first visit, when Jeffrey was three weeks old, 'I'm not what you'd call an instinctive breastfeeder; some mothers really enjoy it. I have to keep an eye on the clock: three minutes feel like ten to me.' She found breastfeeding worrying as she was unable to gauge the quality and quantity of the milk.

Observation at 3 weeks

Nevertheless Jeffrey seemed very peaceful and was lying extremely relaxed with legs froglike and eyes closed. He was sucking gently and spent long times quite still. I could see a round face and soft hair. Mother ended the feed and sat Jeffrey up quite suddenly, supporting him with one hand under his armpit. He slumped forward over her hand, seeming to have no support at all in his own body, opening his eyes very slowly. Mother pulled at the toe of his babygrow and said that he was out of the first size already. Jeffrey was looking up, towards me, and was trying to pull his head upwards, his eyes open and looking across at me intently. I felt sure that he was aware of me as someone unfamiliar. Mother put him to her other breast after a few minutes. She said that she might have to change his nappy to wake him up. He closed his eyes and took the nipple and seemed to suck gently. Mother lent him up against her after only a few minutes. He opened his eyes and stared at the chair back. Then she sat him on her knees and she and Jeffrey looked at one another for a few minutes, enclosed, soft and private. Jeffrey's expression was joyful. After this she continued to feed him the second breast; he now held on to her blouse very tightly, but the rest of him remained completely still and relaxed.

As a very young baby Jeffrey struck me particularly by remaining very still for long periods, but his eyes were active, exploring his environment; it seemed to me as if he only explored through his eyes but that nevertheless he was always aware of the different people around him, and of his family's comings and goings, especially his mother's.

Jeffrey was a sensuous baby who surrendered completely to many experiences, especially the feed, and then later to washes and the nappy change. He adored his baths.

Observation at 4 weeks

Mother laid him, still holding him, on the mat. He lay still, looking about, and then he started to move his arms and legs, continuing while his nappy was removed. Mother went out of the room to fetch water. He got his thumb nearly to his mouth but not quite in, otherwise his arms and legs were almost still and he looked carefully around him. He kicked his legs strongly but not actively while his mother liberally creamed his bottom, and he rested his foot on his penis. Mother cleaned him efficiently and briskly put a clean nappy on him. When the nappy was on him, he began to redden and to screw up his face and to cry with plaintive, whiney noises. Mother picked him up and he settled immediately and began to look around.

Jeffrey seems to be holding his body quite still, holding himself with tightened muscles as he is first placed onto the mat. Is he trying to hold himself together, in one piece, in this spacious expanse, the – perhaps cold – environment of the floor? Next he begins to look about as if trying to place the experience. Then his mother's familiar hands begin the routine, and while washing and cleaning they stroke and soothe him, providing a reassurance so that now, comforted, he can kick out strongly and explore the freedom of his nakedness. When his mother leaves him in order to fetch the water he seeks the comfort of his thumb as a pseudo-breast to suck. When the nappy change and wash are finished, the stroking and arousal end. Jeffrey then cries. This stills when his mother gathers him up.

For the first weeks, until bottlefeeding was established, the breastfeeding seemed to take all day. Mother was clearly unhappy about this. At night too, she reported, Jeffrey wanted to be with her and she 'did not know what to do to comfort him'. When Jeffrey was two months old, she said 'Jeffrey wants to sit with me all morning, looking around, taking it all in, with a few sucks from time to time.' I witnessed many instances of him fiercely resisting being pulled back to feed, and of how one feed could seem to run into the next. Jeffrey successfully controlled his mother's presence very tightly during these weeks.

At two months, 'His uppermost hand fastened around her index finger but after a moment or so his mother absentmindedly pulled it free. Jeffrey's hand felt along her blouse and took hold of a fold of blouse. His eyes remained shut.'

And at two and a half months: 'Jeffrey was feeding, still, eyes shut. Mother talked to me about his sleeping habits. Jeffrey then stopped feeding and looked up at her. His face was puckered, red and cross.'

When he could not hold on to his mother all the time it seemed to me that Jeffrey felt that he could control her movements and also perhaps those of his family, through his eyes.

Observation at 7 weeks

Jeffrey is sitting in the bouncy chair; mother has left him, between breasts, and gone out of the house in order to take Peter to school. Jeffrey looked around, then his hand moved to his mouth and he gave odd mutterings and hummerings. Then he looks at the door that his mother had just gone through. His mouth moves, tongue in and out. He puts a hand to his mouth and licks his knuckles. Father had come in quietly to sit with his son while his wife popped out. When his mother does return and he can finish the feed, Jeffrey fumbles the nipple so that it falls out of his mouth, and then holds himself away. Mother holds her breast so that the nipple drops down into his mouth. He keeps his eyes open, staring up at his mother and then she looks down and their eyes meet. He then begins to suck, while she says, 'Come on, don't play, eat.' He sucked with his eyes open, one foot circling. Was he keeping his mother present, but not letting her disappear again, by keeping his eyes open?

Observation at 12 weeks

Mother stood up and lowered Jeffrey into the baby chair. He looked at her as she stood up and moved away. He watched her go out of the door, but did not show any expression. He played with the plastic figures on his chair; otherwise he was still. He now reached out to one blue figure, holding it with one hand and watching it intently with both eyes.

Reflection and curiosity were often stronger than hunger. Many of my observations describe Jeffrey interrupting a feed in order to look around. It was common for mother to keep the bottle in his mouth as he turned his head. As he grew, she often had to bring him to sit next to me on the sofa, so that Jeffrey could see and perhaps control the presence of both of us. Otherwise he would not feed. He seemed to find that looking around could fill him as well as milk could, as if he could drink in the world with his eyes and deny his need for actual food. This had been hinted at as early as six weeks:

Observation at 6 weeks

As soon as mother went out of the room Jeffrey's face began to crumble. He went pink, and his bottom lip came forwards and wobbled, but he started to look at something (i.e. something 'caught' his attention) and his face cleared. He continued in this way for a while – his lip would come forward and just occasionally, he let out a small cry. Then he would have his attention taken by something, and just as quickly, his face would clear and he would look at what he had seen fixedly for a while.

At three months exactly mother greeted me by announcing that she was now giving Jeffrey a bottle of milk to replace the midday breastfeed. He had accepted it eagerly, but had a lot of wind. Mother said that she was continuing to give Jeffrey a full breastfeed at 6 a.m., and that she would feed him from one breast only at 11 a.m. and 6 p.m. During this visit Jeffrey sucked loudly and noisily at his thumb, and his mother commented that it sounded as if he was hungry, but he refused to breastfeed. I feel that this refusal of the 11 a.m. breastfeed (one side only) could be seen as Jeffrey expressing his anger at the breast which had been withheld from him. Before weaning Jeffrey had enjoyed sucking and exploring with his mouth, but perhaps now his regular sucking of the fingers (which continued through and after weaning) shows Jeffrey inhibiting his own demands upon his mother. He was now regularly placed in a canvas 'babyrelax' chair, as his family came and went about him. Many of my observations record him sitting and either sucking his thumb, or part of his hand, or rubbing his tongue in and out and along his lips, or, on a few occasions, sucking his tongue. Sometimes this seemed clearly linked with his mother's presence, as Jeffrey would watch her intently and suck. After an upset, he often held his hands, as if holding himself together, hanging onto himself quite tightly, and sucked. After weaning he would often suck and chew at small toys.

Mother returned to work when Jeffrey was five months old. This event appeared to pass quietly. One month earlier she had rapidly accelerated Jeffrey's weaning so that he suddenly received three solid meals a day with a bottle in the evening and a breastfeed only in the early morning. This weaning seemed to me to take place very quickly but mother was pleased that 'it had all been so smooth'. A feed was observed when Jeffrey was four months.

Observation at 16 weeks

Mother wrapped a small hand towel around him, imprisoning his arms to his sides. She spooned a spoonful of food into his open mouth. Jeffrey had opened his mouth for the food but was also looking at me. He put his head forward and kicked out his feet strongly but also accepted the food. Mother gave him another spoonful, he squirmed more and made loud 'awk' protests. Mother said, 'It's too hot,' and repeated this as she spooned another mouthful in. I realised that she was referring to his bottle standing in a jug of water on the table behind his head, just out of his view. But Jeffrey was not twisting to see it, he was looking at me and now struggling hard. Mother said, 'Do you want your thumb?' She put the food down and freed his arms and continued. He did not put his thumb in his mouth but lay back and ate with relish, without squirming or struggling. His mouth was opened readily; his tongue came forward between his lips as he licked and sucked and then swallowed the food.

Mother wiped his face with the towel and put him down on the sofa and went to warm his bottle. Jeffrey held the towel in one hand and the other was just about completely in his mouth. Mother returned and, picking him up, held him close; Jeffrey began to mutter, looking at the bottle. As she proferred it he opened his mouth wide and closed on the teat. He sucked noisily and eagerly, breathing rather raspingly through his nose, making panting noises. His eyes were open, looking up at his mother. His feet were still; occasionally one circled slowly. The hand further away from his mother moved a little towards the bottle along her hand; he was spreading his fingers. Mother looked down at him and for a long time all was quiet save for Jeffrey's appreciative grunts.

Mother suddenly spoke and asked about my holiday. I answered. Jeffrey started to mutter while sucking, raising up his left hand to mother's face. She looked down at him, 'What's this? You want me to talk to you?' and she did gently, in a slightly sing-song voice, moving her head in time to her words. Jeffrey looked hard at her, then let the teat go and murmured at her, curling his top lip and chattering, moving his arm toward her face. Then she reset the teat in his mouth and he sucked, watching her all the time.

Jeffrey became more and more relaxed and still. His eyes drooped and he stopped sucking. 'You're nearly asleep, you can't keep those eyes open!' and his mother removed the teat and sat him up. Jeffrey started to cry loudly; his face screwed up and reddened and he passed flatus in a long loud series. Mother rubbed his back, round and round rather abstractedly. She said, 'Oh? Did you want more?' and pushed the teat back into his mouth. Jeffrey accepted it but after a couple of mouthfuls pushed it out. Mother returned him to sitting and rubbed him and he protested and this continued with mother seeming to become more abstracted and Jeffrey more miserable. Then she said, 'I don't know what you want, I'm going to get your changing mat.'

Mother changed his nappy – which was quite clean – and Jeffrey accepted this peacefully.

Once dressed he lay on the floor and mother gave him a plastic 'nappy pin' shaped toy. He looked at it and after a time jerkily reached his hand to it and took hold of it as his second hand began to reach. He brought the pin to his mouth and began to suck it, tongue licking and teeth chewing at it. Mother left the room and Jeffrey watched her leave. He chewed and sucked for some time and his right hand became caught under the bib which fell forward on to his face. He started to redden and I freed him. He resumed chewing and then dropped the pin. I returned it to him. He reached for it and looked at me and then, sucking the pin, looked at the door. Mother reappeared with tea and left immediately to take tea to father. Jeffrey watched her leave and his face reddened and he began to cry out loud, chewing on the pin between cries. Mother returned and Jeffrey stopped crying. She picked him up and talked to him making wind noises near his cheek. Jeffrey watched and began an enormous range of sounds and bubbles and noises to her.

Jeffrey's first toys were these small plastic shapes; there was the pin and also a man and a bird. His mother had introduced them to occupy his hands whenever she changed his nappy. He would suck and chew at these toys. They seemed to serve to inhibit his demands on his mother, and he would hold them tightly when she went out of sight. I feel too that the biting and chewing often occurred when he might otherwise have shown aggression or anger.

Observation at 20 weeks

Mother was outside the French doors cleaning the windows. Jeffrey looked at her, back to me and then repeated this, smiling briefly as he caught my eye. Then he returned the bird he was holding to his mouth and continued to chew on it. I was finding the arrangement uncomfortable, feeling that if I did not talk to Jeffrey he would become anxious. Jeffrey continued to chew the bird and to watch me, his mother and his brother in turn. Then he called out and I looked and he was looking at me. This was repeated a few moments later. Then he would return to stillness except for the chewing. After spending some time quiet and still save for chewing, Jeffrey held out the bird in front of him and spread his fingers wide and the bird dropped on the floor. Then he became even more quiet, he had been watching us now he became dreamy and rested his head on the back of the chair. Mother talked to me and took my attention. Jeffrey shouted and I turned to look at him and he was looking at me, biting at the rim of the talcum powder tin.

Mother came in and slowly changed his nappy. She leant across Jeffrey, lying on the floor to point out something to Peter who was writing next to them. Jeffrey looked up at her, stretched right across him and then reached up a hand to touch her near her breast, and then started to chuckle and laugh delightedly. Mother did not appear to notice and made no remark but sat up and returned to wash him, and Jeffrey started to play with his hands, banging them together, spreading palm against palm, finger to finger. Mother leant across a second time and Jeffrey looked up to laugh and chuckle. Mother did not respond as she was preoccupied by Peter. She wrapped Jeffrey up in a clean nappy and as she did this he tried to put his two linked thumbs into his mouth. This however was in a very jabbing harsh movement and caught his eye once or twice. When they did reach his mouth he did not keep them in but jabbed harshly again. Mother picked him up.

It seems as though potential anger passed unnoticed.

There is a possible link with the way in which the matter of mother's return to work had been dealt with. On my visit the day before she did so Jeffrey was reaching out, eager to take the spoon and feed himself, but his mother briskly fed him, spooning in mouthfuls as he reached out with the spoon. In this way she ensured that he ate quickly and cleanly and perhaps was distancing herself from any pain she was feeling at leaving him the next day through such speedy practical work. She behaved as though acting on mottos like 'don't dwell, up and doing, keep busy'.

On my next visit I arrived when Jeffrey was asleep and witnessed what seemed to me to be a dream recalling a satisfying feed.

Observation at 21 weeks

Mother was talking as we entered the bedroom and Jeffrey opened one eye. Seeing this his mother stopped talking. Jeffrey slowly closed the eye and began sucking on his thumb for four or five seconds. Mother watched him for a short time and then left me alone with him. He sucked his thumb for a few seconds more but was otherwise quite still. His eyes moved behind his eyelids. He seemed gradually to settle into a deep sleep. His periods of sucking decreased into regular five or six second bouts with similar pauses of deep, even breathing. His eyes stilled and I watched him still and sleeping for about twenty minutes. Then I heard mother's voice as she talked on the telephone. Jeffrey suddenly shifted and raised himself slightly on his arms, which remained at his sides. He pushed his face down into the sheet. He wiped his nose into the sheet, face forwards, and pushed right down and moved it from side to side once or twice, and made a grumbly noise. Then he wiped his face, seeming to push into the sheet quite hard. Then he went to sleep once more. He did not put his thumb back into his mouth and settled, breathing evenly and deeply, his thumb a few inches from his mouth.

Mother always wiped Jeffrey's face thoroughly after every feed or meal. Later on in this same visit:

Jeffrey woke and had been placed in the rigid plastic chair on the floor. He looked all around and then at me, smiling and smiling and I felt that it would disturb him if I did not respond so I smiled back. After this he smiled at me and called to his mother, standing at the kitchen doorway and elicited a conversation with her. Then he watched and moved excitedly and called after his brother who was hurling himself about playing an excited and noisy game. His mother shooed Peter out of the room in order to put Jeffrey on to the floor to demonstrate to me his attempts to move. He looked straight down at the carpet and pushed his arms, raising and lowering his body several times. Then he lifted his head and looked around; then, lowering his head, he started to scrabble with his feet and knees, pushing them against the carpet but not very effectively getting them under his tummy or lifting his bottom. Mother was watching him, obviously very pleased, smiling. Later when she lifted him up she talked of this strength.

In this extract I think that there are hints of how Jeffrey managed to find ways that allowed him to be without his mother for long hours after her return to work, and to continue to grow and develop. He continued to work hard at his physical development which was always highly regarded by his family. He developed his ability to call for attention. He also took a great, sometimes even precocious interest in other children, especially his brother, identifying himself with his father and brother as a boy rather than as a needy baby.

In the weeks following his mother's return to work, Jeffrey grew and throve. The bottlefeeds that I observed remained a time of great closeness for both mother and son. They developed a very personal sort of conversation which consisted of a great variety of mouth noises, which were very intimate despite being usually held across the distance of the room.

Jeffrey also continued to be able to assert himself and to make his wishes clear. A month after his mother went back to work:

Observation at 25 weeks

Jeffrey was sucking peacefully on his bottle with his hand on his mother's blouse opening and spreading on the material. His other hand rested on her fingers. Peter talked to me. Jeffrey fought the bottle, pulling his head away. After a few moments his mother said, 'Oh dear, you want to see,' and turned him around so that he could see Peter and me. He beamed with pleasure and lay down to suck again, with both of us in view.

The bottle remained for a long time a satisfying and controllable experience. Jeffrey fondled it and could control his own feeding. On several occasions I saw him bite and chew at the teat if the flow of milk was slow in arrival. After his mother returned to work, Jeffrey took an interest in cups. As early as six months I became aware of his focused attention on any cup that I drank from. Mother habitually made coffee for me on each visit. I felt as if I were drinking his drink. He regularly imitated his family's use of the cup, both with his bottle and with empty cups. I feel that this reflected Jeffrey's own search after growth and a wish to grow up. He wishes perhaps to be Peter or his father. He drinks as if to try to experience the experience of others. I had felt that I was drinking his drink: was he experiencing the drink with me?

Observation at 26 weeks

Mother sat close to me on the sofa. Jeffrey looked at me and reached for my coffee cup. Mother let him struggle to me and, as my cup was empty, I let him take it. He tried to hold it properly, and to look inside. He explored it for ten minutes or so, and then gave me his cheesy triumphant grin.

For many months Jeffrey's toys continued to consist of the small plastic shapes his mother had introduced. He played dropping games. I would see him drop, and look down at the small toy and then lean over the side of his plastic chair and reclaim it. At seven months his mother added several softer toys to his collection and when Jeffrey picked these up he would chatter at them animatedly in the way his mother did to him. It seemed that he was 'being mummy', with the toy as his baby. In this way Jeffrey explored the issue of being separated from his mother; he was now the mother in charge; he could control the presence or absence of the toy baby.

Observation at 24 weeks

Jeffrey was sitting in his rigid plastic chair on the floor. He held out the toy dog and let it fall over the side of the chair. He waited, then leant forward and picked it up. He chewed at the top a little and then let it fall, and it tumbled down over his front on to the floor. He waited and then leant forward between his legs, reaching down with his left hand, but he couldn't reach. Then he leant to the left and reached down his hand looking around for the toy. This time although he could reach it he could not pick it up. After several tries he looked up at his mother and said 'aah! aah!' and his mother said, 'Can't you get it?' and came over to get it. Jeffrey became very excited and happy. He kicked out his legs strongly and occasionally chewed at the toy, between conversation towards me or his mother. He seemed very chirpy and happy with wonderful chuckly conversation. Mother left to make coffee. Jeffrey watched her go out of the room. The instant that she was out of sight he switched his look to me. He smiled and tried to get me to talk with him. I responded. When his mother returned Jeffrey stared intently at the cups.

Once Jeffrey could move, first by rolling and soon by crawling, he would explore the perimeter of the room, touching knobs and opening the doors of the small cupboards. He would carry his bottle, which he dropped from time to time. It seems to me that Jeffrey carried the bottle as if it were a pseudo-mother that he could drop, discard and forget. He was discovering that he did not need his mother with him all the time in the way he had as a small baby. Also in these explorations Jeffrey showed his preoccupations with his brother and father, and his wish to be like them.

Observation at 40 weeks

He turned to Peter's pedal tractor and pulled himself on to his knees beside it. He pushed it across the room by means of first leaning against it until he was at full stretch, and then walking on his knees up to it. He made 'vroom' noises as Peter does, and looked sideways across to me.

Observation at 44 weeks

Other games during this latter part of his first year involved sorting through things, examining, choosing, looking and discarding.

Jeffrey crawled to and sat down beside a wooden milk float. He took the bottles out one by one, looking very hard at each, and then laying them aside. When the box was empty, he searched the inside of the box with his hands, and looked all around inside; then he replaced the bottles one by one.

Many of my observations at this time seem to me to show Jeffrey as being concerned with sorting out the people in his life, their comings and goings and also developing ways of exploring his anger and aggression through his play.

Observation at 88 weeks

Mother brought in a large red apple, and, biting out a piece, gave it to Jeffrey. He happily took the apple and rather wetly began to eat it as he walked around the room. After a while he returned to his mother's knee and held out his apple to her and she took it and offered it back but he urged her on, chattering, so she took a bite. This time he took it back, walked around and came and offered it to me. I took it and offered it back. He took it and ate, then left the apple with me as he chased the cat. Later he reclaimed his apple, then dropped it. Mother picked it up and picked off some fluff and took it into the kitchen to wash it. Jeffrey followed holding out his hand and calling for the apple. Then as his mother held it out of reach and examined it carefully he burst into tears. His bottom lip stuck out and he went very red. Mother crouched down and held him around the shoulder and wiped his nose and mouth. He struggled. As soon as she returned the apple he cheered up and wandered into the sitting room, eating it. He walked around, then dropped the apple, later kicking it about as if it were a football.

Jeffrey feels in charge of the room and so powerful as he feeds both his mother and me. While his mother cleans the dropped apple, Jeffrey becomes upset at its tantalising presence, near but out of reach, out of his control; perhaps he fears that it will never return. When he does have the apple back, it again is in his power and he can choose to kick it and discard it at his will. At times, however, Jeffrey's fragility was evident, and his quiet ways of coping with his distress were displayed. The following extract was when he was six months old.

Observation at 24 weeks

The feed seemed short and quick. Mother stood up and said that she was going to get his bottle, and told Peter to come with her to clean his teeth. They left the room. Jeffrey watched them go. As she left his mother pulled the door to. I was frightened that she might close it. Jeffrey sat very still as she left, hands in lap. Now his face did not change but he began to pick at his right thigh with his hand; the other hand was still.

The right hand was held stiffly to the wrist and just his index finger poked and picked at his tights and leg. He looked around towards me and then at me, and then back to the door. He looked back at me and gave the ghost of a smile, and then chuckled once. I smiled back. He looked at the door. Then he returned his gaze to me, making small low conversation noises at me, slumping to the right of his chair, running his right hand and fingers stiffly up the sides and wings of his chair.

Observation at 32 weeks

When Jeffrey was eight months old I visited when there were several friends of Peter's present. It was early evening, and Jeffrey was tired.

Mother sat Jeffrey on the sofa, near a pile of washing waiting to be ironed. Jeffrey leant forward. He seemed to be watching the children playing energetically in the room. He bounced forwards and backwards smiling and bouncing to himself, very excited and involved in the bustle around him. The three children settled to play Snap. Jeffrey gradually seemed to quieten into a reverie. His left hand started to run over the seats. The velour covers were off, presumably for washing, and he ran his hand over the seams till he found the zip. Then he turned to look, and picked and pulled at the seams until returning into his daydream. Later he jumped when the children shouted, 'Snap' and watched excitedly and then fell quiet and unfocussed again. Other noises roused him less. He absently reached into the pile of washing and pulled out a shirt at random and brought it to his mouth and chewed on the collar. Mother brought in coffee and removed the shirt. He stared at my cup until I felt quite mean drinking it. Mother gave him a toy telephone. He tried to chew the mouthpiece. Then he picked up the string and chewed that and threaded it between his fingers. After a while he slowly sank sideways and collected and absently chewed on several other pieces of washing. He became quite still. Then his face reddened and from the smell I realised that he had filled his nappy. Then he continued to chew the washing. Mother brought in his evening bottle. He snuggled contently on her knee opening his mouth eagerly and sucking with his eyes open. He relaxed, still, looking at the bottle and seeming self-absorbed and dreamy. He held the bottle with both hands and patted it with the flat of one hand. He seemed very content.

Jeffrey was always able to find ways to negotiate compromises with his mother in the daily minor disagreements of ordinary infancy.

Observation at 20 weeks

Jeffrey reached out his hand for the spoon. Mother let him take it and he reached his mouth with it quite cleanly. She rather resignedly let him feed himself and fetched a second spoon. She fed him briskly as he slowly tried to feed himself. After a few mouthfuls he held up his hand, palm outward as if saying 'Stop' and then took a drink. On the next mouthful, he poked his finger into his mouth to suck. Mother said, 'Yes, you use that old finger.' He did not use it again. He opened his mouth readily for every mouthful. Mother fetched a fruit yoghurt; again Jeffrey was not sure. Mother took him on to her knees and tried to spoonfeed him. He refused this and insisted on spooning it for himself. They compromised. Jeffrey fed himself. Mother held his hand so that while he fed himself, he was guided, brisk and clean. Mother was quite rigid and tense but there was something almost comical in her stiffness when trying to bear him feeding himself. I found I was smiling. She turned to me and saw my smile and said amid laughter and in relief, 'I just can't stand mess, I just can't bear it.' Yet she was trying to let him. During the yoghurt, Jeffrey asked for his mouth to be wiped twice and his nose.

Once Jeffrey felt less dependent on the need for help or the cooperation of someone else he could choose and demand intimacy and affection in his relationships with many people.

Observation at 52 weeks

Jeffrey quietened as soon as the mother's help picked him up and then he snuggled into her shoulder, with his hands tucked in front of him, not holding her at all but settling and snuggling against her.

Conclusion

Jeffrey has always been surrounded by an accepting and loving environment. His own assertive constitution has enabled him to struggle for himself, secure in the knowledge that his family will aid him with any difficulty or at his request. This approving, watchful, non-intrusive family allowed Jeffrey time to choose whether to daydream quietly or to play and explore; that is, he had space for both physical and mental exploration. He has determination and concentration and can work until he achieves his end.

Jeffrey's family all eagerly encourage his 'big boy' side and do not seek opportunities to indulge his more infantile feelings or behaviour. They praise his physical development and there has always been a sense of hurry in wanting him to grow up. Every new skill has been met with the introduction of the next stage. For example, in the week after he crawled his mother borrowed a baby walker frame. The week following his beginning to walk, she introduced a potty among his toys. Jeffrey, for his part, always seemed eager to identify with the grown ups, wanting to be grown and independent of his baby needs and of his dependency upon his often absent mother. Jeffrey had perhaps taken into himself and modelled himself upon a picture of a mother who maintained a slight emotional distance, bound up with her own strain and anxiety over his breastfeeding and his early tendency to want to keep her with him, available, all the time. In addition mother was uncomfortable with 'all that mess' which did seem to me to involve 'messy' emotions as well as the concrete messiness of any small baby.

Jeffrey's early wishes to have his mother all to himself, all the time were not met; but his family's qualities, and in particular, his mother's warmth and tolerance, regularity and reliability, and most of all her ability to keep him in mind while expecting him to be separate, and encouraging him to grow up, allowed Jeffrey to grow into and belong firmly and safely in his family.

Notes

Chapter 2

1. The observational setting which is being described in this book is not that of a 'set situation' in Winnicott's sense although it provides the opportunity to see what babies make of the common experiences of infancy – feeding, bathing, being left alone, weaning etc.

2. Esther Bick's importance in the development of psychoanalytic infant observation lies as much in teaching and supervision as in the few brief papers which she published. Magagna (1987) describes an infant observation which she supervised.

3. John Bowlby was at the time the Chairman of the Department of Children and Parents at the Tavistock Clinic. Although his views were later to diverge sharply from those being described here, his role in supporting child psychotherapy in its early stages and in creating, through his own work, a public and professional climate of interest in mothers and infants, was of enormous importance.

4. While those teaching on this course share a common psychoanalytic perspective it is not our intention to imply that all those involved would necessarily agree with all aspects of the model outlined in this book. (There are significant differences between the theoretical positions of Klein, Winnicott, Bick and Bion, to which somewhat different attitudes are taken.)

5. Psychoanalytic ideas are particularly relevant in relation to thinking about the sorts of *processes* which underlie development. Schaffer (1986) cites this as an important gap in developmental psychology. We hope that an interest in underlying processes will provide a fruitful meeting point for these two very different traditions of inquiry.

6. We have paid particular attention to the model which Stern (1985) derives from a comparison of research findings and a psychoanalytic account of infancy. However, the psychoanalytic ideas which underlie our book are in important respects different from the Freudian tradition which developed in the United States and which inform Stern's work.

7. Just as Klein's work developed some aspects of Freud's work rather than others, so psychoanalysts since Klein – e.g. Winnicott, Bick, Bion, Rosenfeld, Meltzer – have taken different aspects of her work and developed it. Spillius (1988) gives a collection of key papers in this development. Meltzer (1978) gives a more personal account of the theoretical changes.

8. These developments arise out of issues raised by Freud in 'Two Principles of Mental Functioning' (1911).

9. This point is easily overlooked since, in working out the implications of her theories, the greater part of Klein's work was devoted to the study of the internal world. Isaacs (1952) gives an account of the infant's mental processes in relation to internal and external reality. Isaacs writes (p. 107): 'The external world forces itself upon the attention of the child, in one way or another, early and continuously. The first psychical experiences result from the massive and varied stimuli of birth and the first intake and expulsion of breath – followed presently by the first feed. These considerable experiences during the first twenty-four hours must already evoke the first mental activity, and provide material for both phantasy and memory. Phantasy and reality testing are both in fact present from the earliest days.' This line of thought was taken further in the work of Winnicott (1945, 1951) and Bion (1962).

10. The theoretical implications drawn from these research findings vary. In some models the physical rhythms and impulses of the baby are seen as being accommodated to by the mother in such a way as to form a 'dialogue' (Kaye 1977) or the infant's behaviour is seen as being fitted into a structure of meaning by the mother. In Stern's model (1985) the emphasis is largely on the infant's perceptual capacities as the original basis for the development of a sense of self. Trevarthen (1979) formulates a concept of 'primary intersubjectivity' and argues 'that human beings are equipped at birth with a mechanism of personality which is sensitive to persons and expresses itself as a person does'. The model to be described here has points of contact with all these positions.

In recent years, there has been an increasing interest in the hypothesis that for infants to be born ready to receive experience, there must already be a rudimentary capacity in operation before birth (Liley 1972; Bower 1977). Piontelli (1987) gives an account of psychoanalytic infant observations which began before birth using ultra-sound scanning.

11. Although as this interest becomes re-cast in terms of the development of communication, rather than in terms of behavioural interaction, the approach can take on an increasingly internal focus (Hopkins 1983).

12. There seems to be a correspondence between Bion's ideas of a 'preconception' and Trevarthen's concept of innate 'motives' (neurological structures) which he sees as underlying the capacity to know the physical world (subjectivity) and to communicate with persons (primary intersubjectivity) (Trevarthen 1980).

13. Mills (1981) refers to the brief periods of time in which the infant is in a state of 'alert inactivity' and the problem posed for research if this state changes during observation periods and these changes are ignored or not reported. Although Stern (1985) acknowledges that experimental research cannot, as yet, address issues concerning the infant in states other than 'alert inactivity', the implications of this for his model of infantile experience remain unclear. Are the infant's capacities thought to remain unchanged regardless of degree of alertness, distress or sleepiness? Is one seeing the *whole* infant through the 'window' afforded by 'alert inactivity'; or do different states give the infant very different experiences of himself and his world which he must then integrate or deal with in some way?

14. Stern (p. 46) maintains that the infant cannot experience states of non-organisation, only the 'many separate experiences (which) exist, with what for the infant may be exquisite clarity and vividness'. Infants cannot know about 'non-organisation' or that they do not know about it. This seems to confuse the cognitive capacity to make something of an experience with the possibility that one might none the less feel its impact. An infant who *was* alert but who, through tiredness or too much stimulation, feels himself to be slipping into a fretful state, may in some sense feel a loss of integration and clarity of perception. An indication as to whether such an occurrence might be

distressing for the infant may be found in the extent to which parents find coping with these states stressful.

15. Winnicott (1945) posits a state of primary unintegration but was of the view that processes of integration started at birth.

16. In Stern's model the processes which carry the infant through the first few months of development are located mainly within the infant's innate and maturing perceptual capacities. In our view this neglects important aspects of the infant's experience as well as underestimating the role of the parents.

17. We will generally refer to mothers and infants (male). However the functions being ascribed to mothers can and are performed by fathers and by other caregivers who are in a close, sustained relationship to the infant.

18. The mother's sense of identity is likely in any case to be more fragile at this time because of the overall emotional social and financial changes which she must accommodate to on the birth of a baby.

19. ' ... the impact of the environment is of major importance *at every stage* of the child's development. Even the good effect of the earliest upbringing can be to some extent undone through later harmful experiences, just as difficulties arising in early life may be diminished through subsequent beneficial influences' (Klein 1952b, p. 96). This is in accord with the resilience of infants and children to which Rutter (1981) and others have called attention as an essential element which must be included in any attempt to understand the effects of early experience.

20. We would argue that this model of the mother-infant relationship offers the possibility of facing 'the challenge of specifying as to what really goes on between parent and child that has such an impact on the child's development' (Schaffer 1986).

21. Stern (1985) has described the mental structures which the baby has for processing *some* kinds of experiences. We are concerned with the whole *range* of states and the demands which they make on the baby's mind.

22. The pain which the mother inflicts on the baby is usually emotional but in some circumstances is physical.

23. The mother needs to be able to have a particular sort of receptive, tolerant relationship to her own states of mind (at least enough of the time) if she is to be able to have this sort of 'containing' relationship to her baby (enough of the time). In Bion's terms an adult identity needs to have the configuration of a container for the infantile and childlike experiences which continue to be stirred up within the adult by their encounters with life in general and by contact with actual infants and children.

24. Hopkins (1983) stresses the role of mother as the interpreter of the infant's behaviour. The capacity for intuition being 'in part dependent on universal, cultural, individual experiences that the mother is exposed to in her own childhood and at later ages'.

25. This seems to connect with Rutter's view of the factors which enable a child to cope with separation – 'it has long been observed that children may be hostile and difficult, as well as clinging, after returning home from hospital, and it appears that the parental response to this behaviour may be crucial' (Rutter 1981, p. 134).

26. This interest and pleasure in understanding the world is seen as a fundamental aspect of the infant's experience. For obvious clinical reasons, psychoanalysis has been more concerned with disturbances in the relationship to reality. However, the relationship to reality and the capacity for thought

and play have a central place in the work of Bion and Winnicott. Alvarez (1988) addresses some of the clinical implications which arise in relation to the child's need for a pleasurable contact with reality.

27. This function is crucially a mental/emotional capacity and is therefore different from the function of a parent as a 'state regulating other' in Stern's model. Here the parents' function in regulating the infant's physiological state seems limited to an external, behavioural role and is in any case more peripheral in his view of the first months of the infant's development (Stern 1985). Similarly, while the model being outlined here is 'interactional', the interaction is conceived of in mental/emotional, rather than primarily behavioural terms. This sort of complex transaction seems to be what Stratton is referring to as the 'total infant environment system' (Stratton 1982, p. 11).

28. The infant of Stern's account is able to use his perceptual apparatus in a way which enables him to feel gathered together. He is surrounded by shapes and patterns which convey emotional meaning. The mother's physical and emotional presence are perceived by the infant, but his *capacity* to digest what is going on around him is not seen as being dependent on the quality of his mother's emotional contact. The mother's impact only becomes a factor after seven months when a more self-conscious relationship begins to develop. However, Stern's account gives important indications as to how some infants may acquire sufficient resources to survive despite difficult early experiences.

29. Stern sees 'vitality affects' – the dynamic contours of emotional life rather than the different 'categorial affects' – as pervading the infant's experience of the world. 'Vitality affects' are perceived by the infant through the intensity, shape and temporal pattern created by human movement, speech etc. This seems of great importance in describing the *form* in which emotionality might exist for the infant. Stern looks at a developing sense of 'self' and 'other' from birth but his model does not seem to account adequately for the development within the infant of a sense of a whole person and a self-conscious awareness of the possibility of communication. This development, which takes place around seven months, he describes as a 'quantum leap'. We hope that the model described here offers some basis for thinking about the earlier stages in this development – when the infant is 'acting in such a way' rather than 'acting in order to' (Mackay 1972; Hopkins 1983).

30. Osofsky and Danzger (1974) demonstrate a relationship between the mother's state of mind and that of her infant. Murray (1988) & Pound (1982) both argue that infants and young children are very responsive to states of feeling in their mothers. Depression, anxiety and hostility reduce the mother's capacity to respond to her infant's needs; but these states of mind are also communicated directly to the child who is then left to cope with them.

31. Stern maintains that the infant's experience of his parents intervening to regulate his state, and his sense of their impact on him, in no way breaches the infant's sense of the integrity and separateness of 'self' and 'other' (p. 105) about which the infant seems so clear in a state of 'alert inactivity'. This seems to be one point at which Stern departs, for theoretical reasons, from his attempt to give an 'experience near' account of the infant. It seems much more likely that, from the infant's point of view, a moment when the mother 'removes' his distress, when her smile fills him with delight, or her preoccupation alarms him, is felt as a dramatic and concrete interchange between them.

32. We are aware that in this chapter we are unable to give a full account of the relationship between Bowlby's work and that of Klein, Winnicott, Bick and Bion.

Bowlby (1969, 1973) stressed the infant's strong instinctual need for his mother's presence and its function in the survival of the species. He stressed not only the dangers of prolonged separation but also the importance of the quality of care which the infant receives. His role in calling attention to the needs of the young child and in generating work which changed the climate of thought about child-care has been of enormous importance.

His interest was not only in attachment behaviour but in the development within the child of 'working models' of his relationship to mother, which allowed an internal sense of attachment and trust to develop. However, his model was one in which emotions were primarily seen in terms of the interplay between biological needs and the pressures of the external situation. Thus, in Bowlby's view, anxiety in children arose from situations of external threat to their security, e.g. separation from the mother, and was fundamentally a biological mechanism promoting behaviour which could be seen as life-preserving in terms of the history of the species.

Klein's focus, and the focus of those who have subsequently developed her ideas, was instead on the internal experience of emotion and the mental elaboration of our biological inheritance. We would see Bowlby's disagreement with Klein over the role of separation experiences in the generation of anxiety as, at least partly, to do with a false dichotomising of their positions so that *either* the external situation was important and the child's anxieties stemmed from that *or* the internal situation within the child was primary and anxiety was really entirely generated internally. It seems to us that, while the quality of the child's external experiences is important, as both Klein (1952b) and Bick (1968) felt it to be, there is also a need to examine what the child makes of external experiences within himself. The concept of an 'internal world' which will be described later allows one to think about how it is that some children *do* survive difficult early experiences while others who have had a benign early upbringing may become disturbed later in childhood or in adult life.

Another area of disagreement concerns Bowlby's view that Klein reduced the infant's early experience to sucking at the breast, ignoring other aspects of his relationship to his mother and discounting the importance of the second and third year of life. Klein's concentration on the breast as the infant's first object was partly a way of gathering a whole range of experiences into one formulation (for which the breast stood as an 'ideal type') in order to draw attention to certain patterns of infantile experience. It was this level of experience at the beginning of life and its continuing manifestations in later development which most interested her. Bowlby has very little to say about the first months of life (e.g. the experience of separation for an infant under seven months (Bowlby 1973, p. 54)), and was chiefly concerned with the particular characteristics of later infancy and early childhood.

A crucial strength of the ethological approach has been its use of detailed naturalistic observations. This has thrown up phenomena such as the tendency of the young child to reject attachment figures on reunion, which have challenged and developed the existing theoretical framework (Main & Western 1982).

33. Schaffer (1986) argues for the importance of this area of experience in understanding child development: 'Thus, the focus needs to swing away from an exclusive concern with overt action to a consideration also of internal

representation.' There are interesting points of contact between the idea of an 'internal object' and the idea of a 'working model of self and others', developed by attachment theorists. However, the concept of an internal object is less cognitive and the focus of interest is primarily on the states of mind generated in relation to particular internal objects rather than external behaviour.

34. The idea is of the infant in a continuous state of identification with different internal objects rather than specific memories being recalled by external cues. In Stern's model, memory adds an extra dimension to external experience; in this model, internal objects are part of the imaginative life of the mind as well as affecting external activity.

35. It is also hypothesised that the internalisations of early experience undergo development over time. Subsequent external relationships are undertaken on the basis of these, now internalised, emotional resources. The model is one in which experience is cumulative rather than simply additive in its effect (Schaffer 1977).

36. The global qualities which are apprehended through amodal perception (such as shape and intensity) and Stern's concept of vitality affects give an external means by which such emotional communication might take place. Meltzer (1983) refers to the communication of states of mind (in projective identification) as the 'song and dance level of communication'. The presence of these modes of communication has been studied clinically through the model of transference/counter transference and through its representation in dreams.

37. Projective identification – a phantasy of concrete exchanges of emotional states – can operate between mother and infant in such a way that both project and receive from each other. It offers an alternative to a linguistic model of early communication. Bullowa (1979) refers to the limitations for an understanding of early interaction of too great a dependence on a linguistic model. The infant's dependence on his mother as the experienced receiver of his concrete communications allows one to think about separation in terms of the temporary loss for the infant of this means of communication (Bower 1977, p. 56).

It has been pointed out (e.g. Schaffer 1986) that a high level of maternal attention is concentrated on the infant in an experimental situation and doubts have been raised as to how far such dialogues can be seen as the pattern of most ordinary mother-infant interaction or as a model of how the infant 'learns'. The operation of projective identification is seen as something which takes place in the midst of all sorts of external activities. The mother may, or may not, be receptive to her baby's projections but this is a largely unconscious activity and does not involve specific 'play behaviour'. Rather, as Stern describes in relation to vitality affects, her response is manifested in *the way* in which she behaves in the course of ordinary routine care. This is not a pseudo-dialogue but a real contact, providing the basis for a more self-aware communication later in the first year.

Stern writes of the development, in the second half of the first year, of a form of communication based on the sharing of different patterns of vitality affect ('attunement'). However, he explicitly limits the scope of this form of communication to the sharing of pleasurable or unthreatening states of feeling (p. 160). We would also want to stress the infant's capacity to apprehend pleasurable experiences, in particular his mother's pleasure in him (Likierman 1988) and his mother's capacity to receive her infant's expressions of delight, as being of great importance in the development of a sense of being loved and understood. However, it seems to us that any model of the development of communication must also address those areas of feeling which are, in various ways, distressing or unmanageable for the infant.

38. Prior to Bion's formulation of a container and the use of the concept of projective identification as a form of communication, projective identification had been formulated by Klein as a process whereby the infant projected aspects of his experience precisely in order to be rid of them. It is still used in this earlier sense. In Klein's view this mechanism of splitting off parts of the self was universal and accounts for the fact that our relations with other people are always to some degree 'disturbed' by our emotional projections. She thought that when used to an excessive degree it was a fundamental mechanism in severe mental illness (Klein 1946). Spillius (1988) gives a collection of papers charting the subsequent development of these ideas.

39. Rutter (1981) refers to the kind of disturbance which characterises children deprived of opportunities to form relationships in early life and distinguishes this phenomenon from those associated with separation. Such children show a tendency to disinhibited, indiscriminate social relations coupled with a lack of emotional depth. However, Rutter dates the crucial period for the formation of such a bond as beginning after six months. This is a position with which we will disagree later in the chapter.

40. There are interesting parallels between Bick's ideas and those of Main and Weston (1982). They have observed the ways in which very young children use inanimate objects as a means of maintaining a sense of organisation during separation and during the impact of reunion.

41. Bick's ideas about the problems for development resulting from certain kinds of adaptation to the environment links to Stratton's view of maternal deprivation, ' … the consequences of any trauma may not be identifiable as directly inflicted damage, but as the result of the attempts of the organism to adapt to the demands of the situation … in the short term, the adaptation is likely to be the response best calculated to preserve the integrity of the individual. It is only with a longer-term perspective and often only with hindsight, that some adaptations can be seen to be maladaptive' (Stratton 1982, pp. 10-11).

42. In situations of deprivation and privation these mechanisms may be thought of as survival measures since the complete absence of experiences of containment is not compatible with mental development and possibly not compatible with life itself (Spitz 1945).

43. We would not wish to argue that this is the only mechanism. It has to be seen in the context of the social and economic factors. Although the infants and their families described in this book come from a wide range of socio-economic backgrounds, the fact that the families were willing and able to sustain the observations implies a degree of stability. It would require a different kind of observational research from that based on the training of students to examine the relevance of these ideas for infants and families in circumstances of extreme social and economic hardship. The methods, however, seem adaptable for this purpose.

44. This might be characterised as the capacity to hold sensations in the mind for a sufficient length of time for this 'raw data' to be digested into emotional experiences which can be thought about. This transformation is seen as taking place largely unconsciously through the related processes of dreaming and phantasy in waking life. This would be in contrast to the always present impulses to abort this process, e.g. through premature action to dissipate the impact of potential experiences or the discharging of feelings into others. This way of looking at mental life, which brings together its various manifestations from dreams and psychosomatic phenomena to the capacity for rational abstract thinking, is the model developed by Bion (1962a, 1962b, 1963, 1965, 1970).

45. It has been argued that because of its origins in clinical work her ideas are not relevant to an understanding of ordinary development (Bentovim 1979). We would not share this restricted view, and Klein certainly intended her model to be seen as applicable to ordinary mental functioning (Klein 1959).

46. A principal argument against Klein's accounts of primitive mental mechanisms operating, and of an internal world forming, from birth onwards has been an objection to the apparent certainty and the precision of language with which she attempted to describe these processes which cannot, by definition, be observed directly. Bion (1962b) has argued that emptier concepts than Klein's are needed in order to map out areas of interest which can be gradually and partially filled as our understanding grows. He was particularly alert to the problems which arise from the fact that, in so far as psychoanalysis uses ordinary language, conceptual models are in danger of getting filled up prematurely with all sorts of meanings, preconceptions and associations.

47. Bower (1977) Meltzoff (1981) Mounoud & Vinter (1981) and Stern (1985) posit the existence of internal representations of experience as existing from the beginning of life. Their concern is centrally with the role of internal representations in cognitive and motor development and in the development of a capacity for social interaction.

48. While processes in the internal world cannot be directly inferred solely from the external situation, it does not follow that we have no means of access to them. In ordinary life we are able to be affected by the ebb and flow of states of feeling in others, even if we are unable to give a conscious account of the source and consequences of such 'communication'. In psychoanalysis, a systematic use has been made of this capacity of the human mind to generate and receive such emotional communications.

49. The concept of an internal world provides a way of thinking about the processes which mediate between influences and outcome in development, which so complicates research in this area, as well as a way of understanding the underlying continuities in personality. It also provides the basis for therapeutic intervention in the present since the current state and vicissitudes in the internal world, the structure of which has developed over a life time, continues to be available for observation (see note 48).

50. This is envisaged as a process similar to that involved in generating images/internal objects to act as mental containers for experience, as occurs in dreaming. Meltzer (1988) refers to this as the metaphor-generating function of the mind to distinguish it from the capacity to aggregate and generalise on the basis of external experience alone which Stern seems to be referring to in his idea of RIGs (representations of interactions which have been generalised) as the basis of memory.

51. These names were chosen because of the different quality of anxiety which she felt was primarily experienced in these two different states. In so far as they carry obvious connotations of pathological states they have not been helpful in conveying her intended meaning.

52. Central to Stern's model of early infantile experience is recent research which indicates the infant's capacity for 'cross-modal perception' – i.e. the ability to match up information of apparently quite divergent sorts which comes through the different senses. But the amodal world of shapes, intensities and temporal patterns is no more a world of whole people than Klein's idea of part-objects. The infant of Stern's account seems to live in a landscape that stands in relation to our familiar, adult perceptual world as does heat photography to conventional photography. It is both more integrated than one would ever have suspected and yet even less like the world of whole physical objects as we know them. This allows a different kind of account to be given of the nature of part-objects; but these are still, in Klein's terms, part-objects rather than whole objects. An account is still needed of the development of the capacity for perceiving whole objects. For Klein it is primarily an emotional development which propels this cognitive development. This has interesting links with Stern's model, since the amodal landscape of shape, intensity and temporal pattern is also an emotional landscape of vitality affects which, long before language, gives the infant a means of communicating his emotional states and grasping those within others.

53. These qualities of experience are, by and large, only expressed by Klein in very cryptic and abstract terms. Stern writes far more vividly about the texture of these kinds of infantile experiences. In Infant Observation, the attempt is made to describe the infants' experiences as fully as possible, rather than reducing them to theoretical entities.

54. These good and bad objects might be envisaged in physical, emotional and cognitive terms. Stern objects to Klein's concept of splitting on the grounds that external experience clearly does not fall neatly into these two categories. The infant has any number of experiences of being fed – all of them characterised by different degrees of pleasure and unpleasure on the part of the infant. It was Klein's view that the infant could not deal with this range and complexity at a stage of development (up to three months) corresponding to Stern's stage of the emergent self. At this stage, Stern's infant is beginning to organise his sense of self on the basis of 'brief islands' of clarity and vividness of perception, achieved in states of 'alert inactivity'. This seems to imply a similar view to that of Klein to the extent that it is only at an extreme of bodily state that the infant can begin to organise his experience. However, Stern does not address the question of other states. Klein's view was that in seeking to sustain a sense of self the infant mobilised himself to shut out experiences of distress and in the process these bad experiences began to acquire more organised characteristics. That infants do in fact avert their gaze from experiences they do not wish to encounter is borne out by research involving experiences of perturbation (Carpenter 1975). Trevarthen (1977) argues for a connection between the child who turns away from his mother at five months, and presumably a mother who can tolerate this, and the development of a co-operative relationship at twelve months.

55. Such processes have become a focus of study by ethologists. Main & Weston (1982) examine blankness and gaze aversion in relation to the older infant (one to two years). They also describe the *apparent* adaptation to a new environment of a separated child as occurring on the basis of an internal shift of attention away from the mother.

56. Klein's ideas about the experience and the origins of anxiety in the infant were the most contentious parts of her theory. She argued that anxiety was generated both from external experiences and internally, and generally arose

from a mixture of both sources (Klein 1948).

We have concentrated here on those experiences of anxiety which derive from real external situations and on anxiety which arises from the effect of the operation of introjection and projection on those experiences. These processes inevitably colour the infant's perception of external reality, creating distress in what might seem benign situations and exacerbating the experience of real difficulties.

However, following Freud's hypothetical formulations of 'life' and 'death' instincts, Klein also argued that, just as there was an inherent capacity in the infant to seek out and make use of experiences which promote an integration of the self and contact with other people, so there was also an inherently aggressive and disintegrative aspect to the psyche. The existence and operation of this aspect of the mind was a source of anxiety in itself; just as the existence and operation of integrative object-relating drives diminished anxiety and led to feelings of wholeness and vitality. She felt that the power of bad external experiences to generate anxiety lay partly in the way they matched with, and gave a focus to, this innate disposition. While this area of Klein's thought has not, on the whole, been much used in thinking about infant observation, it has been important in the treatment of psychotic, borderline, and narcissistic patients (Rosenfeld 1987).

57. In Stern's model, the development of a sense of other is secondary to the development of a sense of self. Thus the infant becomes aware of his own subjective experiences and then aware that they can be shared with another who also has such experiences. This development seems largely driven by cognitive processes within the infant. In Klein's model, this development is primarily emotionally driven and takes place in relation to the infant's experience of his mother, although accompanied by corresponding integrations in his experience of himself.

58. Trevarthen (1980) describes the change in the infant's perception of mother at around nine months in the following terms: 'By some intrinsic integrative adjustment in the cerebral structures that govern motives, the infant comes to perceive the mother in a new way. She is no longer merely a source of pleasure and companionship in games in which the infant's own motives remain central. She has become an interesting agent, whose own motives become something of an object or topic in themselves.' He calls this new basis for the mother-infant relationship 'secondary intersubjectivity'.

59. Klein's theory describes the way in which this first kind of (ideal) good object gradually gives way to a second more realistic, complete and resilient kind of good object within the baby's mind. Her account is largely in terms of the baby's contribution to this development. Klein thought that the infant's capacity to bear a certain amount of uncertainty and anxiety was to some extent innate, although external circumstances determined what the infant was having to cope with. In Bion's terms, what enables the baby to contain some of his painful feelings within himself is the extent to which he comes to feel he has within him a containing object and, therefore, the extent to which such a containing relationship has really been available to him.

60. Included in this would be not only physical separation but a range of environmental 'failures' which result in the infant having to do without mother's presence.

61. This would be in contrast to Rutter's view (Rutter 1989).

62. Thus it might be argued that the infant a few weeks old who is screaming for a feed feels possessed by a *present* bad experience (hunger) rather than feeling deprived of an absent good experience (the feed) (O'Shaughnessy 1964).

63. Infant Observation as part of training is not suited to the study of more serious and overwhelming separations. The aim is to study ordinary development. However, the method has been adapted to the study of infants and those caring for them in various hospital settings (Colloquium: Szur *et al.* 1981).

Chapter 3

1. For relevant reviews of child development literature see Boston (1975); Bower (1977); Murray (1988); Schaffer (1977); Schaffer & Dunn (1979); Stern (1985).

2. See Bowlby (1969, 1973, 1980); Bretherton & Waters (1985); Cranach (1979); Murray Parkes & Stevenson-Hinde (1982); Hinde & Stevenson-Hinde (1988).

3. Evidence of pre-birth attachment to the mother at the foetal stage is discussed by Piontelli (1987).

4. See for example Menzies Lyth (1988); Bain & Barnett (1980).

5. See references in n. 1 above for empirical approaches to child development. Dunn (1977) is an accessible example of work in this genre whose interests in emotional development are close to those of this book.

6. On ethnographic methods in anthropology see Geertz (1973, 1983), and in sociology, see Burgess (1982, 1984), Denzin (1970, 1978); Schwarz & Jacobs (1979).

7. There are several related traditions of sociological theory, derived from Max Weber, American symbolic interactionism, and phenomenology, which give primacy to the understanding of 'subjective meaning'. For overviews of these, see Dandeker, Johnson & Ashworth (1984, ch. 3); Schwarz & Jacobs (1979, part 1). On related approaches in social psychology, see Harré & Secord (1972).

8. The sociology of education is an example of a field in which case-study and ethngraphic methods were employed with good effect to investigate the meanings of social differences in the outcomes of schooling which in quantitative terms were already well established. For a review of this field see Bernstein (1977); for influential examples of qualitative studies, see Hargreaves (1967) and Willis (1977).

9. Rutter (1981) is a well-known example of the use of evidence of longitudinal and other quantitative research methods to test developmental hyotheses grounded in attachment theory, and to a lesser extent psychoanalytical ideas.

10. On the need for openness to the unexpected in fieldwork in anthropology, see Geertz (1983).

11. Donald Meltzer's recent thinking about the timing of the paranoid-schizoid and depressive positions has been influenced by baby-observation. See Meltzer & Harris Williams (1988).

12. George Brown and Tirril Harris (1978) provide much evidence of the vulnerability of isolated mothers left to care for babies with inadequate emotional support.

13. See for example references in n. 2 above; and Tustin (1972, 1981, 1986).

14. Problems of participant observation are outlined in Burgess (1984, ch. 4)

which also contains a guide to further reading on the issue.

15. At this stage of infancy, before independent life is possible either physically or mentally, the functional entity is best seen not as the baby as such, but as the baby-mother couple. On this idea see Winnicott (1965, part 1).

16. See references in n. 1 above.

17. The relationship of knowledge to emotional experience is discussed in Bion (1962).

18. On the transference, see Freud (1912a, 1915) and Hinshelwood (1989); and Laplanche & Pontalis (1973) for further references.

19. On the counter-transference, see Freud (1912b); Heimann (1950); and Hinshelwood (1989) and Laplanche & Pontalis (1973) for further references.

20. See Barnett (1985); and Robertson & Robertson (1953, 1976).

21. The distinction between a process of discovery dependent in the last resort on intuition and imagination, and more rational and routinised procedures of validation (e.g. testing hypotheses by methods of empirical falsification) derives in modern philosophy of science literature in large part from K.R. Popper's work. See for example Popper (1972). Some, e.g. Polanyi (1958), have argued that intuition and subjective judgment play a larger role in all aspects of scientific method.

22. Murray (1988) argues for the importance of this development.

23. On the methods of such work, see M.E. Rustin (1989, forthcoming).

24. For examples, see Boston & Szur (1983); Meltzer *et al.* (1975); Boston (1989, forthcoming).

25. On broader issues of scientific method in relation to psychoanalysis, see M.J. Rustin (1987).

26. On the idea of selection from a value-laden point of view, see Taylor (1985).

27. One influential paper however was Bick (1987).

28. See the essays collected in Menzies Lyth (1988).

29. On the relevance of infant observation to training for work with child abuse, see Trowell (forthcoming, 1989).

Bibliography

Abraham, K (1924) 'A Short Study of the Development of the Libido', in *Selected Papers on Psycho-Analysis*, London: Hogarth (1949) (Maresfield Reprints 1979)

Alvarez, A (1988) 'Beyond the Unpleasure Principle: Some Preconditions for Thinking Through Play', *Journal of Child Psychotherapy*, Vol. 14, No. 2

Bain, A & Barnett, L (1980) *The Design of a Day Care System in a Nursery Setting for Children under Five: Final Report*, Tavistock Institute of Human Relations, Doc. No. 2347

Barnett, L (1985) (film) *Sunday's Child: The Growth of Individuality 0-2 years* (120 mins, short version 60 mins), University of Exeter

Bentovim, A (1979) 'Child Development Research Findings and Psychoanalytic Theory: An Integrative Critique', in Schaffer, D & Dunn, J (eds) *The First Year of Life*, Chichester: Wiley

Bernstein, B (1977) 'The Sociology of Education: a Brief Account', in *Class, Codes and Control*, Vol. 3, London: Routledge & Kegan Paul

Bick, E (1964) 'Notes on Infant Observation in Psychoanalytic Training', *International Journal of Psycho-analysis*, Vol. 45.

Bick, E. (1968) 'The Experience of the Skin in Early Object Relations', *International Journal of Psychoanalysis*, Vol. 49

Bick, E (1987) 'The Experience of the Skin in Early Object Relations' (first publ. 1968), in Harris, M & Bick, E, *Collected Papers of Martha Harris and Esther Bick* (ed. Harris Williams, M), Perthshire: Clunie

Bion, W R (1962) *Learning from Experience*, London: Heinemann (Maresfield reprints 1988)

Bion, W R (1962a) 'A Theory of Thinking', *International Journal of Psychoanalysis*, Vol. 43

Bion, W R (1962b) *Learning from Experience*, London: Heinemann

Bion, W R (1963) 'Elements of Psycho-Analysis, London: Heinemann; also in Bion, W R *Seven Servants*, New York: Aronson

Bion, W R (1965) *Transformations*, London: Heinemann, also in *Seven Servants*, New York: Aronson

Bion, W R (1970) *Attention and Interpretation*, London: Tavistock; also in *Seven Servants*, New York: Aronson

Boston, M (1975) 'Recent Research in Developmental Psychology', *Journal of Child Psychotherapy*, Vol. 4, No. 1

Boston, M (1989, forthcoming) 'In Search of a Methodology of Evaluating Psychoanalytic Therapy with Children', *Journal of Child Psychotherapy*

Boston, M & Szur, R (1983) *Psychotherapy with Severely Deprived Children*, London: Routledge & Kegan Paul

Bower, T G R (1977) *A Primer of Infant Development*, San Francisco: Freeman

Bowlby, J (1969, 1973, 1980) *Attachment, Separation and Loss* (3 vols), Harmondsworth: Penguin Books.

Brazelton, T B, Tronick, E, Anderson, L H & Weise, S (1975) 'Early Mother-in-Law Reciprocity', in *Parent-Infant Interaction*, Ciba Foundation Symposium 33, Amsterdam: Elsevier

Bretherton, I & Waters, E (eds) (1985) *Growing Points of Attachment Theory and Research*, Monographs of the Society for Research in Child Development, Vol. 50, Nos. 1-2, Chicago: University of Chicago Press.

Brown, G W & Harris, T (1978) *Social Origins of Depression: a Study of Psychiatric Disorder in Women*, London: Tavistock

Bullowa, M (1979) *Before Speech*, Cambridge: CUP

Burgess, R G (ed) (1982) *Field Research: a Source Book and Field Manual*, London: Allen & Unwin

Burgess, R G (1984), *In the Field: an Introduction to Field Research*, London: Allen & Unwin

Carpenter, G (1975) 'Mother's Face and the Newborn', in R Lewin (ed) *Child Alive*, London: Temple Smith

Cranach, M von, *et al* (1979) *Human Ethology: Claims and Limits of a New Discipline*, Cambridge: CUP

Dandeker, C, Johnson, T, Ashworth, C (1984) *The Structure of Social Theory: Dilemmas and Strategies* (ch. 3 on subjectivism), London: Macmillan

Denzin, N K (1970) *The Research Act in Sociology*, Chicago: Aldine

Denzin, N K (ed) (1978) *Sociological Methods: a Sourcebook* (2nd ed.) London: McGraw Hill

Dunn, J (1977) *Distress and Comfort*, London: Fontana/Open Books

Dunn, J (1979) 'The First Year of Life: Continuities in Individual Differences', in Schaffer, D & Dunn, J, *The First Year of Life*, Chichester: Wiley

Dunn, J B & Richards, M P M (1977) 'Observations on the Developing Relationship between Mother and Baby in the Newborn', in Schaffer, H R (ed) *Studies in Mother-Infant Interaction*, London: Academic Press

Fairbairn, W R D (1952) *Psychoanalytic Studies of the Personality*, London: Tavistock/Routledge

Freud, S (1909) 'Analysis of a Phobia in a Five-year-old Boy', *Standard Edition*, Vol. 10, London: Hogarth (1955)

Freud, S (1911) 'Two Principles in Mental Functioning', *Standard Edition*, Vol. 12, London: Hogarth (1958)

Freud, S (1912a) 'The dynamics of transference', *Standard Edition*, Vol. 12, pp. 97-108

Freud, S (1912b) 'Recommendations to Physicians practising Psycho-analysis', *Standard Edition*, Vol. 12, pp. 109-20

Freud, S (1915) 'Remembering, Repeating and Working Through', *Standard Edition*, Vol. 14, pp. 121-45

Freud, S (1920) 'Beyond the Pleasure Principle', *Standard Edition*, Vol. 18, London: Hogarth (1955)

Geertz, C (1973) *The Interpretation of Cultures*, New York: Basic Books.

Geertz, C (1983) *Local Knowledge*, New York: Basic Books

Hargreaves, J (1967) *Social Relations in the Secondary School*, London: Routledge & Kegan Paul

Harré, R & Secord, P F (1972) *The Explanation of Social Behaviour*, Oxford: Blackwell

Harris, M (1978) 'Towards Learning from Experience', in Harris Williams, M (ed) *Collected Papers of Martha Harris and Esther Bick*, Perthshire: Clunie

Heimann, P (1950) 'On counter-transference', *International Journal of*

Psychoanalysis, Vol. 31, pp. 81-4

Henry, G (1974) 'Doubly-deprived', *Journal of Child Psychotherapy*, Vol. 3, No. 4

Hinde, R A (1982) 'Attachment: Some Conceptual and Biological Issues', in Murray Parkes, C & Stevenson-Hinde, J (eds) *The Place of Attachment in Human Behaviour*, London: Tavistock

Hinde, R & Stevenson-Hinde, J (1988) *Relationships within Families: Mutual Influences*, Oxford: Clarendon Press

Hinshelwood, R (1989) *A Dictionary of Kleinian Thought*, London: Free Association Books

Hopkins, B (1983) 'The Development of Early Non-verbal Communication: an Evaluation of its Meaning', *Journal of Child Psychology and Psychiatry*, Vol. 24, No. 1

Isaacs, S (1952) 'The Nature and Function of Phantasy', in Klein, M, Heinemann, P, Isaacs, S & Riviere, J (eds) *Developments in Psychoanalysis*, London: Hogarth

Kaye, K (1977) 'Towards the Origin of Dialogue', in Schaffer, H R (ed) *Studies in Mother-Infant Interaction*, London: Academic Press

Klaus, M H & Kennell, J H (1982) *Parent-Infant Bonding*, St Louis: Mosby

Klein, M (1921) 'The Development of a Child', in *Contributions to Psycho-analysis 1921-1945*, London: Hogarth (1950)

Klein, M (1928) 'Early Stages of the Oedipus Conflict', in *Contributions to Psycho-analysis 1921-45*, London: Hogarth (1950)

Klein, M (1946) 'Notes on Some Schizoid Mechanisms', in *The Writings of Melanie Klein*, Vol. 3, London: Hogarth (1975)

Klein, M (1948) 'On the Theory of Anxiety and Guilt', in *The Writings of Melanie Klein*, Vol. 3, London: Hogarth (1975)

Klein, M (1952a) 'Some Theoretical Conclusions Regarding the Emotional Life of the Infant', in Klein, M *et al*, *Developments in Psycho-analysis*, London: Hogarth

Klein, M (1952b) 'On Observing the Behaviour of Young Infants', In Klein, M *et al*, *Developments in Psycho-analysis*, London: Hogarth

Klein, M (1959) 'Our Adult World and its Roots in Infancy', in *The Writings of Melanie Klein*, Vol. 3, London: Hogarth (1975)

Laplanche, J & Pontalis, J B (1973) *The Language of Psychoanalysis*, London: Hogarth

Likierman, M (1988) 'Maternal Love and Positive Projective Identification', *Journal of Child Psychotherapy*, Vol. 14, No. 2

Liley, A W (1972) 'The Foetus as a Personality', *Australian and New Zealand Journal of Psychiatry*, Vol. 7, pp. 99-105

MacFarlane, J A (1975) 'Olfaction in the Development of Social Preference in the Human Neonate', in *Parent-Infant Interaction*, Ciba Foundation Symposium 33, Amsterdam: Elsevier

Mackay, D M (1972) 'Formal Analysis of Communicative Processes', *Non-verbal Communication* (ed. R A Hinde), Cambridge: CUP

Magagna, J (1987) 'Three Years of Infant Observation with M Bick', *Journal of Child Psychotherapy*, Vol. 13, No. 1

Main, M & Weston, D R (1982) 'Avoidance of the Attachment Figure in Infancy', in Murray Parkes, C & Stevenson-Hinde, J, *The Place of Attachment in Human Behaviour*, London: Tavistock

Meltzer, D (1978) *The Kleinian Development*, Perthshire: Clunie

Meltzer, D (1983) *Dream-Life*, Perthshire: Clunie

Meltzer, D (1988) *The Apprehension of Beauty*, Perthshire: Clunie

Meltzer, D *et al* (1975) *Explorations in Autism: a Psycho-Analytic Study*, Perthshire: Clunie

Meltzer, D & Harris Williams, M (1988) *The Apprehension of Beauty*, Perthshire: Clunie

Meltzoff, A N (1981) 'Imitation, Intermodal Co-ordination and Representation in Early Infancy', in Butterworth, G (ed) *Infancy and Epistemology: an Evaluation of Piaget's Theory*, Brighton: Harvester

Menzies Lyth, I (1988) *Containing Anxiety in Institutions: Selected Essays*, London: Free Association Books

Middleton, M P (1941) *The Nursing Couple*, London: Hamish Hamilton

Mills, M (1981) 'Individual Differences in the First Week of Life', in Christie, M J & Mallet, P, *Foundations of Psycho-somatics*, Chichester: Wiley

Mounoud, P & Vinter, A (1981) 'Representation and Sensorimotor Development', in Butterworth, G (ed) *Infancy and Epistemology: an Evaluation of Piaget's Theory*, Brighton: Harvester

Murray, L (1988) 'Effects of Post-natal Depression on Infant Development: Direct Studies of Early Mother-Infant Interactions', in Kumar, R & Brockington, I F (eds), *Motherhood and Mental Illness 2*, London: Wright

Murray Parkes, C & Stevenson-Hinde, J (eds) (1982) *The Place of Attachment in Human Behaviour*, London: Tavistock

O'Shaughnessy, E (1964) 'The Absent Object', *Journal of Child Psychotherapy*, Vol. 1, No. 2

O'Shaughnessy, E (1981) 'A Commemorative Essay on W R Bion's Theory of Thinking', *Journal of Child Psychotherapy*, Vol. 7, No. 2

Osofsky, J D & Danzger, B (1974) 'Relationships between Neonatal Characteristics and Mother-Infant Interactions', in *Developmental Psychology*, Vol. 10, pp. 124-30

Piontelli, A (1987) 'Infant Observation from Before Birth', *International Journal of Psychoanalysis*, Vol. 68, Part 4

Polanyi, M (1958) *Personal Knowledge: Towards a Post-Critical Philosophy*, London: Routledge & Kegan Paul

Popper, K R (1972) *Objective Knowledge*, Oxford: OUP

Pound, A (1982) 'Attachment and Maternal Depression', in Murray Parkes, C & Stevenson-Hinde, J (eds) *The Place of Attachment in Human Behaviour*, London: Tavistock

Richards, M P M (1979) 'Effects on Development of Medical Interventions and the Separation of Newborns from their Parents', in Schaffer, D & Dunn J (eds) *The First Year of Life*, Chichester: Wiley

Robertson, James (1953) *A Two Year Old Goes to Hospital*, Ipswich: Concord Films Council

Robertson, James & Joyce (1976) *Young Children in Brief Separation: Five Films*, Ipswich: Concord Films Council

Rosenfeld, H (1987) *Impasse and Interpretation*, London: Tavistock

Rustin, M E (1989, forthcoming) 'Clinical Research: the Strength of a Practitioner's Workshop as a New Model', *Journal of Child Psychotherapy*

Rustin, M J (1987) 'Psychoanalysis, Realism, and the new Sociology of Science', *Free Associations*, No. 9

Rutter, M (1981) *Maternal Deprivation Reassessed*, Harmondsworth: Penguin Books

Rutter, M (1989) 'Pathways from Childhood to Adult Life', in *Journal of Child*

Psychology and Psychiatry, Vol. 3, No. 1

Schaffer, H R (1977) 'Early Interactive Development', in Schaffer, H R (ed) *Studies in Mother-Infant Interaction*, London: Academic Press

Schaffer, H R (1986) 'Child Psychology: the future', in *Journal of Child Psychology and Psychiatry*, Vol. 27, No. 6

Schaffer, H R & Collis, G M (1986) 'Parental Responsiveness and Child Behaviour', in Sluckin, N & Herbert, M (eds) *Parental Behaviour in Animals and Humans*, Oxford: Blackwell

Schaffer, H R & Dunn, J (1979) *The First Year of Life*, Chichester: Wiley

Schwarz, H & Jacobs, J (1979) *Qualitative Sociology: a Method to the Madness*, New York: Free Press

Segal, H (1957) 'Notes on Symbol Formation', *International Journal of Psycho-analysis*, Vol. 38, pp. 391-7; also in *The Work of Hanna Segal*, New York: Aronson

Spillius, E (1988) *Melanie Klein Today: Developments in Theory and Practice*, Vol. 1, London: Routledge

Spitz, R A (1945) 'Hospitalism: An Inquiry in the Genesis of Psychiatric Conditions in Early Childhood', in *The Psychoanalytic Study of the Child*, Vol. 1, New York: International Universities Press

Stern, D N (1985) *The Interpersonal World of the Infant: a View from Psychoanalysis and Developmental Psychology*, New York: Basic Books

Stratton, P (1982) 'Significance of the Psycho-biology of the Human Newborn', in Stratton, P (ed) *Psychobiology of the Human Newborn*, Chichester: Wiley

Szur, R *et al* (1981) 'Colloquium: Hospital Care of the Newborn: Some Aspects of Personal Stress', *Journal of Child Psychotherapy*, Vol. 7, No. 2

Taylor, C (1985) 'Neutrality in Political Science', in *Philosophy and the Human Sciences: Philosophical Papers 2*, Cambridge: CUP

Trevarthen, C (1977) 'Descriptive Analyses of Infant Communicative Behaviour', in Schaffer, H R (ed) *Studies in Mother-Infant Interaction*, London: Academic Press

Trevarthen, C (1979) 'Communication and Co-operation in Early Infancy: a Description of Primary Intersubjectivity', in Bullowa, M (ed) *Before Speech*, Cambridge: CUP

Trevarthen, C (1980) 'The Foundations of Intersubjectivity: Development of Interpersonal and Cooperative Understanding in Infants', in Olson, D R (ed) *The Social Foundations of Language and Thought*, Toronto: Norton

Trowell, J (1982), 'Effects of Obstetric Management on the Mother–Child Relationship' in Murray Parkes, C & Stevenson-Hinde, J (eds), *The Place of Attachment in Human Behaviour*, London: Tavistock

Trowell, J (1989, forthcoming) 'The Use of Observation Skills', in Central Council for Education and Training in Social Work, *Post-Qualifying and Advanced Training for Social Workers: the New Priority*

Tustin, F (1972) *Autism and Childhood Psychosis*, London: Hogarth

Tustin, F (1981) *Autistic States in Children*, London: Routledge & Kegan Paul

Tustin, F (1986) *Autistic Barriers in Neurotic Patients*, London: Karnac

Willis, P (1977) *Learning to Labour*, Aldershot: Saxon House

Winnicott, D W (1941) 'Observation of Infants in a Set Situation', in *Collected Papers*, London: Tavistock (1958)

Winnicott, D W (1945) 'Primitive Emotional Development', in *Collected Papers*, London: Tavistock (1958)

Winnicott, D W (1949) 'Mind and its Relation to Psyche-Soma', in *Collected*

Papers, London: Tavistock (1958)

Winnicott, D W (1951) 'Transitional Objects and Transitional Phenomena', in *Collected Papers*, London: Tavistock (1958)

Winnicott, D W (1960a) 'The Theory of the Parent-Infant Relationship', in *International Journal of Psychoanalysis*, Vol. 41, pp. 585-95; also in *The Maturational Processes and the Facilitating Environment*, London: Hogarth (1965)

Winnicott, D W (1960b) 'Ego Distortion in Terms of the True and False Self', in *The Maturational Process and the Facilitating Environment*, London: Hogarth

Winnicott, D W (1971) *Playing and Reality*, London: Tavistock

Index